THE SKEPTIC

PSYCHIC

An autobiography into the

acceptance of the unseen

by Suzy Graf

Copyright 2007, 2010 by Suzy Graf

ISBN 978-1-60910-097-1

All rights reserved. No part of this publication may be reproduced, stored in a retrieval system, or transmitted in any form or by any means, electronic, mechanical, recording or otherwise, without the prior written permission of the author.

Printed in the United States of America.

BookLocker.com, Inc.
2010

This book is dedicated to

those that exist within my current scheme of

reality...

Greg and my children,

my friends that shared and grew during circle,

my guides, teachers, healers, mentors

and any who choose to expand after reading

this text

...thanks and Namaste.

Table of Contents

CHAPTER 1: An Introduction 1

CHAPTER 2: Fairies - August 2005 9

CHAPTER 3: Dimensions and Realities- late Aug. 2005 42

CHAPTER 4: Shapeshifter - September 2005 77

CHAPTER 5: Healing with Hidden Deer - Oct. 2005 111

CHAPTER 6: Digesting the Possibility – late Oct. 2005 138

CHAPTER 7: Conversations with Yellow Dog – Nov. 161

CHAPTER 8: Aliens - The Delphi – Dec. 2005 198

CHAPTER 9: Aliens – The Corona – Jan. 2006 222

CHAPTER 10: Huichols and Egyptians – Feb. 2006 259

CHAPTER 11: In Conclusion 309

EPILOGUE 329

DIARY OF RESOURCES 331

~ CHAPTER 1 ~

AN INTRODUCTION

FEAR is an emotion necessary for the survival of the human species. If man would see a tiger, man would fear the tiger, man would run away from the tiger and then man would survive. If this logic has sustained the existence of mankind for centuries then why change? Why would fear ever be considered not beneficial? These were some of my struggles as I progressed through my psychic development. I discovered that although fear may be a necessity while living through my lower self, a part of me that exists fully within my human form. My senses that see, taste, hear, smell and feel are not all that I am. No, I am more, for there is a higher self that is locked within my consciousness, waiting to emerge once I can overcome old phobias.

I was raised Catholic and within this religion I learned habits of fear and guilt. "Don't do that or you will go to hell." Or "How do you think that makes the other person feel? If you continue on that path, you will go to hell." Or "Stop wanting that item, don't you know you are being selfish and if you continue to behave that way…you will go to hell." Catholicism did not teach me to love God but rather threatened me to behave or, you guessed it, I would go to hell. So I drifted away from the religion and learned to let go of my fear of hell. I learned that hell was what people envision it to be, an existence of the human mind and not a place. I learned that society's concept of the place called hell was perpetuated by an author called Dante in the year 1321 through his writing of *The Divine Comedy* (also known as *Dante's Inferno*.) I learned that witch craft was not evil but was the Christian religion's competition. Before Christianity there was Paganism and by condemning the rituals and practices of pagans and by labeling earth religions as evil the Christian religion encompassed a larger population and could prosper. I discovered that I was living in an existence similar to the Pagans of old, trapped by the dogma of Christianity through my own fears of retribution. Then I learned to let go of my fear of hell and thus allowed my mind to wonder about other possibilities and my consciousness started to expand. I began to understand that there was much more than what my physical eyes could see. I started to read about psychic phenomenon, especially animal communication, and I began to experience another world of existence. Yes, I no longer feared that delving into the unknown was wrong then I butted into old phobias that I never realized I had.

Although I began to learn about Paganism, Wicca or Witchcraft I knew the practice was not for me. My Catholic roots were too deep. I was happy to let go of the rules and the fear but I needed a Sunday service, not a circle or a private ritual. I happened across a Spiritualist Church and there is where I found my religious answer. Spiritualism offered a Sunday service not unlike the masses I grew up in but better. Instead of receiving Holy Communion I could receive a Spiritual Healing and instead of listening to a priest berate me for not being good enough a Medium, a person who could talk with the dead, would stand on the podium and give messages or share impressions of what the congregation's beloved relatives in spirit form wanted to share. Yes, the Spiritualist service was interesting, peaceful and best of all the belief system of the religion fit into what I needed. Spiritualists believe in Infinite Intelligence and that God is part of each of us. God is a spark within every human, every animal, every plant and the whole universe. There is no hell and hell is simply a state of mind that

THE SKEPTIC PSYCHIC

one chooses to experience in order to learn a lesson, or to help another learn their lesson while living here on earth. Yes, Spiritualism was what I was searching for except for one thing, I did not like thinking of myself as part of everyone else. I was raised in America, I thought of myself as an individual and I did not want to be part of everyone else. This was where my next fear surfaced, the fear of being one.

I am a "Trekkie." As a teenager I watched late night re-runs of *Star Trek* and fantasized about being with the suave Captain Kirk or the charming Russian Chekov. The character Mr. Spock with his Vulcan ability to filter out human emotions, he was my idol. The concept of new races of humanoids and new places of existence fascinated me. I was hungry for more and became an avid reader when the topic revolved around aliens and until I stumbled across the possibility of alien abductions. Alien abduction stories were not the fairy tale adventures between aliens and mankind exploring "where no man has gone before". No, the aliens in these stories were evil deviants that looked down on humans as nothing more than lab rats. I found the idea of being helpless and captive to the prodding of evil aliens terrifying. To add to my suspicion of aliens and their intent a new *Star Trek* series introduced the concept of the Borg, a fictitious race of aliens whose mission was to assimilate any humanoid into one consciousness. A common theme from this *Star Trek* series would be that a being would be encountered, the being would then be altered and the being then lost his or her individuality and became a Borg, an evil race munching its way through the galaxy, consuming all of humanity's individualism and shaping all humanoids into one evil consciousness. My simple phobia of alien abduction expanded into the fear of being assimilated into a common consciousness of evil. I realize this sounds silly but think of the theme of the Science Fiction movie *The Matrix*. In *The Matrix* humanity is a mass of sleeping people who are being farmed, sustained in a suspended state with wires and plugs emanating from the human form and that the human brain, as a collective, is being used as an energy source to support evil machines. Once again the heroes of the movie are the individuals, the humans that are not part of "the matrix," and these people that do not join in a common consciousness are the only characters that retain their individuality. When I speak to spirit and sense beings that are not visible to the human eye I wonder, could I be sensing evil aliens that want to abduct me and change who I am?

Fear, my fear of the unknown, of unlabeled or labeled unseen beings, of what they want, of what they may do to me, this is the purpose of my story. Fear of the unseen beings is a phobia that may boarder on insanity to most people but this phobia is something that I needed to confront if I wanted to experience communication with the other side. And my desire to communicate with the dead and to understand more than my eyes could see was something that I wanted to develop and NEEDED to develop. As a Spiritualist I wanted to learn how to communicate with those that exist on the other side of the veil, those that are in spirit or what most people would call ghosts or dead people. In order to develop this ability I would sit in a development circle for mediumship, a sort of séance, and try to receive images, and would concentrate or meditate with the purpose of speaking to spirit and I was making progress. But at home when I tried to meditate or even during my dream state I rediscovered that I had this block, this fear and this lack of trust for those that exist within other dimensions. To put it simply, I would wake up because I sensed there was a spirit in the room and that brief instant when my consciousness first understood that there was a spirit in the room I would panic and ask it to go away. Then my thinking mind, my awake state would start to emerge happily searching for the chance to talk with spirit but the spirit would be gone, having been banished only moments earlier by my fear. My fear was stopping my progression into the possibility of mediumship. But this was 2005, allow me to back track in time.

I did not always want to speak with the dead, or animals, or aliens or anything else that was "just in my imagination." But I've had the ability to sense other people's feelings for most of my life. When participating in a group's conversation, often I would find myself assuming the tone of the people. If they were acting petty, I would find myself joining in. If the conversation centered on a tragedy, I would stifle back tears. On some occasions I would even pick up the accent or the dialect of an individual which sometimes would become quite embarrassing. This ability, a knowing of the mood of those around me, could be labeled as being psychic. I wasn't concerned over labels, I was who I was and I accepted how I perceived the world. I gravitated towards a somewhat solitary life and I was happy.

I was living in semi-solitude and fully enjoying my existence as a stay at home mother of three raising my children on the family farm. Happily married to the same man for over twenty years, my days were filled with clipping coupons, tending a prolific garden and raising sheep. My life was simple, almost invisible with my only socialization being through the showing of my Arabian horses, first by myself and later as a shared experience with my daughter. Being an agricultural student, an Animal Science major in college, my world was bound to the laws of science. Life was not a question of imagination but a predictable expression of the rules.

I never would have changed had I not suffered a back injury in 1999. Chronic pain was a catalyst for change but I was stubborn and not willing to give up my routine of existence. Then my ailing mother-in-law had moved in with us and stress precipitated from physical as well as psychological causes made me miserable. In 2002 my in-law was in a full time care facility but my mysterious physical pain remained. I struggled through the trials of traditional medicines and concluded that my healing needed to come from within myself. This was when I started to practice yoga. Besides coercing my crooked body to become straight once again through breathing and gentle postures I also started receiving a therapeutic massage twice monthly and a chiropractic adjustment monthly. 2002 turned to 2003 and as the pain slowly eased from my body I began to learn that the body didn't end with what I could see. Part of my yoga instruction was learning that the aura surrounding my body and energy centers called chakras existed as part of my human form. These concepts challenged my scientific mind but I listened to the wisdom and allowed myself to wonder on the possibilities. As did I allow my mind to wander during the meditation that ended my yoga practice. It was during these brief, five or ten minute meditations, that I started to experience lapses into imagination that proved coincidental to what I was experiencing in life. Could psychic powers actually exist? Intrigued, I explored further.

My psychic development began during the fall of 2003 after I attended a workshop on animal communication. In the spring of 2004 I stumbled upon a class regarding mediumship which also exposed me to Spiritualism and instruction on Spiritual Healing. I then took classes in the Reiki method of natural healing and by May of 2005 I had completed four months of study with an animal communicator who also taught me my Master level of Reiki. While advancing through my Reiki classes my psychic abilities became more acute. I wasn't aware at the time but as I was using energy to heal myself, or others, I was opening myself up to being able to understand, or read, others' energy as well. I was becoming a Psychic.

I began learning, through dreams, about ancient races of people and thus gleaned knowledge, through these dreams, that I couldn't possibly have learned. Crystals came into my life and I learned how to use the stones to aid in energy healing as well as helping me to meditate. I also learned to travel through my meditations or how to journey, with crystals that were somehow connected to animal guides. Through these meditations I could follow a boar, a hare, or a horse into a pantomime of an experience into another world of existence. I would retain memories of this strange silent movie I shared with an animal and learn a lesson from the experience. Through meditation, dreams and my development circle I learned about a race of people that called themselves Ancients and I began waking up at night to find myself with an ability to write beautifully composed prose. I discovered that I could stay in a semi-conscious state and actually interact with myself. I could ask a question, achieve a semi-conscious trance state, and write an answer. The answers were, quite frankly, too smart for me to be formulating. I felt I was confiding in more than a guide, this new entity, energy, was a teacher, a friend. Circumstances led me to call my new guide "Yellow Dog", while he referred to me as "Little One". It was through my conversations with Yellow Dog that I began to journal my experiences, almost daily. And as Yellow Dog shared with me the wisdom of the ancients as well as insights regarding the fragile state of our planet earth I also started to develop the ability to trance and allow Yellow Dog to speak through me. As I learned with my writing, I would zone out, relax, and allow the wisdom to come through. But instead of allowing my fingers to type or write I would allow my voice to speak in a foreign tongue that sounded somewhat Native American, somewhat Hawaiian, then I would understand the intent behind the words. I also used this strange foreign language to enhance my ability to heal. In keeping with my spiritualist teaching I referred to Yellow Dog as my control, my gate keeper guide or my guardian angel. But when I shared my ability to heal I would chant and feel differently then when I channeled Yellow Dog's wisdom. The healing energy working through me felt different, as if it was emanating from a different source. I came to understand that my healing guide was named Hidden Deer.

By August of 2005 I was quite comfortable with my two guides, Yellow Dog and Hidden Deer yet I was still awkward with sharing my newfound Reiki skills with other people and I struggled through my mediumship. To relieve my doubts and insecurities in working with unseen beings that didn't feel like my guides I began to learn and read about Angels. I begin my story after a long weekend course based on the teachings of Doreen Virtue. I went away for the weekend to learn about Angels and I returned home wondering about Fairies and Aliens. Share my memories with an open mind and challenge yourself to accept the possibility that, maybe, unseen entities could exist beyond your current scope of reality.

~ CHAPTER 2 ~

FAIRIES - AUGUST 2005

August 8, 2005: All summer long we have not had any trouble maintaining our family pool. When my husband, Greg, complained last night that the water had turned green I started to rethink what could have gone wrong with his pool maintenance routine to precipitate this overgrowth of algae. Yet in my heart, I knew what caused the water to turn green. I explained to my family what I have been experiencing over the course of this past week. I have met fairies and they turned the water green.

A few days ago I decided to take the time and relax in the family pool. Before I jumped into the pool I pulled a few weeds in the surrounding flower garden. I smiled at my finished handiwork as I noticed how pretty the gladiolas looked weeded against the large sage plant, the oregano bush, and the chives. The power of the filter pumping water caused the raft to lazily float around the perimeter of the pool. I grabbed the raft and pulled myself aboard and settled onto my back. I know I should have shielded my face from the sun, but the spontaneity of being outside felt so good and so right, that I risked getting a few more age spots. I simply closed my eyes and floated around to the hum of the filter motor and the bubbles it created in the water. Bliss!

I shaded my eyes with my palm to have a look around. Everything was so bright in the sun! I felt wonderful. I decided to enjoy an impromptu meditation. I placed a protective shield around my body, envisioned my chakras, my energy centers opening, and enjoyed a floating sensation while simultaneously feeling the water pulsing underneath the raft. I felt wonderful with the water coursing under my body. Relaxed and happy after my brief meditation, I opened my eyes and lazily watched the vivid colors of summer float by; the blue sky, the green pasture, the flowers.

I watched the gladiolas peaking over the pool's rim as I floated by them. The scene changed as I floated past the pool deck. Then I was by the far side of the garden where the corn stalks where visible, their tassels stirring softly in the wind. Past the grape vines I glided only to return to the gladiolas once again. Around and around I drifted when my attention was drawn to little bright lights by my thighs. I reasoned that the sun must be too bright and closed my eyes as a smile stretched across my face.

I could hear the barn swallows singing on the power line across the street, only twenty feet from the pool. I opened my eyes to watch the barn swallows as they sat, talking and chirping on the power line. I watched one swallow take flight and swoop down to get a drink from the swimming pool and vigorously beat its little wings and arc back up into the sky. I love watching these birds.

I noticed that a few swallows were still sitting on the power line so I decided to project my consciousness into one of the birds. I concentrated and felt myself leave my body. I was in the bird. I could feel the roundness of my body, the body of the swallow. I could feel the weightlessness from being perched on a swaying power line. I felt totally relaxed and my energy felt squashed into the plump frame of the bird. But I could not see or hear anything through the bird. I could not seem to access sight or sound through this little animal. I decided to break the connection and I allowed my consciousness to return to me.

I opened my eyes and looked up at the bird and sent out silent thanks for the experience. Then I floated past the gladiolas. Again I saw the little bright lights. I closed my eyes. I could see fairies hovering above my legs. Their dragonfly wings were buzzing in flight as they hovered, looking at me. I opened my eyes. Fairies? Did I just see fairies as clearly as I have experienced seeing dead people in the past? I've caught moving images behind my closed eyes before but these were of human forms. This seemed too unreal. But, then again, so was the idea of my consciousness jumping into a bird and now I accept this ability as a fact. Curious, I floated another lap around the pool as I rethought this short burst of sight, this glimpse into another reality, that I had just experienced.

I saw little beings that were not as skinny as Walt Disney's Tinkerbelle but were stockier in build with dark straight hair and pointy ears. The one I saw the clearest was a male with a page boy hair cut that resembled the "Mr. Spock" character from the original *Star Trek* TV series. I had the image of these fairies in my relaxed mind. Then the image disappeared as my mind registered the unbelievable. Was I picking up these images in a meditative state or was I really asleep and dreaming?

My mind wrestled with these questions as I floated past the deck, the corn stalks and the grape vines. As I was approaching the flowers I closed my eyes, cleared my mind, and centered myself. Fairies landed on my legs and were looking at me. I could actually feel them on my thighs but I was not too freaked out. It was too hot and I felt too relaxed from floating around in the pool. This did not make sense. There were fairies sitting on my thighs! As I floated towards the deck the fairies took flight and left.

Wide awake from this reoccurring visitation I decided that the pool no longer offered the respite I was searching for. My garden was infested with fairies! Or, at least, the gladiolas were. Or was I finally going nuts! I needed time to think this through. I left the pool and returned to the house to eat lunch. As I was chewing on my sandwich my mind reeled with possibilities. Could the Angel workshop have planted this fantasy into my head? Or did the Angel workshop open my mind up to a reality that I haven't experienced before?

Later that night my encounter with the fairies resumed. I was in my bed enjoying a deep sleep when suddenly I woke up to a terrible dream that I was being squashed like a little bug. I had no memory of the dream's content, just the way the nightmare ended. I awoke to a sensation so real and life like that I thought I was killed, smashed, squashed, flattened. I jolted to consciousness confused, my heart beating. I opened my eyes to a still, dark, room.

I didn't understand why I just had this horrible nightmare. It was late and I wanted to return to sleep. Still agitated by the fright sleep was not returning so I decided to do one of the exercises I learned in my Angel class from this past weekend. I envisioned Archangel Michael sticking a vacuum hose into my crown chakra and sucking out all the agitation I was feeling, that yucky energy. Then I asked Archangel Raphael to fill up my body with green healing energy and asked that this loving green energy fill the void left by the agitated energy that was sucked out of me. This process took ten minutes and upon its completion I tried to return to sleep but something was wrong. The emotion was still there. I could feel it in the room, pressing its presence next to mine. I knew this invisible being wanted to communicate. I've learned from past experiences that I wouldn't be allowed to return to sleep until I understood what this being wanted so I decided to automatic write into my journal. I asked my guide, Yellow Dog, what was in the room with me and why did I have this horrible dream?

Yellow Dog answered me: "You have traveled with the elementals. You have seen the fairies, danced with them, worked with them. They want you to know they are real. They will work with you if you wish. But their tests and trials are severe. They tolerate not. They are strict. Yet their powers are so strong. Their reality can overcome ours. Do not play with them. Respect! Remember to follow the rules, learn and listen. They teach. They are unyielding. Provide for them and they will reciprocate. Harm them and they will remind you of your mistakes."

I then felt the energy start to shift, to change. This time when my hand wrote I knew the message was not from Yellow Dog for that loving feeling was gone. I felt that this message was coming directly from a fairy as I wrote; "*I can see you too now. I am watching. Honor my space and I will honor yours. I may be small but there are many of us. And we will try to understand.*" I also wrote down the name "Thomas." I felt the energy leave and I knew my nightly visitations were finished. I put down the pen, rolled over and fell back asleep.

When I woke up the next morning I was curious. Before I got out of bed I asked Yellow Dog to enlighten me as to who visited my room last night. He explained that they were fairies and that they did not appreciate the chlorine that we used in the pool. I accepted this explanation but I wondered what I could do about the chlorine. After all, the pool needed to be maintained. A few days passed and I had forgotten about this incident until the pool water turned green.

Now that I shared my fairy story with my family last night and watched for their reaction. Surprisingly my two children and husband patiently listened to the possibility that fairies could exist. When I shared that the fairies said that they didn't like the chlorine in the pool and the coincidence that today the pool water had turned green, my husband's reaction surprised me. Instead of balking at my suggestion of the existence of fairies, he became argumentative towards his use of the chlorine. He started talking to the air, spewing: "The fairies better get over their problem with me using the chlorine. They've had it pretty good here, living in our garden. They can put up with me using a little chlorine to maintain the pool!" My husband was talking to the fairies as he would to our cats. He was talking to beings that exist with us, but remain independent in their choices. Greg's reaction to the fairies challenging his use of chlorine in our pool had sealed my new found belief. Fairies really do exist!

As I am writing this into my journal, I wonder if the fairies are actually living in another dimension. Is this why I can see them when I meditate? I have the ability to see the deceased that exist in another dimension. Could it be possible to naturally interact with the fairies within my dimension? Perhaps their metabolism, their existence, is so must faster than mine. Is this why most people usually don't sense them? Could the existence of the fairy realm be to humans like the flapping of a hummingbird's wings so sped up that the human mind can't comprehend its existence? Humans accept that dogs can hear pitches of sound that humans are unable to detect. People also accept that cats can see images in the darkness where the human eye cannot see. I wonder if a whole species of being co-exist on this planet without humans being aware of them? Could there be a fairy sitting right next to me and I wouldn't be able to naturally hear, smell, see or sense them? This was an interesting theory that I'll have to think about some more.

I bought the Doreen Virtue book titled *Earth Angels* last week. This book talked about incarnated souls and I found the section concerning incarnated elementals very interesting. As I read about the attributes of elementals, I am reminded of a friend I know. I wonder if she could be an incarnated fairy. I asked Yellow Dog about this and wrote the following answer.

YD: *"Your friend is very wise and very, very old. She has existed on your planet in the woodlands for centuries. She travels underfoot, amongst the toadstools and the moss. She is fleet and loved hitching a ride on a mouse or large cricket. A wingless Brownie was she; happy in the moist soil and amongst the dense moist foliage. Burrowing into the earth or into the hollowed tree or log for warmth, for comfort, for home. She is friends with all the small creature and master of her realm. Like a beetle, the Brownies are distasteful to most wee predators. Yet common sense must prevail. For the Brownie's size does put one at risk. They are borrowers. They allow Mother Nature to provide a toadstool bench. They harvest a spool of thread as a table, a shard of glass as a mirror. Like the earthly known pack rat, all of these items are stored, or rather used, in their homes.*

Curious that the pack rat is one of the Brownie's favorite mounts; part dog, part horse in personality. The pack rat helps the Brownies to move and obtain objects. For the Brownies fear humans. Humans have enslaved the Brownies in the past. These humans have used the Brownies, forced them to harvest riches or re-claim lost artifacts. The Brownies see and know what is in their territory. They know what is in their 'backyard', their 'homes'. Why wouldn't they? This is where and how they live. But Brownies are unfamiliar with objects that are not around them, the objects not within their normal region of existence. This lack of understanding is what led to the human persecution of the Brownies. How can a Brownie or Leprechaun know of a 'Pot of Gold' if such riches don't reside in their regions?

So stupid the humans! (OK, I know this is not Yellow Dog speaking. This feels like the fairy called Thomas that I met the other evening. Thomas continues to channel through my hand.) *They believe that we know all! The end of the rainbow! This is not about a tangible rainbow meeting the Earth! This story has to do with the light spectrum! What human eyes can see! It is so obvious! Why don't you get it! When there is enough water in the air to refract light, see a rainbow, the light may be refracted enough to see us! Do we have a pot of gold? No! But humans in the past learned the knowledge to alter their sight to detect us and then rely on us for our help in recovery for objects. Of course silly humans would hide their riches within our territories and then get killed, be moved or forget about these 'human riches'. Gold, silver, jewels, they change little with time. We know of their existence, use them as land marks, but care little for them otherwise.*

It was the wizard who was able to detect us with the rain in the air and the sunlight who was able to produce these riches that started this fable. We cared little about the riches and just wanted to play with the humans. But we do not like to be controlled! We fear enslavement! It is foreign to us! It is wrong! We play tricks on humans, torment them, put fear into them, to keep them away! Your psychic friends are ready. You may open THEIR eyes. We can enlighten them. They are not so driven by greed or power. Spirit has humbled their souls. They understand, co-existence, co-respect. For without this they would have no beings to channel. Yes-open their eyes today and we eagerly await the meeting. Thank-you-Thomas."

That was an interesting channel. I enjoyed reading the logic behind the refracting light that allowed a rainbow to be seen could also allow the human eye to see a fairy. I don't think my mind could have thought of this as I was writing it because my consciousness was surprised at this insight. I could definitely feel a shift in the energy when Thomas started to write through me. He felt so cold, so hard while Yellow Dog's energy feels loving, like a beat from my heart. This was a curious channel and I am looking forward to sharing this with the development class today. One more thing I need to journal before I stop. I saw the fairy that is called Thomas in a dream when I was waking up this morning. I took a pencil and drew a quick sketch and I will share this picture with my classmates as well. Thank you Yellow Dog and Thomas and any other unacknowledged beings that helped to enlighten me this morning...Namaste.

Still August 8th: As I drove into town with my journal earlier today I expected to read Thomas' channel. I was fully charged and eager to share my story about the swimming pool, the fairies, my nightmare of being squashed and the green pool water. My mind reeled with just exactly how to tell my tale in the shortest amount of words so I could highlight my experiences before getting cut off by another eager classmate vying to share their adventure first. But all my mental preparation as I drove the half hour to class were for naught because our teacher began her lesson plan early and we had no time to share our experiences of the week past. The class started with a guided meditation and we later were coaxed to describe and share our experience. One man in our group described a strange-looking child like person with cropped black hair. Thomas! This was when I saw my opportunity, so I quickly passed around the picture and told my story. The man agreed that my picture of Thomas was the figure he saw in his meditation. And as I was wondering why Thomas followed me to development class I realized that another classmate had approached me. He shared his experiences and beliefs about fairies with me as I was still pondering the coincidence that a fellow student would be able to accurately described Thomas the fairy.

(I can sense the presence of Yellow Dog as I am writing this down. But before I allow Yellow Dog to come through allow me to continue to write what happened after class today.) The same class mate that approached me after class about fairies asked me if I wanted to go with him and his friend to a place where he, too, had "seen" fairies. I agreed and the three of us piled into my SUV and drove to this spot across town. We ended up at a dog walking park, an empty field on a back road of town called Asylum Street. We parked next to the fenced off Dog Park and got out of the car. I followed my two friends across a grassy path that led to a newly installed monument. The rectangle of granite was inscribed in memory of the 212 people that died at this site during the 1890's through 1912 at an asylum for the mentally and chronically diseased located on these grounds. This place was a little creepy but interesting. I wondered where the fairies where.

My male friend led us out and around the grassy lawn then down a winding stone road. Sitting in the middle of the road was a woodchuck. At the sight of us approaching the animal sat up, looked directly at us, then quietly lumbered across the road to a mound of dirt and disappeared. I found the little animal charming but my friend was concerned over the close proximity of the "wild animal." With the animal out of sight the three of us walked past the hole in silence.

I noticed that the dirt road had a retaining wall to my left that supported the lawn I was standing on moments before. Wooded scrub land dropped down to a railroad bed and a small river to my right where trees and bushes grew haphazardly. These were plants not seeded by man but rather planted by nature. I stopped by an interesting cluster of second growth trees. At one time there was an older, single tree growing in the center. The original tree was gone leaving a grouping of seven younger trees which formed a cluster around a circle of barren space. I stopped by this group of trees and said; *"Oh, look at the sister trees. They have fed off the mother and now have formed their own circle"*. I am not sure why I said such an odd statement. Nor did I understand why I needed to walk off the dirt road to touch the group of trees. The man leading me wanted to show me something in the embankment. So I reluctantly turned 180 degrees and went to the opposite side of the road, following his lead.

Off to our left, embedded into the retaining wall, was what looked like a cave? I became excited and ran over to the hole in the wall. My companion was a little concerned that more wildlife might have taken up residence and appeared eager to reach the end of the road. Something inside me was excited and I wanted to stay by this hole in the wall. I tried to explain and blurted out an excited explanation about this space, but I was not talking in English. The woman that was with me was smiling at the fluid Native American language I was babbling. I was frustrated that I couldn't get my point across. I was frustrated that I didn't know what my point was! The man was irritated because we hadn't reached the end of the road yet. I heard myself say *"English, in English"*. I started to talk in broken English. The man was insistent that we go on. I recaptured my composure and the three of us moved on.

We walked past another grouping of second generation growth trees where I noticed that again, the center, older tree was missing. The dirt road took one more turn and then we were at the end where, off to the left of the dead end road, stood one very large ancient tree. This tree stood alone. Surrounded by a few vines but not yet surrendering its life to the next generation. Together, the three of us walked towards this behemoth and as I walked towards the end of the road and the base of this large tree, I noticed a little hole in the embankment to my left. This opening was similar in shape to the cave I hesitated at earlier but it was in a scale much smaller. Was it a ground hog hole I wondered? I pointed the hole out to my female friend and we were about to investigate the hole but our leader was agitated. He wanted us to see this tree for we were now less than ten feet from its base.

Before I closed the last few feet to the base of the tree, I looked down. There, at my feet, was something shiny. I reached down and picked up a pebble, a man made pebble of opal colored glass. I gave it to my friend for she had described this color during the meditation that we did during circle that morning and she seemed pleased with the stone of glass. Our other friend was still agitated that we were not paying any attention to the tree. He wanted us to step back and look at the tree. He told me he had seen little beings in the tree that he called Gnomes or Tree Fairies. I listened to his story but I couldn't "see" spirit or any fairies. Being more clairsentient than clairvoyant I wanted to touch the tree so I walked back to the base to lay my hands on the bark. I looked over and saw that my friend was assuming a similar pose on the other side of the trunk while our leader chose to stand back and look up at the tree. There was poison ivy around the base of the tree but I ignored my friend's warning about the ivy and laid my right hand on the tree's rough bark. I relaxed and let the energy flow and felt a wonderful, powerful, grounding energy. I closed my eyes and immediately started to journey, to imagine another place: *My feet were falling into the earth. I was weightless, light but firmly rooted. I could sense others. A whole community of little people bustling around my feet. They were happy; working together as a community and building something. Little trucks were moving about.*

I was hearing a noise and came out of the meditation wishing I could sense more for the image was too brief. Then I noticed that a real dump truck had just lumbered down this road and dumped a load of fresh dirt opposite of us. I looked at the piles of soil. The town must be planning on forming a turnaround space, a lollipop shape, to the end of this road. The driver of the truck showed no signs of acknowledging us and simply dumped his load then drove away. The mood was broken with the noise of the truck so instead of returning to my meditation I joined my friends to exchange experiences and I learned that my friend that was touching the tree with me also sensed the parallel community. My other friend, our leader for this excursion, commented on the smell of a skunk. We were near the swampy ground of lowlands and I questioned if he could be smelling skunk cabbage? I looked around and didn't see the familiar vegetation growing and started to wonder if we all imagined the smell when our conversation was interrupted by yet another truck. It dumped the dirt, and then drove away. It was time to leave so we started to retrace our steps back to my car.

As we walked back I listened to my friends talking about the gnome that lived in the tree. Like a chameleon, this gnome can disappear at will by causing his body color to change and blend into the tree. I learned that the gnome was the reason for our walk today and even though I didn't see the gnome I am grateful for experiencing the community that was existing in another reality that I, somehow, accessed by touching the tree. I am also grateful for having other people that are willing to believe in the seemingly unbelievable to share my experience with. So...now that I have journaled these experiences down allow me to question Yellow Dog further.

Question: "What happened today at the asylum site?"

YD: *"You were at a cross over place; a place where the veil between the worlds is thinner. A place where magic can seem to happen. For what we think of as magical is, to the others, common place. Nature, the animals, the trees, must live in two worlds here. This place where a tree exists in our plane and that of the others is where magic appears. Yet this is not magic. This is the reality of the others. This is how the tree would behave in their world. So do not be surprised or consumed by variations in nature for the stage is set for both sides to enjoy, both sides to use and learn from."*

Q: "I think I understand. Why do the animals and nature, the trees, feel they must behave differently around man then how they act around the others?" (I am not sure exactly what an "other" is but I know this is a group of beings and I'll allow the reader to assume a title. Also, I am not sure if this is Yellow Dog answering so I recorded the rest of this conversation as an answer or A.)

Answer: *"The others are no threat. They co-exist, they may even provide. The others will warn a swallow about a cat. Man will watch. The others will hitch a ride on a cricket, man may step on him. Man is careless, clumsy and heartless. The others are non-threatening, playful and recognize and appreciate how helpful the animals and the foliage really are."*

Q: "Who was in the big tree at the end of the road?"

A: *"He was an 'other' that can use the tree's energy to materialize. The other hugs the tree and becomes barely visible to man and facilitates an energy shift that bridges the two worlds. This way he can better ascertain why you were there? What you were doing? And whether you and your two friends were a threat? Acceptance and trust is not easy. Ambassadors for the other ones have 'sold out' on their own species before. Allow time. Allow Thom to act as an ambassador and consult with the others. If they so choose they will materialize and enlighten your male friend. You however Little One, you must keep traveling your own path, seek your own truth. Go into your own garden to meditate. Read literature and find knowledge from your own people on this subject. Learn to understand your own truth. For it is with truth that you will grow, blossom and prosper. Enjoy traveling this path."*

Q: "A few more questions please. Was there a minnie cave, a ground hog hole, at the end of the road?"

A: *"The reality of what you saw is up to you."*

Q: "Why didn't I recognize my male friend's need to share his vision of the tree dwelling gnome while I was at the trunk of the tree?"

A: *"You were channeling, sensing your own experiences. Don't feel you need to always do for others. Allow yourself to be useful to yourself."*

Q: "What was it about this cellar that my spirit guide wanted to communicate when I first walked down this road?"

A: *"The cave, the coolness, the hominess was so familiar to Hidden Deer. She is very ancient and has called cave like dwellings her home. She was trying to explain this. And she was aware of this basement storing food, of its abundance. It is a good place to explore and feel different energies."*

Q: "What is the fable of the Mother and Sisters trees?"

A: *"Long ago a wise old oak grew. She was abundance; providing home and shade, protection for many animals. As she progressed in years and her trunk became weak. Her mighty branches broke. She bore less leaves. Like an old woman her size diminished, her leaves, her hair thinned out. Her gnarled old branches broke short and her delicate under bark was exposed. A cluster of small seedlings started to grow around her trunk. This gave the mother much support but she still aged and grew weak. But she smiled as the sisters grew tall and straight and strong.*

Soon they towered over the mother's broken branches. She died happy, knowing that the sisters would gain nutrients from her rotting trunk. They would forever circle around the ghost of the mother. For she is now gone in body, having physically rotted away, but forever immortalized in spirit as the sisters dance and encircle her sacred space and so life goes on, ever changing, ever wise and everlasting."

Q: "Thank you for your wisdom. That story was beautiful. Namaste"

A: *"Namaste"*

August 10, 2005: Today I worked with Angels. Allow me to explain. My daughter takes weekly horseback riding lessons across town. This morning I was hitching the trailer to the truck while my daughter brought the horse out of the pasture. I pulled in front of the house. We wrapped the horse's legs in her shipping boots, dropped the ramp to the trailer, loaded the horse into the trailer and we all drove off to the lesson. It was just after 9:30 AM.

Just a mile down the road, at a four way stop, I noticed the trailer bouncing more than usual. I wondered what my mare was doing to cause the trailer to rock. I thought about pulling over to investigate but the noise subsided after the trailer settled into the stop so I drove on. We took a right at the stop light, a left turn off the road at the next village, then up a steep road where I usually accelerate but, for some reason, my daughter spoke up and cautioned me to slow down. I knew that I would lose momentum before I reached the top but I instinctually drove more cautiously. After cresting the hill my daughter's voiced concern caused me to be more conscientious while descending down the other side as well. At the bottom of the hill I pumped the brakes earlier than I normally would and I sort of rolled through the three-way stop. The trailer was rocking again as we made the left hand turn. What was my mare's problem today?

We proceeded the half mile down the road where I slowed for the right hand turn. We made the turn and accelerated down the narrow country road where the riding stable was located. With only another mile left in our journey I suddenly felt the truck pull as I tightened my hold on to the steering wheel and heard a horrible, skidding sound. My daughter yelped that we must have a flat tire but my mind raced as to how the trailer wheels somehow locked up. It felt like I was dragging dead weight as my truck and trailer finally skidded to a stop along the side of the road. Instinctually, I flicked on the flasher lights, put the truck in park and pulled myself out of the truck to analyze the situation. My disabled truck and trailer were all alone, on a desolate country road with only a few houses to break up the endless corn fields flanking the roadside. Just as I was stepping onto the pavement I heard a voice say; "Your trailer wheels are locked up." Surprised I turned to see the smiling form of a lone man walking down the road towards us.

By the time he reached my truck I was inspecting the trailer's emergency brake system. My hopes for a quick fix were dashed when I realized the battery pack had not been activated. Since the automatic emergency brakes were not engaged what was dragging? I turned my attention to the kind stranger standing in front of me. He introduced himself as the father of my daughter's classmate who just happened to be driving home in front of our rig on this last road. The man shared that he heard the same noise I did as he was getting out of his own truck and that my truck became disabled only yards from the driveway to his home, one of the few homes on this country road.

Having turned our attention to finding answers the Kind Samaritan told me to back my truck and trailer up slowly for this may disengage a faulty lock mechanism on the trailer tires. I settled behind my truck's steering wheel, shifted into reverse and slowly started to back up. Immediately the skidding sound resumed amidst the voice of my new friend yelling "Stop! The sound is coming from your truck, not your trailer!" I felt a pit in my stomach forming upon hearing this news as my mind started to rationalize the situation that was unfolding this morning. With no time to panic I settled my mind towards the task at hand and walked around with my new found friend to examine the front end of the truck where the problem then became obvious. The tire that was closest to the shoulder of the road was pointed inward while the other front tire, the left tire, still pointed straight. The tie rod that held my right tire straight had somehow broken.

Before I could think what I should do next I looked up to see my helper was walking back to his home. Watching him leave allowed me to notice that his wife had pulled in front of my truck with their own truck. I looked past the stranger's Ford's flashers and saw the woman's face and noticed her knowing, sympathetic smile as I was thinking; "What am I going to do with a broken truck and trailer and a horse?" Then I noticed the Samaritan had returned with a heavy duty truck jack. He was able to lift the front end of my truck and temporarily stabilize and straighten my wheel. As he worked on the tire I realized how lucky I was that we broke down on level ground for there was no need to block my truck's tires or worry about my rig rolling down a hill.

The husband and wife team helped me to unhitch my trailer which still housed my horse who was standing obediently in the trailer, munching on hay. My friend instructed me to get in my truck and drive it the few yards into his driveway. When I was walking back to my trailer I noticed his wife and my daughter's riding instructor were directing traffic around my lone trailer sitting in the road. I had forgotten that my daughter had called the barn as soon as we stopped for we didn't want the riding instructor to wonder where we were. I didn't think she would drive down to help us…I didn't even see my daughter's riding instructor drive up in her car.

Then my new friend, the Kind Samaritan, who just happened to drive a full sized truck with the proper sized ball hitch, backed up to my trailer and hitched it to his truck. My daughter and I piled into our new friend's truck who towed the horse and trailer down the road to the riding stable. The Samaritan unhitched my trailer at the horse farm where I left my daughter and horse in the care of the riding instructor as I returned with this friend to his home to further assess fixing my truck.

Without me expressing concern, options or opinions, the Samaritan offered to call his mechanic whose garage just happened to be less than a mile down the road. The Samaritan then instructed me to get in and drive his truck to the garage while the Samaritan jockeyed my truck, lest the temporary strap he installed give way. Carefully I followed this stranger as he navigated my ailing truck the half mile to the garage. Once at the garage my friend explained this tie rod stuff to the mechanic, I handed the mechanic the keys, I got in the Samaritan's truck and he drove me back to the riding stable. Somehow all my truck problems seemed to be answered. Before leaving me at the riding stable I thanked this kind stranger profusely. His reply; "Someday it will be my wife whose truck is broken down and will need help. I believe that by helping you today another will repay this same kindness to my own family." Not wanting any payment I watched this man drive off.

I walked into the indoor arena and saw that my daughter's lesson was over. The realization now hit me that I had my daughter, a horse and a trailer to transport back to my home without a truck. Our riding instructor assured us her boyfriend would be back soon with the farm truck. As we were talking he pulled into the driveway. I soon discovered that he happened to have the right sized hitch for my trailer and as he was backing up to hitch to my trailer I noticed his license plate number. The numbers 444 were tripled within the six digits of the farm plate. I smiled for I had learned that this was a sign from the Angels.

Allow me to elaborate. During my Angel Messenger course we learned that the Angels communicate in subtle ways one of which was through numbers. I purchased a small book written by Doreen Virtue entitled *Angel Numbers* and included in this book was the teaching that the number 444 was a strong sign that the angels were near. To quote the writing from page 146 of *Angel Numbers* concerning the number 444: *"Thousands of angels surround you at this moment, loving and supporting you. You have a very strong and clear connection with the angelic realm, and are an Earth angel yourself. You have nothing to fear-all is well."* My husband had teased me about my *Angel Numbers* book having pointed out that ALL the messages in this little pink book were concerned with loving, positive messages from Angels. He said that he would believe the correlation of the numbers and messages if, just one entry, was negative. I knew that all the numbers in the book were positive, but I also knew that they differ and that the number 444 was special. I was taught that this was the most loving, positive sign of the presence of Angels. Was it coincidence that this man's license plate had the triple four?

My daughter, horse, horse trailer and I were home by lunch time. All of this morning's events proceeded as if orchestrated. Yes, it sucks that my truck broke but it could have been so, so much worse. I never had a chance to worry. The Samaritan was there to help facilitate getting my truck fixed. The riding stable provided the ride home. Even the garage cooperated by being located close by and willing to assist. I was very, very lucky today.

Thank you Angels, guides, spirits, God for not allowing my truck to harm someone when it broke for I could have skidded through three different busy intersections on my drive to the barn this morning and have been the cause of an accident with another vehicle. Thank you for having that wheel collapse with it pointed inward for this stopped my truck without causing it to steer off the road and jack-knifing my rig. Thank you for having my daughter mention that I was driving too fast which caused me to drive cautiously, breaking sooner and softer. Thank you for having my truck break down in front of a kind family's home and for timing this event when they were outside of their home, in a place where they heard my truck skid. Thank you for the Samaritan, for him being adept at fixing trucks, for him knowing the local garage mechanic. Thank you for the garage being so close and the willing to fix the truck. Thank you for providing the Samaritan to hitch and drive the trailer and horse to the barn. Thank you for the riding instructor who watched my horse and child while I tended to the truck and then thanks for providing the transportation for me, my daughter and horse. So many, many thanks for so many blessings. Of course I would rather not have to fix my truck at all but since it was failing, thank you for your watchful loving guidance in this domino of events. Now I know what my friend meant the other day when she said, "Don't worry, his guides will protect him." For some strange reason this whole incident has given me confidence and reconfirmed that there are unseen beings, guides, angels, whatever they are called, that are watching and helping me. I feel strangely empowered; self assured and well cared for. Pretty Cool! For Now…Namaste.

Still August 10th: My "luck" continues for my husband, Greg, came home early today to drive me to retrieve my truck from the garage AND the garage happened to have the proper parts to fix my truck…today! As I write this my truck is now in my driveway and I never had time to contemplate how and when I was to get my truck back from the garage. Everything fell into to line, as though pre-ordained or pre-planned. Not only is this weird but if I think back as to what I had originally planned for yesterday I am grateful of the change in yesterday's itinerary as well. I had originally planned on driving to church last night but felt too tired and cancelled my plans. I wonder...would my tie rod have broken when I was on the highway? Now that I think of that possibility and back track in time I had originally planned on trailering a friend's horse to a horse show last Sunday but they cancelled the night before. Could the weight of an extra horse have caused my tie rod to break sooner and thus precipitated a more tragic accident? Thank you, thank you guides for your impeccable timing in allowing this truck to break when and where it did! For now...Namaste.

August 12, 2005: I saw two deer in the north field this morning. I was cleaning the stalls and noticed the horse's demeanor change as their heads flew up, their ears pricked forward and all four nostrils were flaring. I followed the sight of their vision and saw that standing around thirty feet away from the barn was a white tail and her child staring back at us. Our eyes met briefly then the doe and fawn turned tail and bounded effortless over the fence and disappeared into the woods. As a rational person I realize that deer live in Connecticut. But lately I have started to interpret strange events as signs, paths of communication used by angels, spirits or fairies. If the appearance of the deer was not a manifestation meant for me, then why did I get the opportunity to stare into this doe's eyes? Why were these deer so close to my barn this morning? What does this all mean? I can sense Yellow Dog near me.

YD: *"I laugh Little One at your skepticism. Your connection to nature is great. Man has been receiving signs from the mother for eons. It is just recently that he (man) chooses not to see. Not to hear the voice of the mother. Not to care about her concerns. The deer are the mother's scouts, the mother's senses. They see, hear and smell for her. Then the*

Great Spirit can understand better. Understand what is happening on your side.

The fox that came yesterday also watches for the mother. The fox views from ground level. The deer view higher up. The birds can see from the sky and the fish from the sea. Even the hummingbird you saw was watching you, evaluating your progress.

We, the ones in spirit, can tap into the mother and see. We can use the animals to sense. So do not be concerned. For the animals help us to speak. The animals help us to know. Know the environment around you so we may help. We listen to the fairies. We heard their view of your world. We needed a closer look. Embrace the hummingbird, the moth, the fox and the deer. For through their senses we can better understand your world and how to best assist you.

Take care Little One. Namaste."

This conversation made me think of Ted Andrews' reference dictionary which is the section at the end of the book titled *Animal Speak*. I asked Yellow Dog if I should use this book to further enlighten me as to the meaning of seeing these animals. To which Yellow Dog answered: *"I do know about this book. The ideas stem from our teaching. Use it Little One to achieve a greater understanding."*

Even though I had much to accomplish before the day became too hot I took that time to sit and refer to the chapter on "Deer" in Andrews' book and from page 264 I gleaned the following: *"...it is time to be gentle with yourself and others...are you trying to force things?...Are you being too critical and uncaring of yourself?...There is an opportunity to express gentle love that will open new doors to adventure for you."*

As I record this wisdom from Andrews' book I am reminded of the message I received from the worker during last night's service. There is a Spiritualist Camp that hold's evening services during the summer months and it was here that I was told that I had a man in spirit who was looking over the back of a horse and down at me. The medium during this camp service told me that I was surrounded by horses and was sharing a message from spirit that I should relax more, just go for a trail ride and don't take everything so seriously.

The show season is starting to drag. My daughter and I have competed in eight shows and are planning on attending four more. I enjoy the horse shows yet I am frustrated that I haven't found my niche, a way of helping the horses. I can feel the equine stress when I am at a show but I feel helpless. My original plan was to practice Reiki healing on horses at the horse shows but my daughter has become an obstacle in that she is embarrassed by my eccentricities. Also I need to devote much of my time to my daughter and her riding abilities while attending these shows. And now that I am having such a difficult time splitting my responsibility between my daughter and any would be clients I wonder…could the Angel Messenger course that I attended recently be more than just a coincidence in timing? When I started studying psychic phenomenon I intended on working with horses, not healing people and certainly not turning into a medium. Am I destined to work mostly with humans and only communicate and heal horses as a secondary practice? I can sense Yellow Dog wishing to answer.

YD: *"Ahhh. I know you don't respect your own kind. Your old knowledge is too great, your patience with others too thin. Yet it is your destiny to help man. He is the sick species. He is what causes the horse harm. Cure the man and the horse will always benefit. Use your horsemanship for respect. Use your skill as a healer and medium for monetary means. Be patient. We understand you are concerned about not doing enough 'practicing'. The time will come when the time will be right."*

Thank you Yellow Dog. I knew it was getting late and I should have been outside riding but first I needed to research one more animal in Andrews' book. Earlier this morning I had walked into the living room and I saw a hummingbird buzzing outside my bay window. My mind acknowledged the bird as cute and its behavior as somewhat unusual when I realized that this hummingbird appeared to be mirroring my movements, following the pane of glass as I walked across the living room floor. I hesitated at this peculiarity and stopped to look more closely at the bird who responded by darting away from the window, zigzagging a path out across the lawn until he disappeared. After the deer incident and Yellow Dog's words I wonder if the appearance of this morning's hummingbird could somehow be significant. On page 157 in *Animal Speak* I read about hummingbird: "*...reminds us to find you in what we do and to sing it out...has the ability to move its wings in a figure 8 pattern-a symbol for infinity and links to the past and future...the laws of cause and effect.*" This infinity symbol has been surfacing a lot during our development class lately. I read on: "*....it has also come to be associated with the Faerie Realm. One species has been called the wood-nymph hummingbird and another the purple-crowned fairy.*"

Hmmm...I wonder...I have been considering registering for an evening class regarding fairies being held at a local metaphysical shop. Could seeing this strangely attentive hummingbird be a sign that I should sing out and learn more about fairies? I wonder if the moth I saw this morning could have some significance through Andrews' book.

This moth was huge with a wing span four inches across lying partially under the door latch of the feed room barn door. It didn't move as I opened the door which caused me to almost smash it...come to think about it...the moth was still on the door when I closed it after finishing my barn chores. Weird.

About the moth from *Animal Speak*, page 339: "*...there has long been an association in folklore of a relationship between those of the Faerie Realm and butterflies or moths.*" Again, a mention of the Faerie Realm! I don't have the time to look up any more animals right now for I have to ride the horse before it gets too warm. For now...Namaste.

Still August 12th: It is now 11:30 AM. My daughter just practiced riding my mare, Ginger. Since my other mare, Heather's, breathing has been labored lately I did not ride her and opted to spend my time keeping an eye on the riding ring while cutting burdock bushes down in the pasture. As I pushed the wheel barrel into the pasture I took notice of all the animal species that were enjoying the purple flower heads of the burdock plants. A pretty monarch butterfly floated off one of the first clump of weeds I was cutting. Honey bees were buzzing around the next batch of weeds. Then a persistent goldfinch flitted off the next plant I intended to hack down but instead of flying off this bird landed on another burdock plant a few yards away. The goldfinch worked fairly close to me, frantically feeding off the purple flower heads and chirping as if to complain about the flowers and prickly plants that I was intent on destroying. I made a mental note that it was strange that this wild yellow bird would challenge me instead of flying off. And after my daughter was through riding the horse and I was back inside the house I looked up "Goldfinch" on page 143 of *Animal Speak*: "*Black and yellow are the colors of Archangel Auriel. These colors...used to invoke that aspect of this being that oversees the activity of nature spirits-the fairies, elves and divas.*" I flip to page 144: "*The presence of goldfinches usually indicates an awakening to...activities of...beings...relegated to the realm of fiction. Goldfinch can help you to deepen your perceptions so that you can begin to see and experience the* *activities of the nature spirits yourself...in those areas where they (finches) are found, you can also find the fairies and the elves...*" The book then explained how goldfinches make their nests out of thistledown. Thistle (what produces burdocks in the dried flower state) had an association with nature spirits and healing aspects of animals. This section mentioned, several times, about the association of the goldfinch with that of the Faerie Realm. Curious that fairies would again be mentioned in Andrews descriptions. I wonder, do all the entries in Andrews' book refer to the fairies? I have to take care of some chores. For now, Namaste.

Still August 12th: It is now around 2:30 and I just finished gathering the laundry off the clothes line. As I was pulling the clothes in I noticed a dragonfly sitting on top of one of the clothes pins holding the laundry. I jerked in a few feet of rope and the dragonfly fluttered off the clothes line only to resettle on top of the clothes pin. I removed the laundry, jerked in a few more feet of rope and again the dragonfly stirred only to resettle on the line. A third jerk brought the dragonfly so close that I could almost touch it then the insect finally took flight and sped across my lawn.

Now that the laundry is put away and I am, once again, sitting down to look through *Animal Speak*, on page 341 I read about Dragonflies being connected to dragons: *"...the fantastic creatures of the Faerie Realm often come in many shapes and sizes..."* Again, more reference to the fairies. I can think of only one more animal to research in this book. Yesterday morning I saw a red fox drinking out of the stock tank. I sometimes see fox in the winter when the trees are bare and the snow offers a contrast against their sleek form but never before have I seen a fox go down to the barn to get a drink from the horse's water trough in the summertime. Thinking this as unusual I turned to page 272 of Andrews' book: "...*often most visible at the times of dawn and dusk, the 'Between Times' when the magical world and the world in which we live intersect...it can be a guide to enter the Faerie Realm. Its appearance at such times can often signal that the Faerie Realm is about to open for the individual.*"

OK, now I believe that most of the animals reviewed in Andrews' book must be associated with the Faerie Realm. To challenge this thought I looked at the section concerning birds. I thought about all of the birds that I commonly saw at the bird feeder in the morning and made a list; barn swallows, cardinals, crows, doves and robins. I then read what Andrews has to say about each and if there was a reference to the Faerie Realm. Out of these five birds I read no mention of fairies with the exception of the dove where Andrews does talk about 'Between Times' but no mention of fairies. I'm curious, out of all the birds listed in Andrews' book, how many have fairies in their description? For now...Namaste.

Still August 12th: It is now just after 4PM. I just skimmed over the listing of almost sixty birds and discovered six birds that mention fairies in their descriptions, three shore birds; the gulls, the loon and the stork plus three land birds; the goldfinch, the hummingbird and the swisher. A seventh bird, the vulture had a brief association with the mythical creature the griffin but it was not associated with fairies. So, I read the descriptions of nearly sixty different birds that Andrews has critiqued in his "Dictionary of Bird Totems" section of *Animal Speak*. Only three were known for their shoreline association with the Faerie Realm and three were known for their between realm association on land. The latter are the goldfinch and the hummingbird which I did see today. The last species is the swisher, which I wouldn't know if I saw it. Statistically I would think that my seeing these two birds out of sixty must be significant. Yes, I just wasted a few hours looking through this book simply to prove a point to myself. But it was a very hot summer afternoon and this little research experiment was more productive than watching re-runs on TV. I now know that the fairies are with me. My tea bag this morning even read: "*Laughter lives within freedom*". I guess the fairies are enjoying my torment over their existence...Namaste.

Still August 12th: It is now 10PM. I had to do it. I spent the evening perusing the "Dictionary of Animal Totems" section in Andrews' book. Out of the 45 animals listed only the fox, the hare and the seal are associated with fairies. Three out of 45 animals and I saw one of them. Is this another statistical significant find? Looking through the "Dictionary of Insect Totems" I learned that out of the eight varieties of insects listed the butterfly/moth and the dragonfly are the only insects associated with fairies. I guess I've beaten this point to death. Statistically speaking, within the last 24 hours I saw many wild creatures that were unique because they were the few creatures listed through Andrews' book as being associated with fairies. Strange...for now...goodnight and Namaste.

August 16, 2005: I find myself still recovering from the near 100 degree horse show this past weekend. I never knew I could sweat like that. Yuck! But I'm happy for the experience for I had the opportunity to share the possibility of the existence of fairies with a few friends. I asked one friend and her answer was a wry smile as she coyly pulled down her pant waist to expose a hidden tattoo of Tinkerbelle on her hip. I guess some people do believe.

My Christian friend who had shared angel stories with me in the past gave me a blank stare when I asked about fairies. I sensed that she did believe in angels but felt uncomfortable when confronted with the thought of fairies so I changed the topic and shared my recent experience of talking fluently in a native language. I was surprised to learn that in my friend's church fellow worshipers talk "in tongue" and that a few of the "believers" seem to have the ability to understand the language they were speaking. Interesting! I wonder if while I channel Hidden Deer's voice during a healing, as I seem to have the ability to do now, if maybe there was someone out there who could interpret what it was I was saying. Or, perhaps, I am destined to just ramble along, allowing the energy to flow through me, content with hearing the sound of her voice. Am I to find a way to understand the meaning of the words? Yellow Dog, do you have any comment?

YD: *"Good morning Little One. You're trying too hard to understand. You're trying too hard to predict. Just allow. Allow what needs to flow to flow. The information will be interpreted if it is necessary. The song of a language will be used if it makes the energy work, if the Native words have an established harmony with the powers.*

Do you not use foreign language with your Reiki? This is good. This is effective. So allow Hidden Deer's language to activate her talents. She knows much. She calls upon the earth in many ways and forms. Allow her to work through you. Allow her to teach, to heal, to help make your new reality acceptable to other skeptics.

Relax, enjoy, practice!"

Thank you Yellow Dog. Back to my story...after reading Ted Andrews' book before going to bed last night my evening meditation was set with the intention of traveling with an animal totem. I placed my large quartz point which I call Big Bertha on the mattress under my right hand and allowed my consciousness to drift. I went through a barrier of plasma then plopped into a grassy field that I call the Other World where I experienced playing with a fox. I was a fox. Then I was me. At the same time the scenery would change. I was in the Other World. Then I was in my own south pasture, running along my stone wall. The meditation was fun, interactive and playful. I wished I could have experienced it longer but household noises kept bringing me back to my body and left me staring into the blackness behind my closed eyes. Then I noticed a swirling purple color forming inside my closed eyes. Curious, I laid still and watched this color take the cartoon shape of a lion. A purple outlined face of a lion turned and stared right at me! The realness of this animated violet form startled me into a full awake state. No longer sleepy or in the mood to meditate I got out of bed to settle in front of the TV for around an hour before returning to my bedroom to sleep for the night.

Questioning the purpose of the violet lion I saw last night, I wonder, Yellow Dog, what is the difference between Animal Spirit Guides, Power Animals and Animal Totems? Ted Andrews has one opinion about Animal Totems but another author talks about Animal Guides. I'm confused.

YD: *"How much are you willing to write Little One? You understand more than you allow yourself to believe and your belief, your understanding, is your truth. Do not feel you need to read about other's beliefs. Believe in yourself. Form your own opinions. For these will be the right path for you."*

Thank you Yellow Dog. Now that I am contemplating, allow me to comment upon an early morning channel. When I woke up this morning I felt the need to journal. I wrote: *"Over lapping realities transcend"*. Then I got an explanation: *"One species may not see a species within our reality. A sparrow may see fairies but not a dragon. An elephant may see dragons but not a fairy. We see the elephant and sparrow but not the fairy and dragon. Where is the reality?"*

Along with this explanation I saw overlapping circles. Each circle representing a species and how its reality overlaps that of another species. This was an interesting concept that caused me to question exactly what reality are humans living in and what reality do animals experience? As I journal this into the computer I sense Yellow Dog...

YD: *"The answer differs from animal to animal. Dogs, they can see much that humans and other predators can. Dogs can see many celestial beings. Their world, their vision, is large, all encompassing. The circles you drew were too even in size. The circle for dog compared to human would appear like this."*

I find myself drawing a large circle engulfing a small circle one tenth its size. I label the large circle as dog's reality and the smaller circle as our human reality. I then continued to channel Yellow Dog's thoughts: *"Humans choose to see only that which they can understand. Dogs see all and don't need to understand everything. Dogs share much with humans but experience much with nature also. They are domesticated but are still of the earth. They know the energy of the earth and of the sky.*

Humans have tried to evolve towards the sky. But their body, their vehicle in this life, is of the earth. If humans want to continue to use the earth and want to continue to experience lives as they have over the many centuries. They must open their eyes. They must re-learn to see the unseen. Experience the edges of their realities. For it is through these expanded realities that they will learn respect. Respect for other beings that share this earth and beings that exist in other dimensions.

How to explain...The earth, you do believe it is round, even though you see it as flat? Reality is multi-dimensional also. Not a linear line as shown in a diagram of the colors of the spectrum. The colors of the spectrum should be visually represented within a sphere with the blackness of nothing being the center of the sphere and a white glowing aura the outer perimeter. All the colors of the rainbow would then be bands around and into the ball similar to the multiple gasses encircling a gaseous planet."

Q: "I don't understand what you are explaining."

YD: *"I am trying to get you to think three dimensionally. Think in spheres, not planes. Think in depth, in fluid, liquid motion. Do not think in distance and surface touch. Think from the inside of your being to your outer aura. Not from your nose to five feet away from your body. You are energy. Vibrating, circling, existing in a very complex web of realities. Another being, say the dog, vibrates slightly different. The dog's realities are slightly altered from yours; the more basic the organism, the more basic its needs and its realities.*

On-na-kia-see-na-ko-sha-neigh, sha-neigh so ma na tem...How to explain...you are a difficult one to explain to. You simply do not believe. Do not have faith. I know I am to teach, to light the way. But I am hindered by language. How to explain my knowledge to you? I know this is necessary. Both for you as a student who needs to understand and me as a teacher who needs to enlighten. Give me time Little One. I will think of a way to illustrate a dimensional idea that is easier to understand, I hope....Namaste."

~ CHAPTER 3 ~

DIMENSIONS AND REALITIES - LATE AUGUST, 2005

August 17, 2005: I've been thinking about the forces that humans draw upon and I am struggling with the meaning behind these philosophies. Many theories abound regarding the hybrid nature of my current human reality: part earth and part sky?, part ego and part angel?, part animal totem and part alien soul? I know that I am a combination from God. That my intellect and soul energies are evolving. But I feel the need to function within my matrix of cells, nerve endings, reflexes, instincts. This is why I can't simply "trust in God." I still feel the need to observe and react to my physical surroundings. I need to protect my three dimensional form from harm within my three dimensional reality.

I will learn how to honor my past. I will learn to honor my evolutionary beginnings. I will make peace with my vessel, my earth bound body. I will tie into the loving matrix of energy produced by the earth. Earth has many secrets to reveal and share. Earth has so much energy that man has not used. (This was when I realized it was actually Yellow Dog channeling through me. For these thoughts were beyond my usual way of thinking. I allowed Yellow Dog to continue...)

Not energy that is tangible. Such as oil, wood, coal. But energy that is unseen. Life energy! Man is energy. Man is a spiraling tornado of chakras emanating out of a soul. Our reality, what we use our earth body to see, to hear, to smell, to touch, to taste. Our reality is only the surface of what truly is.

The energy of me, the present life around me on earth, the lives before me on the other side, the lives in other realms, other dimensions, we are all intertwined. A complicated set of notes laid out into a beautiful melody. The human soul is out of balance with nature, out of balance with its own human ego, instinct, essence.

The body and soul must evolve together. This is the true destiny. Learn Little One. Learn to tap into the true resources of the earth. Learn to manifest her wealth of energy. Teach others that this ability is also within their grasp.

Help man to evolve. Help man to reach his destiny. For then he will start to understand. He will understand the balance of energies that is so necessary for survival. For survival is just not a single life on this earth. Survival is the continuation of the soul. Survival is the preservation of the soul's existence in all realms, the soul's existence with and without the human form.

Develop your mediumship so other humans can further understand the immortality of the soul. For with this understanding others will learn respect. Other humans will learn to respect earth. For the importance of the planet Earth is paramount for the survival of the humans and many multitudes of other species.

Be pure of heart. Learn of the energy potentials. Develop and share this knowledge. For this is your destiny Little One. Learn from the fox. Be brave, live your life to its full potential...Namaste".

"Thank you Yellow Dog...Namaste."

August 17, 2005: Notes from a workshop I attended regarding Fairies. The woman that gave this talk, this discussion about the "Fey", was very respectful and cautious about fairies. She does ritual often and cautioned about "evoking" the help of fairies. She believed that even though fairies were very playful their humor could border on dangerous. I was fascinated by my fellow students and it was cool to be in a room of people that believed in the existence of fairies.

The woman teaching had studied ancient writings and mythology in college. The information we learned that night was derived from folk lore. Fairies predated humans as existing on this earth and were long lived, but perhaps, not immortal. There were many stories that mention "fairy rings", a sort of porthole into the fairy realm. Humans that step into the world of the fairies somehow lose time as in the famous story, *"Rip Van Winkle"*. I found this difference in time within the different realms a fascinating concept as well.

We learned about the many herbs that attract or repel fairies. That fairy energy could be a great help in establishing a bountiful garden or curing sick animals. We learned about fairy etiquette. Never thank a fairy for this was interpreted as a brush off. Thanking was like saying no thanks. We learned never to eat food offered by a fairy and that there was significance in the number seven. The lecture then turned to rituals and using a seven pointed star or the existence of seven entrances into fairy land.

I learned so much information, opinions and..."Facts?" What did I glean from all of this? I learned that there was some sort of dimensional difference between the fairy realm and ours. This had to do with the difference in our aging and the way it affected humans when eating their food. I learned that not all fairies were happy with humans and that there were some fairies that could harm humans. Great, just what I needed, more information to feed my paranoia!

One interesting topic discussed last night was fairy healing. We learned that the higher "Fey" were without bodily form and existed as pure energy; ever changing light patterns, shapes and colors. They could assist as guardians or healers when asked and approached with proper respect. We were guided to meditate on these energies, to open our inner self; listen, believe and ask. At the end of class I drew a fairy card from a deck authored by Brian Fraud. The card was that of a being of light. The message offered assistance in healing. I was flattered to be noticed by these bodiless fairies and I wondered if I could learn to work with these advanced beings of light? Before we left that night we were cautioned not to force interaction with fairies. They either will come or they won't. To work with a human was their choice, not ours.

What do I now think about fairies? I think they consist of various species of inter-dimensional, or perhaps even extra-terrestrial, beings of which many pre-date man in development and intelligence. More pure in essence than humankind, the fairies are either pure earth energies or they may vibrate to higher, angel like energies. Where man is but a hybrid formed by the marriage of a heavenly soul and an earthly body.

August 18, 2005: I just got back from service at the summer Spiritualist camp. Just hours ago I had resigned myself to a quiet evening at home because my husband and son went to a football game and I didn't want to leave my daughter home alone. Then the phone rang and my friend suggested that I would enjoy the worker, the person holding service. I politely declined and hung up the phone when it rang again. It was a friend of my daughter who invited my daughter to spend the night at her house tonight. I guess spirit had other plans for me for I would be able to attend service after all!

Besides the invitation to attend service tonight my first phone call was amusing. My friend was recalling the way I tranced when we were walking on the old Asylum Street site a few weeks back. He said that the monologue I did when I was by the old basement, the struggle between myself and Hidden Deer's voice was pretty funny. He understood that I was channeling, but he shared that I looked like Anthony Perkins from the horror movie "*Psycho*" when I was talking to myself in two different voices. I hung up the phone laughing from his description. It was nice to have others to validate and share my psychic experiences with.

My friend didn't make it to tonight's service. In fact tonight's service attracted a small congregation which was fortunate for me because everyone that attended received multiple messages from the worker. I have never met this worker before and was looking forward to something different. The message that I received was interesting for I was told that I had a beautiful glowing woman with a crown and scepter next to me who worked with natural medicine or was an elemental. The medium then described this being as an image painted by the fairy artist Gilbert Williams. This medium had no idea that I was interested in fairies so I found this part of her message more than coincidental.

I was also told that I was a Star Child or an incarnate alien. The worker saw me as a gifted healer and I was told that I could work with stones, herbs or any venue. She saw many guides around me offering to help with this healing. She also saw my maternal grandmother knitting who shared the phrase *"One stitch at a time"*. Lastly she saw me with a single humped camel in the desert. The medium interpreted this as a sign that I may be traveling to India to study?

I found this rather lengthy message both flattering and troubling. I liked the idea that spirit sees me as a healer. I found the information about my grandmother to be rather general and besides, I never knew either of my grandmothers. My yoga practice was the only link I have to India. I was disturbed when told that I might be an incarnate alien because although I have grown accustomed to the idea of fairies around me the prospect of invisible aliens around me still scares me! Receiving messages from mediums has become a common occurrence through my Spiritualist church and I realize that not all the messages are accurate. So, perhaps, this medium is wrong about the alien stuff. For now…Namaste.

August 19, 2005: My mind is curious about last night's message. "Yellow Dog, was the worker at church last night correct? Am I a Star Child?"

YD: *"You know, you have always known. You are different than others. You have always been attracted, accepted and a little fearful of the extra-terrestrials. This was your true memories. Yes, your soul is from another world. You came here to help enlighten as to the wonders and the joys of Mother Earth.*

Teach, teach about the earth's glorious energies. Light the way for the rest of humanity so they may appreciate that for which is their birthright. Enlighten humanity so they may embrace the earth's natural energies. Your path is widening, your choices becoming clearer, you destiny is unfolding. Embrace, Enjoy and Love the adventure…Namaste."

Q: "Thank you Yellow Dog. One more question before I go. Can you tell me if my friend will win the lottery this Wednesday?"

YD: *"What you see as reality can be. If she is meant to achieve her dream, her millions, then she will. The goal in life is not the money but the experience of life. If she won money would this change her goals, her aspirations, her pre-chosen lessons? If her destiny is not on this path then the lottery will not be awarded. It's the lessons learned in trying that are the true reward. Enjoy the game. Enjoy the experience. Namaste."*

August 27, 2005: It has been a very busy and productive week. My father and brother visited for the week and helped to mend my ailing old horse barn. Four trips to the lumber yard and five long days of working has produced a barn that is much sturdier.

Having guests in the house and long obligations during the day didn't afford me much time to meditate. I practiced a brief daily cleansing meditation where I focused on healing and balancing my body, separating my essence from my guests, and allowing any worries I may have to evaporate away. During these meditations I held my two crystals, Big Bertha in my right hand and my candle quartz in my left. My goal was to achieve a quick floating sense of bliss, just enough to "smooth out" any aches and worries I had about my guests and overworking my body. Thank you guides for assisting in these mini-healings and allowing me to stay busy during the week.

I've been reading Doreen Virtue's book *Healing with the Fairies*. On page 49, Virtue talks about how she would receive a message during a dream that made perfect sense and she was sure she'd remember the details of the dream upon waking up only to find herself forgetting it completely when she did wake up. I have experienced this as well so I was fascinated to learn another's perspective of why the thought would be so fleeting. According to Virtue this type of a dream was actually when one would travel to a fourth dimension where realities were not easily transferable into our third dimension world. I am not sure what this means. What exactly would the fourth dimension feel like? Then I experienced a dream this morning. In my dream I saw myself lying on my back and I could see a profile of my own body and my own aura. I was fascinated with the beautiful light bluish color of my aura when, BAM, I was back, fully into my body. I awoke confused as to who and where I was. Then realized I must have been traveling off somewhere and was just jolted back into my human form. I wonder, was I, somehow, jolted back into my three dimensional reality? Fascinating!

August 28, 2005: I've enjoyed reading Virtue's fairy book and have a question for you Yellow Dog. If fairies protect and are guardian angels to the animals, then do they watch over horses? Is it the healing energy of the fairies that I feel when I ride my horse?

    YD: *"Yes, Little One. The horses are guarded by the wee lights. These lights flit around and mend the horse's aura. When you ride, when your aura combines with the horse, the wee ones heal you both. But you also must consider that your own guardians struggle to help and heal you too! Open up and ask. Ask for your own healing energies to flow and balance. You can self heal. Trust and try and you will succeed! Namaste."*

August 29, 2005: I had a disturbing dream last night, a nightmare. I was in the center of my town but the buildings were developed differently. The post office had two stories and the donut shop was not there. In the dream I was being threatened by some men. I was trying to use my key to get into my truck before they could reach me. I was being grabbed. I woke up trying to scream but the pitch was too high for my voice to sound.

    When I woke up I asked Yellow Dog about this place. I wrote in my dream journal the answer I received from Yellow Dog last night: *"Yes, you were in a parallel plane. You have traveled here before. This is the familiarity that you felt. This parallel world is more dangerous. The downtown area more city like...."* I stopped writing. Something about this channel didn't FEEL right. The energy did not feel like Yellow Dog, I couldn't sense the love. I rolled over and returned to sleep only to be awakened by another disturbing dream.

    In this dream I was confronted by an acquaintance. I felt threatened so I began chanting, willfully sending negative, hurtful energy his way. Once again I woke up because my voice was unable to articulate the sounds from my dream. Only this time I wasn't looking to scream, I was trying to chant negative energy. When I woke up I realized what I was doing and immediately felt remorse and horror at unwittingly channeling hurtful energy to another person. To remedy the situation I laid in bed sending the acquaintance from my dream positive healing energy. I started to drift back to sleep when I saw a large rabbit. A big rabbit like the character from the old Jimmy Stewart movie "*Harvey*". Could spirit be sending me a message that I have a "Pooka", a mischievous fairy or spirit, in my room? Even though the vision of a big rabbit is far from threatening it was the feeling around this rabbit, the negative energy that I found unsettling. I tried to ignore the rabbit. I tried to relax and allow healing energy to flow into me so I could fall back to sleep but I couldn't establish a sense of peace. So I rolled over and retrieved my pen and notebook from my bed stand and allowed the energy to write through me.

"*Will protect you. Surrender yourself for you will channel our protection. We will not allow harm to come to you. Accept our offer, for it is through goodness that you will be able to do the most good. Surrender your animalistic self preservation ways. Allow us to show you the light. Allow us to help you to evolve past your body, past your environment. Trust in us. We will do no harm. We will guide with love. Please learn to trust.*"

I tried to roll over and fall back to sleep but I needed to write more. "*Please remove my ability to harbor ill will towards any other human.*"... and also the phrase... "*Please do not allow me to unknowingly inflict harm upon others.*" At this point I felt deeply troubled and unsettled. I just didn't feel safe so I relied upon my Christian upbringing and started to recite the "Our Father" prayer but for some reason I couldn't seem to remember the words. So I started to chant a healing chant. Then I could feel the healing, loving energy start to course through my body. The chanting in my mind brought in a loving healing energy from the heart which unlocked my memory for the words to the "Our Father". As I silently recited the prayer I could feel the imbalance. I could sense an intruder close to me.

Sensing an unknown spirit in my room caused me to go into a defensive mode. I placed a protective shell around my aura and peered through my third eye. I could clearly sense a being in my bedroom. With a feeling of love and caring I asked him if he was from God. The second time I asked I sensed the being leaving my room and when this being left, so did my anxiety. I could then hear the words of the "Our Father" trailing through my mind and I was able to feel a loving energy pour into me. Able to once again achieve a state of bliss I fell back to sleep.

Now that it is morning I am a little pissed off that I had to go through last night's ordeal. Yellow Dog, couldn't you find a more peaceful way of teaching me? How can I trust you as my Controller, my Guardian Angel, if you let a negative being into my aura? Aren't you capable of protecting me from "evil" spirits? Are they more "powerful" than you? I don't like being scared and last night really pisses me off!

YD: *"Calm down Little One. You need to see the dark side. We have to expose you to some of the 'evil' possibilities. We are not here to hurt, but to teach. I look for the best methods with the strongest memory attachment. You will remember last night. Life is not all good. It is a fool who believes so. Overcome, fight, these are good traits. Think-do not fear. I am with you. Harm will not come to you. But you are right. Total surrender (to anything that channels through you) is stupid.*

Your free will allowed the Pooka access. I can only aid and suggest. I did suggest the 'Our Father'. Do not be angry. This lesson must be learned. Your natural fighting instinct is a plus. It makes you strong. I am proud at how you handled this situation. I am proud of how you fell back upon our earlier teachings of scanning, then requesting proof of God's support.

You are correct to want to live in the gray. Your course is correct and true. You are loving and have the right intension. Otherwise your guides would not be with you. Be brave, continue on. This was an unfortunate hurdle we had to cross. Sorry for the unhappy feelings. But the destination, the result of this lesson, is the true positive goal. Now you understand. Be yourself and together we will accomplish much. Go for your ride and enjoy. Namaste."

Before I go ride the horse allow me to talk about the "Ego". I have been struggling with what Virtue defines as negative, or lower self attributes. I define my need to preserve and protect myself and my family as part of my lower self. I read in Doreen Virtue's book, *Divine Guidance*, on page 73, that the undesirable lower self characteristics are: "jealous, insecure, unfulfilled, delays tasks, guilty, manipulative, dreams only about future, inconsistent, abusive, greedy, and clumsy." I believe I am confusing this author's opinion with lower self which is negative, with another author's opinion of lower self, which is primitive. I have to stop relying on opinions in books but I am hungry for information for which to draw my own conclusions from. I just finished writing this and I found my answer. My tea bag reads: *"Recognize that you are the truth"*. So much to learn and think about. Namaste.

August 30, 2005: It is a rainy day and I got up early. I can sense Yellow Dog near and I have the time to journal. "Good morning Yellow Dog."

YD: *"Good morning."*

Q: "Two nights ago, my dream about being grabbed. Was that dream caused by the pooka also?"

YD: *"Yes, Little One. He has been amongst you since your house guests left. They have brought with them spirits and this mischievous fellow, that you call a pooka, was with your brother."*

Q: "Am I correct in calling that entity a pooka?"

YD: *"Yes, humans have called these inter-dimensional beings pooka. He is a lost soul, hanging out at bars, looking to do mischief to those that are unawares. If allowed to manifest he could be dangerous to one who is naive. Never work with a spirit whose soul is not pure. Never assist an entity whose purpose is not for the greater good."*

Q: "Please tell me your version of the human emotions. I am confused about the negative attributes contributed to the human ego."

YD: *"The human ego is the part of you that wants to control. It is the emotions that are produced in an effort to control. Not all emotions are produced by the ego when it wants to exert its dominance. Many of these emotions are transparent, many are easily visible.*

A smile on the face with forced talk of encouragement. This is how humans may suppress anger or frustration. Is this reaction being true to one self? Or is it better to just say 'I am angry with this situation' or 'I am frustrated with you'. Why must humans cover up a truth with a lie?"

Q: "When done out of love is this acceptable? Is it ok to tell a child he is doing great in a game while he is truly horrible at it?"

YD: *"The adult to child relationship is precarious. Even some adult to adult relationships can differ greatly in abilities to understand. So the question still remains. When is it ok to basically lie? For lying is not only passing on an untruth to another but also letting an untruth pass on through you as well.*

Perhaps the old adage 'If you have nothing positive to say, don't say anything at all' comes into play here. Avoid untruths for they precipitate same. One who stays in the light of truth will avoid all the problems with ego that you are struggling with.

Jealousy is normal, human. Embrace the feeling, confide in its counterpart. Adjust your own goals. For isn't this what jealously truly is, a goal for which you too wish to achieve?

If a competitor beats your daughter at a horse show do not feel ill will at the competitor. Enjoy the joy they are experiencing. Appreciate the harmonious job the horse and child had. Yes, you feel protective of your own child. But your child is showing the horse in order to experience the win AND the loss. The horse show is designed to help all children, and adults, to grow.

Use this loss (of a first place ribbon) as a lesson. Analyze why your child/horse combination did not win. And if you still feel your child's ride was flawless. Then embrace the idea that it was another child's turn to be lucky and win. For perhaps the winner truly needed the boost in self esteem. Competition is not important. Camaraderie is the goal. Enjoy the people, the energy.

Do not feel bad that your jealousy has a horrible twinge. Explore your own negative energy. Embrace then release it. Acknowledge and let go. With time you will be instantaneous. Do not fear or be ashamed of your human emotions.

Jealousy is a signal, a signal that you too can achieve this. Jealousy can be a boot in the butt. Saying 'Hey-try harder, Hey-practice more, Hey-learn more'. Jealousy can spur you into an adventure; can lead you towards new insights. Do not be frustrated or embarrassed to be human. The human body, its emotions, its ego, has a purpose. Find your own path of acceptance.

Of course, do not nurture the negative. Fear, pain, hatred are wake-up calls for change. Acknowledge the emotion and modify. You are in a frail vessel. Honor and protect it.

Acknowledge your human emotions. Acknowledge your body's silent language. Then use our brain to modify the situation.

Seek the positive. Seek out love, peace and happiness. But respect the negative as a signal. For the negative is necessary as a basic form of communication. Just do not embrace and cultivate negative emotions. Say to yourself. 'Ok, I am jealous. I recognize this. How can I change this?' This would be a proper step towards a solution. Do not brood for this holds the negative within. Jealousy was not intended for manifestation. Jealousy was intended as a catalyst for change.

Do not gossip for this spreads the negative energy. Like a virus, gossip leaves you and infects another. It feels good to gossip because this is a form of diffusing negative energy from the person initiating the gossip. Unfortunately the recipient is accepting this negative energy just as readily as she is listening to the juicy tidbits of the gossip. Gossip eventually dilutes negative energy as it is passed on and on amongst people. Yet wouldn't it be healthier to see the object of the gossip and help it to change? If change is too difficult, than offer this issue, offer the negative energy of the gossip to us. Send it off to the heavens for a healing.

Why is gossip fun? Why is it common to take pleasure in another's pain? Why is it entertaining to watch a human suffering on a television program? These are all forms of promoting human self esteem. Watching others suffer is a primitive way of humans releasing their own negative energies. Can this be accomplished without the ill effects of the gossip vehicle? Yes. You do know how. Teach, teach about the 'archangel/energy/vacuum technique'. Teach others how to dump their negativity safely, without causing other people harm.

This will not be easy but you can do it. People develop routines, habits that are difficult to change. Coax, set an example, be patient. People will learn. If you teach one person who can truly reform another then this new philosophy will spread. We are proud of your efforts and confident of your new path. Until next time...Namaste."

Still August 30th: It is raining outside. The blacksmith is not coming to shoe my horses today. I have time to continue with my journal entries. Yellow Dog, can you teach me more about my negative, ego feelings, and how to best deal with them?

YD: *"A purpose for gossip? A negative situation exists. A friend tells a friend about another's unhappy home life. Pity is felt. Pity is a form of positive healing. It is a mini-prayer of intention sent to the unhappy situation. So any pity precipitated by the gossip sends healing energy into this open wound of a situation.*

The chain letter of growth through gossip also dissipates the negative energy. The troubled family is dumping their negativity, through gossip, and dissipating it. This is why it feels so good to complain. You are releasing negativity. But we must be more careful upon whom we release the energy to. This is the real education. Time to grow up and learn how to handle energies-both negative and positive but I am getting off track- back to the gossip.

Another positive result of gossip is realization. A person may hear the gossip and react by stepping in and personally altering the situation such as offering the original friend money or a solution to the problem. Overhearing the gossip may offer realization to help the friend manifest her own solution. Over hearing the gossip may be the catalyst for the friend to desire a change. Is gossip hurtful, yes? Does it spread negativity, definitely? Is it necessary, no? Are there other options, of course?

Self empowerment! Learn how to work with energy. Learn how to embrace and invite the positive. Learn how to repel and dump the negative in a safe, non-contagious way. Recognize your emotions as normal and healthy. Recognize your emotions as signals. Recognize your emotions as a primitive form of cause and effect. RECOGNIZE YOUR EMOTIONS!

Envy is a form of flattery. But recognize why you are envious. Then accept how you may change yourself. Accept how you can modify your behavior, modify your looks, and modify your method of achieving goals. You have so much power, so many resources! Use your mind, set a plan, and then act upon it. Act upon it to achieve your own goals. Be grateful to others for illustrating your unhappiness in a situation. Be grateful that you can feel and understand envy. Then act upon a resolution.

Negative emotions are a primitive language. Recognize, analyze and act upon the feeling. Recognize why you are feeling angry or anxious. Recognize why you avoid a person or situation. Recognize why your own behavior shifts. Analyze exactly what it is about the situation that makes you unhappy. Do you fear that people will not like you because of other's popularity? Do you feel ashamed because your appearance is not as you perceive you should look? Do you want to possess items or things that another has?

If the last question holds true then go a step further and ask why. Why do I want a new car? Why do I need to own this rare coin? Why do I want my child to have that well schooled horse? Why? Why? WHY? Then act. Act upon your realization. If you feel that a new car is safe to drive and my old car is unreliable and the old car is costing money to constantly fix. Then the true issue here is money. So act further. Analyze your income. You can legally earn more if you truly want something. Curious thing about working with positive energies and working with loving spirit helpers is that; 'Ask and you shall receive' becomes a reality. Or perhaps it is the mindset of a chronic positive outlook does not allow any other results?

There are many ways to develop a positive energy flow towards a specific goal. The ancients would rely on their earth religions to convey a desire. A fire would be lighted, herbs burned, humans would dance a circle of movement. Perhaps substances would be offered towards icons or deities. All of these visual, aromatic and energy movement are a way of communicating; communicating with us on the other side, communicating with the Divine, communicating with God.

You deserve your true heart's desire. You must first find what it is you truly want. What it is you truly need. Then ask. So many humans accept defeat and drown in its negativity. Many learn how to feed off the pity they can siphon from others. Do not accept defeat. Change your situation. Outsmart the situation. Acceptance is defeat.

Humans are marvelously diverse. Use this adaptability to enlighten your own soul. You may rely on each other. Ask other humans for help. Read other's books. Look up answers on the internet. Watch a related television program. Or you may ask us. Ask God. Pray to Jesus, Allah, and Buddha. The form of religion is not important. The asking, the understanding, the resolution of a problem, this is what is important.

You are here on this earth to learn, grow and develop. If you fear evil then ask why. Look at what is evil to you. Feel what is in your heart. For you will truly know if something does or does not feel right. If you feel the advice from the other side may be 'evil' then question it. Ask if it is from God. If you ask three times then any lower forms of beings, any entities with un-pure ideals, will leave."

Q: "Why? Why does this work?"

YD: *"This is a complicated question Little One. We are without body. We are pure thought. We are empathic. So we cannot lie. You read our thoughts as we read yours now. We share thoughts. Your human brain must convey these thoughts into language so you may understand and communicate with others. We don't need the language. We are using the source. We cannot lie with words because there is no middle man. Our thoughts go into your words. We don't think first then use the words to convey a message. This is where humans have the ability to lie. We simply convey the message in its pure thought form. And this is how you receive it, as pure thought.*

When you ask 'Are you from God?' you are asking 'Are you pure in thought?' This is how we understand your question. This is how we are taught to interpret your questions. Spirit guides are not magically transformed. We must be taught, taught about the human psyche, the human emotions and the human ego. Then we are taught methods of communicating and understanding you. It is this teaching that ensures continuity in us assisting you.

Any spirit who is not a guide that gives you advice will not have had our teachings. Because they cannot lie, because they 'speak' to you telepathically, you will always be assured when using the question; 'Are you from God'. Go ahead Little One. I can feel you trying to formulate a way spirit can get around this question. Roll this over in your mind and let me know your opinion. For it is through your mind using your human emotions that we spirit guides can better understand how to assist the human race."

Q: "Please clarify this more. When the entity of two nights past told me; 'Allow us to help you to evolve past your body, past your environment. Trust in us. We will do no harm. We will guide with love. Please learn to trust.' Weren't these pooka lying to me?"

YD: *"No, they wanted to help you but they lack the training, our training. We ARE trained as spirit guides. WE are trained to guide HUMANS. The fairies are trained to guide and protect the plants and animals. Most fairies are NOT trained to guide humans. The teacher of the fairy workshop you took was correct in her caution. There is no evil intent with the pookas of a few nights ago. They were not TRAINED in the human way."*

Q: "Yes, Yellow Dog, I do understand. I am so sorry I am continuing on with this questioning but if you cannot explain and prove why. Then I will not accept an idea as true. Thank you for your patience."

YD: *"We enjoy your attitude, your personality, Little One. It is the combative ones like you that challenge our abilities. If everyone was a nun our job would be truly boring. Namaste."*

September 1, 2005: It has been three days since hurricane Katrina hit New Orleans. This was such a horrible and sad event. I think I watched too much news coverage before going to bed last night. Was this why I had a hard time falling asleep or was I was sensing heartburn, probably due to the potato chips I ate before I went to bed? Sometimes I have a difficult time separating what is physical pain and what is emotional yet I don't feel I carried sad emotion into the bedroom with me. I decided to try a brief meditation to settle my stomach. I placed myself in an imaginary egg of protection then I envisioned my chakras opening. I waited to sense an energy flowing through my chakras which feels like a line of energy traveling down my spine. But I couldn't access the energy and experience a state of bliss. Sensing that something was wrong I pushed energy out of my third eye. I sensed spirits in my room. These felt like wanting or wandering spirits. Could these be the newly deceased from the hurricane that I was sensing? Being tired and not in any mood to interact with lost souls I concentrated on myself and my desire to sense bliss and drifted off to sleep.

In and out of sleep I passed without ever achieving a state of bliss. My body was restless, echoing little aches and pains. Frustration was starting to overcome my stomach ache. All I wanted was to sleep. I thought of Archangel Michael and asked him if he would please escort these spirits to the light. Not feeling any change in the room I peered out of my third eye and could still feel the presence of beings. They were still there! At this point I really didn't care if they were lost spirits, if they were friendly spirits or if they were evil spirits. All I wanted was to fall sleep! My frustration blossomed into anger as I threw out a harsh "Get lost!" thought and envisioned Archangel Michael leading these spirits out of my bedroom. I didn't care if these beings found the light or not! I just wanted to go to sleep! Finally, I could feel that they are gone and immediately sensed a healing energy flow. My stomach gurgled a peaceful song and my heartburn was gone. I slept peacefully the rest of the night.

This morning I awoke to memories of something that I was learning during a dream state that I would OBVIOUSLY remember when I woke up only to wake up and remember nothing. I looked at the clock and it was too early to get up so I rolled over and returned to sleep. I started to dream and was awakened by a bright clear lightning bolt under my closed eyelids. A horizontal bright spider web of a flash against a black background that was so clear that it startled me awake. This was not a pleasant way to wake up but I did remember the message I was learning and wrote it in my dream journal: *"Think three dimensionally but heal in a sphere."*

I retained part of the dream I was in and I understood what I just wrote down so I tried it on myself. I placed myself in a protective egg as I usually did and I opened up my chakras and allowed an energy to flow up and then down my spine as I usually do as well. But I added another step by envisioning myself existing in the center of ball of light, a ball of electricity or a ball of glowing energy and the result was wonderful! I could feel a healing energy, my sinuses started to clear and I felt a blissful floating sensation. Now that I am out of bed and am writing this down I can sense Yellow Dog near. I have questions about this dream state I awoke from.

Q: "Does the human soul evolve from that of a lower life form and evolve many lifetimes through animals before reaching the state of human? Or are humans seeded onto earth from another source?"

YD: *"Evolution is true and yet false. Earth was seeded. But these seeds were left alone to evolve and then, occasionally, tweaked when circumstances would warrant.*

The planet earth has had catastrophes. We would use these opportunities to introduce new species or hybrids. Man and mammals are mostly influenced by us. We chose these lactating, nurturing species for their ability to host soul development. With communal caring instincts evolve into emotions. Emotions evolve into the love and trust that the universe needs.

To us earth is a Garden of Eden. We cultivate souls as they shed one physical body for another. We watch the center energy of light grow and expand. We watch the matrix of memories develop. A sensitive caring being eventually emerges.

We welcome and adore our new brothers and sisters. We encourage them to use and re-use the Eden of earth. We encourage them to re-establish lost or underdeveloped pieces of their true life force. Some of us choose to cultivate souls from afar as guardians of your planet. Some of us choose to partner up with a soul that is living a renewal. We will guide this soul and help it re-touch lost memories if it should require them.

The animals, they too have souls and guides. Their purpose is more simplistic, their guides more protective and nurturing, less analytical and instructive. What you call fairies enjoy and love the animals. The fairies choose to live slightly out of your human dimension. But the animals see and sense the presence of the fairies.

This is one of the reasons why an animal may act strange around the spot where another animal suffered a tragedy or a death. A fairy may be nurturing and guarding the negative lost energy or the sorry soul of the tortured animal. The fairies cannot help but keep a fierce guard over these souls or energies."

Q: "What do you mean when you use the phrase 'negative lost energy'?"

YD: "I know that negative or positive energy is a hard concept to grasp. Refer to the example of matter or anti-matter. If a negative energy ball gets stuck, it is stuck. How can I explain this? What I am referring to is a complex, multi-dimensional reality.

Think of the lost soul of a ghost, a ghost that stubbornly repeats the same pattern, forever replaying an existence that no longer exists. This is how the animal may remain as a negative energy, feeling the same experience over and over again. With the fairy compelled to guard the energy until it is freed.

Think of the pony in the barn your daughter takes lessons in. She died fighting to free herself. So violently did she fight, so stubborn and steadfast was her convictions that her soul would not accept that she had died. Her soul would not allow time to go forward. Her guardian fairies were also stuck in this quagmire of time and dimensional suspension. A being existing without an existence. A little black hole of negative energy tucked off in the corner of the barn. By doing a releasing ceremony you opened up a vortex of energy. You helped to start a tornado of energy to flow. This tornado vacuumed up this stale pony energy and swept it into the heavens.

I realize this is an abstract idea for your mind to grasp. We are talking about multi-dimensional realities. Realities not only *concerned with time and matter but realities of multi-dimensions concerning light, energy and vibrations as well.*

Do not confuse soul evolution with energy vibrations. Simple souls learn and start off evolving in simple plant and animal forms. These simple forms, however, vibrate higher than humans. The human body must vibrate lower in order to counteract the brighter, larger human soul.

Do not use lower and higher vibrations as a guide in comparing evil or good. Or in evaluating stupid or advanced. Animal's souls, their light, vibrate lower. Animal forms, their mass or physical being, vibrate higher. The soul must complement the body. An evolved human soul needs a heavy, low vibration to stay as one.

I believe this answers all of your questions. Namaste."

September 4, 2005: I was taking a relaxing bath and I was thinking about the symbols I had received last April that corresponded with my chakras. I closed my eyes and followed a meditation that used these symbols then I enjoyed the white light beaming down into my crown. It was while experiencing this energy that I felt compelled to write:

"Allow the white light to fill the body. Then allow the source of the light to come from you, your solar plexus, and emanate outward. You are the source, the center of a sphere of energy. Enjoy your perfect spherical shape as you breathe in fresh energy and exhale the stale. Relax, enjoy, and refresh your soul...Namaste."

(At this stage of my development I understood chakra alignment as the linear placement of energy centers up my spine. I did not learn that I could heal as a ball of energy until later in 2005 when I took a class in sound healing. As I edit this entry I find it fascinating that I am receiving messages or writing wisdom about a healing technique that I haven't been taught yet, well at least not within this three dimensional reality!)

September 8, 2005: I just had a neat experience as I was walking up the road after my daughter caught the school bus this morning. My house sits several hundred feet off Main Street. My road snakes over a bridge and rounds a corner before climbing up to the little white Victorian cape that I call home. The road is paved but is very overgrown and if two cars should meet on my road they would have to slow down to pass without getting scratched by the weeds protruding out of the road's shoulder. At the bottom of my hill, the bus was on time and my daughter was off to school and having no obligations for the day I was in no hurry to return to the house. I meandered up the road and took the time to notice how large some of the trees that line my road really were. As I was staring up at a huge old shaggy bark hickory tree, I could feel the tree's energy, the tree's presence. Inspecting the tree from the road my mind reeled at the possibility that this tree must be over one hundred years old. The base of the tree, its trunk, was thick with huge flaking masses of shingling bark. The knots that remain from the branches falling off or being removed by the power line company, these knots or scars looked like faces. While staring at one large knot situated around ten feet above the ground I could see an elongated face that resembled a dragon or perhaps the shape of a dog head. Not wanting to be influenced by what my eyes could see I decided to close my eyes and open my energy. I allowed myself to feel the tree and I felt weird. I felt very, very small then I felt the presence of the tree. I'm not sure how long I was standing there but something made me come back. I pulled back into my body, my full consciousness and found that I was still standing in the middle of my paved road. Somewhat confused I struggled to gain my composure. The thought crossed by mind that I could have gotten hit by a car as I was tranced in meditation. Not a bright idea! Now that I am back in my house and journaling this experience I have some questions.

Q: "Yellow Dog, what can you tell me about the soul, or the entities, that reside within a tree?"

YD: *"Little One, you ask many good questions. You search for much truth. The tree draws upon the mother's energy for her strength. But the tree also needs the spirit, the energy from the sky, for its existence. This sky energy utilizes a spirit form, a gnome or elf, as a conduit to transfer the energies. Put another way, the gnome has a symbiotic relationship with the tree.*

The tree synthesizes oxygen, a chemical reaction which the tree can do with the help of the mother. The gnome then harvests the reaction of synthesis in his dimension. The gnome uses the tree as a renewable energy source. Unlike man who harvests the tree to burn as fuel, the gnome cultivates the tree to harvest its ability to change sunlight into energy.

Man kills the cow to eat its flesh. The gnome keeps the cow to enjoy her milk. The gnome can even tap into the methane expulsions of the rumination of the cow. These are the renewable energy resources of the fourth and fifth dimensions.

Think of the advances man could make if he was able to tap into the energy of a tree. A large tree can easily host many parasitic plants and still survive. What if man were to farm the tree? Care for the tree by weeding out the parasitic vines and seedlings. Then man could learn from the gnome the secrets of the tree's true energies.

The sun can beat on a solar panel to convert energy into electricity for man. The sun is used by the tree for conversion into energy also. The tree requires the help of natural substances such as chlorophyll that is contained within its leaves and tender stems to produce the energy giving life force to the tree. The tree converts energy.

This energy pulsates just beneath the bark of the tree. Here is where the gnome lies. He transposes into the tree's bark and receives some of the tree's life energy flow. The gnome does not harm the tree. The gnome cherishes the tree as a human would nurture a bee hive. The gnome energetically absorbs the honey of the tree. Then he can exist happily in his dimension. The gnome exists in a state slightly altered than that of the human realm. The gnome has wisdom and some socialization within his own realm. To you humans the fairy realm appears as a Science Fiction tale. Beings exist that know how to create their energies from strange renewable sources.

In the human realm there is substance ingesting, substance digesting. Humans and animals receive their energy by eating each other or by consuming plants. Yes there are some oddities that may not fit into this mold. But your realm is different than that of the gnomes. The idea that gnomes do not eat, the idea that they can derive some energy from a tree and function normally throughout the day, this idea may seem foreign.

Think about your five human senses. Think about how you can sense more now. How you can see the unseen. Then take this one step further. Believe that you can learn to believe the unbelievable. All that is holding you back is desire. Namaste."

Still September 8, 2005: I had this gnome/tree issue on my mind when I went to yoga class this morning and I experienced a wonderful meditation that clarified, solidified, this new reality: *As I laid on my yoga matt I envisioned a lone tree. I was able to feel mother earth's energy travel up out of the ground. The energy from the earth was pulsating, like a human heart beat synchronizing with the beat of my own heart that I could hear resounding in my mind. I could feel the earth's energy in* my veins and I was one with the earth as she coursed her energy through me. I, like the tree, was part of this planet. I had a soul that emanated out of my solar plexus. My soul energy was a sphere. A sphere transposed over my human form.

As I am documenting this experience into writing I start to wonder if the gnome that lived with the tree was the soul of the tree. Or was this tree gnome simply a beneficial being supporting the tree as would a honey bee pollinating the flower blossoms? Is the tree gnome sharing its own energy with the tree? Is this why fairies are known to help gardeners grow their plants into stronger yields?

YD: *"The fairy realm is a dimension of different physical laws. It is a dimension of varied norms. Whereas the average human thinks of him or herself as having a physical earthly body, the gnome's body is influenced, driven by ethereal soul energy.*

The plant may survive on the earth alone. This survival would mimic that of a comatose human existing on life support. Living yes, but not living. To truly flourish the plant needs varied energies. The plant is an earlier form of life. The plant's soul is mobile. The gnome provides the needed additional energy for the plant to thrive. The energy needed for a plant to grow and reproduce.

The celestial sun energy is a catalyst yes. But the gnome provides something more. The gnome provides a link, a missing link of energy that helps the plant to reach out and touch both the earth and the sky.

And when this tree should die, when the earth energy is no longer able to course through its existence, when the biology of cells and membranes cease to function, this is when the gnome shall leave the tree. The gnome will then choose a new tree to inhabit. The gnome will seek out a new home to enhance his existence. And so life continues. The gnome casts off a used up earthly body for a fresh tree."

Q: "Who cultivates the youngest of seedlings? How old is a tree before a gnome moves in?"

YD: *"The other beings of the fairy realm, the sylphs in particular because they are small. They are the gardeners of the frail plants. They twit from plant to plant blessing each with a burst of energy. The little plants visited by the sylphs respond with vigorous growth.*

All plants benefit from the energies of the fairies for the fairies are the souls of the earth's plants. The fairies are little souls that live as separate happy beings. But they choose to lend their soul, join in their existence, with the plants. They nurture the plants with the milk of their own celestial energies. They enjoy the earth essence, the planet's energies, by briefly joining with the plants.

As the earth's plants have evolved, so have their detached souls of the fairy realm. Like a hermit crab searching for a shell home, the gnomes seek out a host tree. The gnome's peaceful methodic energy co-exists nicely with the lumbering pulsations of an older stoic tree.

The spirit of the gnome does materialize to our eyes. He does take what we see as humanoid gnome forms. This is when the gnome wishes to view us. This is when the gnome is curious about human intervention upon his tree, his current home.

If you stare upon a tree, when you're human soul locks its energy upon a certain tree, do not feel startled if you see a gnome looking back at you. For when your soul wishes to contact the spirit forms, when your intent is sent upon the fairy realm. So you may actually, consciously, see the gnome.

This is when you cross between the dimensions. This is when you allow your soul to travel. You allow your celestial being to experience and yet process through your earthly body.

This is what the fairy is like. Pure energy that can inhabit, or rather interact with earthly bodies at will.

The fairy needs not an earthly body, be it the form of a plant or an animal, to exist. The fairy only needs the energy of self. This is not to say that the fairy do not benefit from other energy sources. As you can feel the energy from the sky during a meditation. The fairy can also draw upon celestial or even earth energies. The fairy can touch a being surviving on our earthly plane and tap into, or draw up the earth's balancing vibrations.

The fairy has evolved beyond the humans. The fairy has the knowledge, the self assurance, and the empowerment of self. The fairy can function without a constant tie to the earth. The fairy can exist as our bodiless spirits exist."

Q: "If the fairy is bodiless how can it exist forever? Why do humans have to have a limited time in a body to exist on earth?"

YD: *"How to explain...We are talking dimensions again. In your dimension there is mass and form. Fairy can enter your dimension and tap into the energies pulsating through a plant that exists as one of earth's three dimensional forms."*

Q: "Are humans forever tied to an existence within a three dimensional body?"

YD: *"Not exactly 'tied to'. Humans have chosen three dimensional bodies as a vehicle of existence. Your life in your current body was pre-chosen as an adventure, as an experience of enlightenment, as the ultimate 'amusement park ride'.*

The earth, however, cannot survive if she is not respected more. This is why we've 'turned off the amusement ride'. This is why the human soul has to re-awaken while occupying the human body. Humans have to enlighten, teach and show each other the importance of mother earth.

Earth is NOT DISPOSABLE! Earth supports many beings. Beings that are visible in your dimension and beings unawares to most mankind in other dimensions, planes or realities. This is your mission Little One. Teach, enlighten, and convince the public of the importance of these other worlds....Thank you and Namaste."

Still September 8, 2005: It is now around 8:45 PM. All of this talk about energies set me to wondering about a woman I channeled Reiki energy to last weekend. She did not seem to feel the energy nor did she seem to benefit from the session. Why?

YD: *"This woman did not want to be healed. She does not want to be fully whole. Because with sound health comes the realization of your dreams. If health is an obstacle you always have an excuse, a reason as to why you cannot achieve. This woman enjoys the attention of being hampered by medical calamities. Do not let yourself feel that you are not practicing properly. Remember that you are simply a vehicle for the healing to travel through. That which is not truly desired cannot be transmitted."*

"Thank you Yellow Dog for your wisdom. This puts my mind to ease. Namaste."

September 11, 2005: I've been reading a book about Shamanism, about the four directions and its correlation with the four elements. This has caused me to ponder the relationship of the elements to Druidic energies. The elements as listed in the Shaman book were Earth, Fire, Air and Water. I was taught by my Druid guides last year that energies come from three sources; Earth, Self and Sky. I wonder if there is a relationship between these two theories.

In thinking about the three Druid energies, I've experienced what I would call Earth energy. This is what I would describe as the warm hug of energy that I feel when I ride a horse; a motherly energy from the earth that emanates up through my root chakra. I would describe the energy from the sky or heavenly energy as the sense I feel when I pray to God; the same energy that I was brought up feeling when I prayed in church. These two energies I understand and can differentiate the feelings but I don't understand what the Shaman book means when talking about the four directions because this book I was reading identifies North with the earth energy. Is this the same energy that I have felt? Is the earth energy from the north the same as the earth energy that I feel through my root chakra?

YD: *"Oh, Little One. You ask good questions. We enjoy your analytical mind yet you are comparing apples to oranges. The directional earth is different than the energy you feel through your root. If you stood on your head you could receive celestial energy through your root. So do not lay specific energy paths, do not map directions out on a human body. The human body is mobile. Planet earth is not. Mother Earth's relationship to the cosmos is basically stationary. North is north. North is not 'up'. For 'up' can be 'down' if the human body were to rotate.*

Air energy radiates from the East, towards the rising sun. Here the light of day is in favor of living. The East celebrates a new day, celebrates the breath of life, and celebrates Air and its life giving purpose. Each new day begins in the East. Celebrate with deep breaths. Celebrate by reveling in the intake of oxygen. Breathe in the air and enjoy being!

It is to the West that the cooling waters quiet the earth; the promise of evening, the promise of dew, the enveloping of a deep night, as dark and cool as a still pond. The West can be felt as; the setting sun entering in a lightless place, a place under the sea, a moonlit night, barely piercing the darkness, seeing in the depths of a lake. The West is a slow, peaceful energy, lapping, soothing, and undulating like the rhythmic peeps of the early nighttime creatures; the crickets, the frogs.

The West may have the feel of evening, a feel of rest, or a feeling of returning to the waters of the womb with the steady thub, thub of the heart. The lap, lap of a rolling tide is a welcome when sensing the West and her cool, nurturing, comforting, restful water energies. Beginning or rejuvenation coinciding with the new day of the East is very different when compared with that of Water; a rest, returning to motherly comfort and the association with the West, the setting sun.

The magnetic pull of the North is Mother Earth's energy. Her strong surface energy stabilizes the human interior blood waterways. Her northern pull helps maintain our gravity, our mass. Her rotation insures the stabilities of the East and West as well as the stabilities of Air and Water. The gentle pull of Earth's energies sets the stage for all other life's integrations and stabilities.

Enjoy the mother's energies. Enjoy the mother's delicate ecosystem. Enjoy the stability the mother offers us. Humans choose to vary their lifestyles yet always count on the stability and strength of the mother. Humans can count on the mother's strength to hold together the sky and waters while delicately supporting our fragile human bodies.

Emanating deep from within the mother is the fire. As does the fire of the Sun bombard the earth. The heat and excited energies of the fire pull opposite from Earth's North; the heat of the equator, the fire of the sun."

Q: "Yellow Dog; I do not understand fully what you are saying. I want to know if I can transmit healing energy as Fire or Water."

YD: *"Little One you are working with ancient lore in a three dimensional reality. The energies of Fire and Water are not easily processed through the human body. Air, celestial* energies, is easily processed through your human body. If you were a fish the water energies would come more natural. For now the water only offers you a remembrance of what once was.

To achieve a comfort of human beginnings bathe in water. Allow the water to undulate around your skin. A comfort as it did when you were in the womb. Allow a gentle rain to wash away your worries. Allow water energy to comfort as its droplets absorb and bind with any negative energy and whisk it away.

The Fire of the Universe may conflict with the human's homoeostatic abilities. The human body creates its own heat. The human body has its own delicate balance in temperatures. The frail human form is unable to sustain great heat influxes. Be content with bathing your exterior in the energy of Fire. Bathe in the sun's rays. Warm yourself by a fire. Rejuvenate in a hot bath or the steam of a sweat lodge. Fire is strength. Fire is powerful. Fire can be destructive. Fire can, in small doses, provide the energy for many tasks. Is it not Fire that runs the internal combustion engine in your automobiles? Is it not Fire that runs your power plants?"

Q: "Where does Nuclear Energy fit into this? Is it another form of Fire? Was it a natural form of energy available to the ancients?"

YD: *"No. This technology is beyond natural. This energy emanates outside of three dimensional realities. Nuclear energy is a peek into a new dimension, a dimension for which the human mind does not fully grasp. Let us not include this under the natural conversion of Fire energies. Do not agonize over the four directions. Rather, feel and understand the energies and their attributes.*

Air; appreciate the life giving energy of Air. Essential in your human life form, breathe in Air's essence. Allow the air around you to cleanse your body from the inside out.

Water, your breath of life from whence you arose; remember its comfort, its protection. Allow Water to wash away any negativity.

Earth, the commonality of your humanly cells. Feel her heartbeat rhythm. Allow Earth energy to vibrate within you. Allow Earth energy to align with your human DNA. The human body has arisen from Mother Earth. The cellular component of your three dimensional earth form loves to realign to Earth's comforting low vibrations. Enjoy Earth's steady, low beat. Rejoice in Earth's tender motherly energy.

Fire is the chaos of earth, the impetus of change. Allow gentle waves of Fire to touch your aura, your shell. Allow your cells to speed up, to excite, to re-energize. Allow negativity to be baked away. Allow negativity to leave under the gentle warming of the fire energy. The chaos can be dangerous so choose wisely.

Be familiar with your possibilities. Understand the language of the ancients so we may better communicate with you. Formulate your OWN conclusions. There is no right or wrong. This is YOUR reality...Namaste."

As I am typing this into my computer I question Yellow Dog's accuracy and I am confused with his parable way of speaking. I wonder why he can't just come out and answer my questions with blunt, hard facts. Then I looked back at what I had written into my dream journal last night. A channel that, coincidentally, just answered my question:

"*What is fact? A truth based on a reality. But if the reality base is different, if the physical laws are different. The world, the dimension, is different. Then wouldn't the truth be within the base of the beholder's reality? Yellow Dog is doing his best to form a model, an illustration, an example to explain a theory. A truth within his reality, a truth he is trying to transcribe into yours."*

Perhaps, with time, I will learn to simply trust and follow where I am guided. For now...Namaste.

~ CHAPTER 4 ~

SHAPESHIFTER - SEPTEMBER 2005

September 9, 2005: I purchased a new book at the metaphysical store called *The Magic of Shapeshifting* by Rosalyn Greene. Greene describes shapeshifters on the back cover of her book as *"people with animal medicine, people who connect with and use their animal powers. Those with access to this magical power can shift mentally, astrally, or even physically into their power animal or totem."* I enjoyed this author's unique view point such as, on page 32, Greene's description of "sense shifting"; *"Sense shifting occurs when shifters receive information from a real animal's senses...Shifters usually receive information simultaneously from their own human and animal sense. While seeing what the animal sees, they still see out of their human eyes."* Finally, another person who shares what I have experienced! I am fascinated to have a vocabulary, to assign; a name, a title or a phrase associated with a technique that I stumbled upon last year. I thought that "shifting" was a natural extension from animal telepathy. Perhaps this "sense shifting" could be a uniqueness I can somehow market? I wonder if Yellow Dog has any wisdom to share regarding shapeshifters?"

YD: *"Little One, read further into your book. You will see all that can be done. I too am a shifter. This is where my totem name, Yellow Dog, comes from. I had keen senses; could 'smell' trouble, could track any game, could out-think, out maneuver a herd that I would follow. Others realized this and were agreeable to my directions. I could easily organize a group of hunters into a dog pack moving in for the kill.*

Yes, I also yelped and howled. Just like you did at the séance circle held at your church last winter. The earth energy stirs the old soul. The earth energy awakens old memories of the wolf within you too. Do not fear these attributes. Embrace them for they give you strength, courage, abilities beyond your human body's normal function.

When you were a child you played as an animal. This was your natural abilities surfacing. You always had the ability to communicate with animals. You just chose to shut it down, as an attempt to conform, fit in with the society around you.

Embrace, embrace your re-discovered self. Yes, use some decorum, but use your abilities. Recognize your uniqueness. Explore your possibilities. Now-go outside and work the garden before the bees and hornets awaken. Until later...Namaste."

Hmmm...much to think about...for now...Namaste.

September 12, 2005: As I type this into the computer on this Monday evening I feel fortunate to have found a psychic development circle through my Spiritualist Church. I have the opportunity on Monday mornings, from 10:30 until noon, to sit in circle with likeminded adults who are willing to cultivate their own imaginations into the exploration of other dimensions, other realities and the possibility that we are much more than what we were brought up to perceive. Today's class theme was to pair off with a partner then listen to our teacher as we were led through a guided meditation in search of mythical creatures. I stilled my mind and allowed my imagination to soar as I searched for mythical creatures around my partner. The only image that appeared to me was a pastel colored unicorn. At the end of the meditation I shared my image with my colleague as she confessed seeing a ring of swirling animals around me of which she could remember a pig, a unicorn and a goat. Now that I am reflecting upon today's experience I wonder if Yellow

Dog has any wisdom to share about unicorns or "mythical creatures."

YD: *"Unlike the hoofed animals in your realm, the unicorn has a deep understanding of healing and energy work. They glow in pastel colors as a reflection of your chakras. The soft hues of the rainbow echo their soft demur attitude.*

More closely related to the shy deer than the horse, they are at home in the woodlands and frequently travel alone. They merge and heal with many forms of animals in your realm. They prefer to stay invisible and private as do most fairy folk.

The unicorn understands what it is to be four legged and having to move on hooves. They think as your herbivores would think. Yet they have little fear of natural predators for those in the fairy realm do not feed upon each other as in your ecosystem."

Q: "Thank you for your wisdom but I am curious about my experience in this morning's development class. What was this significance of the unicorn I saw around my partner?"

YD: *"The unicorn was curious about you Little One. He can sense your abilities to shapeshift and communicate with the animals. He could help you to better understand the diagnosing of the hoofed beasts in your world. Do not fear the unicorn. They are shy and would sense your fear as a warning. Try to open up, as you would to a fallow deer. Allow yourself to be touched. Trust that you are well protected as you journey tonight with your large crystal. Journey with the intent, with the question about unicorns then ask the beasts themselves and see if they can help you in your quest for answers. Namaste."*

September 13, 2005: I was tired last night and fell asleep before I experienced a sense of meditation so I can't remember traveling with any unicorns. Instead I woke up this morning with broken ideas regarding the fairy realm. Sensing more questions than answers I decided to visit my local book store today where I bought more books. I have this need, this craving, to absorb more ideas or facts but I can't seem to formulate the proper perspective. Unfortunately this overwhelming desire for knowledge has caused my mind to flit from one book to the next so I've temporarily abandoned reading Greene's shapeshifting book and am now enjoying reading my newly purchase book entitled *A Witch's Guide to Faery Folk* by Edain McCoy. And with this new text I have more questions: "Yellow Dog, are fairies really offended by humans thanking them?"

YD: *"Hello Little One. You have chosen your books wisely today. Make the time to cherish and absorb their wisdom!*

The fairies are brave and proud folk. They do a task for themselves or because a task needs to be done. Fairies do not perform for notoriety. By thanking a fairy you imply that their actions are destined to illicit a counter reaction. A thank you implies that a task was completed out of showmanship, not meek necessity. This is one of the many cultural differences between your worlds.

Do not fear trying to make contact. I will act as your ambassador. I can help you to better communicate. Fairies are interesting folk, are extremely adept at energy exchanges and are excellent shapeshifters as well. You will learn more about fairies for they can help you immensely. Read, learn, practice- you will achieve beyond your imagined potential. Namaste."

September 14, 2005: I woke up around 2AM this morning because of my allergies? My throat felt sore and my nose was dry as I rolled over to return to sleep. I made a mental note to adjust my nasal spray in the morning and sent healing to my nose. Finally my mind started to drift and I almost returned to sleep when a bright flash lit up the inside of my closed eyelids.

The light was so bright that I thought a light was on in my room. I opened my eyes. The room was dark.

I have experienced this before so I was not afraid and I instantly knew that this light was from beings in another dimension of existence that I couldn't see with my eyes. In the dark room I could sense the group of beings and could feel perhaps five, six or maybe seven separate individuals. I closed my eyes and allowed myself to visualize the source of the light, the presence that must be in my bedroom and was surprised to learn that these beings were not lost souls or "dead people." No, these beings were not human at all!

I saw little beings that resembled bull dogs but with humanoid faces. They were smiling broad, strange smiles on their wrinkled aged faces and their bodies were small and round. I was surprised at their unusual appearance and instantly recoiled in fear. I then opened my eyes to the dark room thinking; "Damn! It did it again! Why am I so afraid of little smiling people? I know Yellow Dog is near and I am well protected."

Having regained my composure I closed my eyes to see if the lights were still there and instantly saw the brightness. Just to be sure I opened my eyes and the room was dark. I closed my eyes to enjoy the light show and tried to fall to sleep but my mind was awake. I wondered if these could be the same beings that I saw in the shaggy bark hickory tree alongside my road. I was tired and wanted to return to sleep and didn't feel like conversing with gnomes, or little fat aliens, or whatever these smiling beings were. I decided to send healing energy to my sore throat so I grabbed my Big Bertha crystal off the night stand, pushed the grumbling dachshund away from my side to allow room to hold my candle quartz in my left hand, and with a crystal in each palm, I laid on my back and allowed myself to drift into bliss.

Normally I never would open myself up for a self healing meditation if I sensed other beings in my room but for some reason I FELT that this was safe. I allowed the Reiki energy to flow and envisioned healing entering my sore throat. I was enjoying a blissful energy flow and started to fall asleep when I was startled by something jumping up on the bed. I was confused at first because I was dreaming, or journeying, with a wolf. In my dream state I saw a wolf pouncing and at the same time I sensed a form jumping on the bed. I felt the wolf pounce twice off to my left. I've journeyed with a she-wolf in the past and recognized her energy. I woke up wondering why my wolf was in the room and reasoned that she must be scaring or chasing the chubby beings away. I looked at the clock and it read 2:52. Tired and wanting to return to sleep I acknowledged the wolf and returned to my self-healing meditation.

I was enjoying the meditation or journey and had to force myself to awaken enough to scrawl some words into my dream journal: *"When you do your Reiki you continually work with those of the other world. They are with you now. See their energy. Feel their presence. Acknowledgment is enough for now. Namaste."*

After writing this down I was able to return to sleep. Now that it is morning and I am typing this into the computer I wonder if Yellow Dog can tell me why my wolf totem chased away the portly beings that were in my room last night.

YD: *"She has not been introduced to them. She has an ego too. She was partly protecting you but mostly protecting her possession-you! Go now. Journey with your wolf crystal and invite the Brownies to return. See if your totem can accept the wee folk. Discover if the Brownies have a message for you. Go now and meditate."*

I had the time this morning to meditate so I followed Yellow Dog's advice. I usually meditate in the early morning light or in the evening so the upstairs felt very quiet with me being the only one in the house and my bedroom strangely bright in the light of day. I decided to use the method of meditation that I perfected just last year so I reached for the quartz points that I store in the little table by my bed. I laid on my back in my bed with the intention of using my body as a human crystal grid and carefully placed a quartz point on each of my seven chakras; the first on my panty line, the second in my belly button, a third at the bottom of my rib cage, a forth over my heart, the fifth laid in the hollow of my throat and the sixth balanced on my forehead. The seventh chakra crystal was placed on the pillow above my head and I held an eighth crystal point in my left hand. In my right hand I held an Included Quartz crystal point that I journeyed with months earlier and determined that I can contact a she-wolf with. With all my crystals in place I was able to achieve a meditative state rather quickly. This is what I could remember of my journey:

I was in a mist then in a clear field. Coming towards me was a big black wolf with pendulous teats and bright yellow eyes. I recognized her as the wolf that I've traveled with before and reached my hand out towards her to which she responded with a whine and sniff in greeting. We then walked side by side along the open field where I felt my human form changing as I shifted into the body of a wolf. Together the she-wolf and I trotted across the meadow, side by side, wolf to wolf. We stepped into a fog and when we emerged out of it the scenery had changed. We were in woodlands inside a dense growth of underbrush and trees. It was here that we met other wolves. I could sense myself as a wolf, greeting the others by gently biting muzzles. I was amidst a swarm of warm fur, yellow eyes and shiny teeth with a friendly feeling of camaraderie all around.

I felt an overwhelming sense of belonging, safety and of being one with the pack then the scene changed. I was with my she-wolf at the base of a particular tree and understood that something was buried under this tree. I knew that the wolf's cache was under those gnarled tree roots as I watched her use her large paws to dig. She dug and exposed what I thought was a hidden kill, a stored meal for us to enjoy. When I looked into the hole I was surprised to see a cavernous entryway to a hidden village. My wolf had exposed a fairy village that existed underground!

Upon seeing this fairy village I became aware of some deeper knowledge and understood a conflict between the fairies and my she-wolf. The fairies didn't like the wolf putting her cache in their space. The wolf didn't like her cache being moved by the fairies. The misunderstanding was now exposed and a compromise was made. The wolf will find a space to store her meat elsewhere. The fairy will not cast aside the wolf's possessions, promising to inform the wolf if she is trespassing on their property. With this agreement reached the scene once again changes.

At first I saw a memory of six years ago, a memory of a cartoon that I used to watch with my young son called "David the Gnome." I saw a brief glimpse in the cartoon when a small, mouse sized gnome would sit between the ears of a fox and ride on its head. Then I returned back to the reality of my own wolf journey. I was a wolf and I turned to look at my companion, the she-wolf, and saw that one of the portly fairies that was in my room last night had crawled aboard her head and was settling between her ears. Then I sensed a weight on my own head and knew that a fairy was sitting between my own ears as well. Once more my journey shifted and the scene changed.

I was back in time, my own time, my own childhood memory of the 1960's. I remembered this place. I was walking on the sidewalks of Washington DC. I was five, maybe six years old. This was the year my family went to Washington on a vacation. I remember that Kennedy was in office. What was the meaning of this memory?

I could see the city people passing me. I could see their bodies from a low perspective as though I was seeing through the eyes of a person very short. I could only see knees and skirt bottoms, everyone around me felt so busy and hurried. I felt uncomfortable with this towering sea of human legs and knees.

Then I saw a vision of an elf's face. He was smiling and felt so endearing. He was trying his best to smile a large human smile but his facial features were so foreign that the smile appeared grotesque. Frightened by the vision of this clown like smile I was startled back to consciousness. Weird! As I lay in bed feeling my heart beating I allowed myself to relax and could feel my heart slow. Somehow I sensed that I was just reacquainted with a long lost friend. I wonder…were the fairies in my room last night around me when I was a child as well? I can sense Yellow Dog near as I am typing this into my computer.

YD: *"Yes Little One. You did play with the fairies when you were a child. The fairies that accompanied you were not the beautiful Tinkerbelle winged fairies that most children dream with. The fairy you played with lived in your back yard and resided under the trees that shaded your play house. You spent many hours playing in the dirt with these wee folk.*

Ickaba was the name you assigned one of these beings. He remembers you and traveled with you to Washington DC when you were a child. You both had a wonderful time on the vacation. You enjoyed his company and your parents will verify how you often chatted with him.

You and Ickaba shared many memories together that your young mind could not retain. Remember the story your mother tells of you stealing a stick of butter out of the refrigerator? Your mother was surprised to find you under the bed, hiding. She assumed you were eating the butter yourself. You were actually sharing the treat with your fairy friend Ickaba.

When you were a little older do you remember how the light had to stay on in the closed closet at night? You knew there were fairies in there. Your family did not believe. So your mind perceived the fairies as beings that were wrong or frightening.

Ickaba is happy that you want to work with him again. He loved the butter. Leave him some tonight. Your wolf totem has made peace with the fairy clan. Travel with the fairy. Learn of their secrets. Learn of their knowledge. They understand your thoughts and intent are pure. Namaste."

After I recorded all of this I also drew a picture of Ickaba's face. Looking at it closely I can understand why I was freaked out by clowns as a child. Ickaba's smile is huge and overcomes his facial features but I would assume I could become accustomed to this face. I wonder why I learned to fear the fairies. What happened? Yellow Dog, do you have any answers?

YD: *"After the butter incident you were angry about being punished by your mother. You were angry about being blamed for stealing the butter when it wasn't your idea, it was Ickaba's. You were angry about being accused of intending on eating the stick of butter. You weren't going to eat it, Ickaba was. You were angry at being misunderstood. You were confused that the adults and your siblings did not believe in Ickaba.*

At first you hid your relationship with the wee folk. You would crawl under the bed to visit with them or squeeze into the back of a closet. But this behavior was not accepted by the family. With time the friendship with the Brownies was too difficult. You started to ignore them like the rest of the family did. The Brownies were hurt. They would purposely try to scare you at night. This was when you started to sleep with the lights on. For the Brownie's nocturnal antics continued to scare you for years."

Thanks Yellow Dog for this wisdom and insight. I don't remember having any attraction to fairy memorabilia as a child nor do I remember having imaginary fairy friends. Could I have had a traumatic experience with fairies when I was very young that had clouded my memories? This all seems rather silly but then why did I experience a flash back to the 1960's? I didn't lie down to meditate this morning with a conscious memory of a vacation I experienced when I was five years old. I was surprised to follow the progression of the meditation. First I was with the wolf, then I was a wolf, then I saw "David the Gnome" cartoon which explained why I was feeling the fairy touching me as a wolf. Lastly I fell into this memory of Washington and the story of Ickaba. Could this all be my imagination? I am not completely convinced but will remain open to the possibilities that Brownies may exist. I turn to pages 189 through 191 in *A Witch's Guide to Faery Folk* by Edain McCoy and read the section devoted to the Brownies.

From McCoy's book I learned that although Brownies originated from Scotland they are also known in the United States, certainly brought over with Scottish immigrants. They are described as being "...*one of the most benevolent and kind fairies you could hope to meet...small dwarf faeries who always appear as males with coal black eyes. They wear little suits of green, blue or brown and small caps of felts. Their ears are slightly pointed and they have long, nimble fingers.*" This description does fit how I saw Ickaba in my journey and what brief glimpses I can remember of him from my experience last night. I wonder if other people do experience Brownies enough to describe them and that I am tapping into this knowledge in my dream state. Or am I remembering descriptions that I have learned about Brownies in the past such as the workshop I attended on August 17th? Or are there really little invisible men that walk on my bed at night?

Curious to discover if my mind is simply regurgitating memories and turning them into a reality I read more in McCoy's book about the lore of the Brownies. In this section McCoy describes how the house Brownie searches for a deserving human to aid and prefers to live in the attic, woodshed or cellar of a human home the best. I wonder, if they actually prefer small uninhabited spaces could this include the closet and under the bed which Yellow Dog shared with me earlier?

I read about the Brownie's favorite foods; milk, honey, ale and cake. Although McCoy did not list butter, being that butter is made from milk I think it would qualify as a variety of the Brownie's favorite foods. If my imagination was creating a story about invisible Brownies would my mind remember an old memory of a "butter incident" that happened to me as a child. Hmmm...could Ickaba be real?

McCoy also writes about how Brownies are active only at night and may turn into roosters during the day because they choose not to go abroad in the daylight. This rooster shifting theory stirs another memory from when I was six years old. I freaked out when I learned that my father butchered the two roosters that we raised when I was little. They lived in the back yard, not far from my play house. Strange to think that those roosters were living in an enclosure only feet away from the play house where Ickaba and I played. Could Brownies have the ability to shapeshift? Why am I pursuing two topics, shapeshifting and fairies, at once? Are all fairies shapeshifters?

Why did Ickaba go to Washington DC with me? I remember being afraid when I was put in the car. I knew nothing of the trip ahead of time. I was the youngest of three children and my parents decided it was easier to plan the trip without including my curious, questioning, mind. Was Ickaba volunteering to travel with me and my family to protect me? Did Ickaba believe, as did I, that the family was moving? I could not offer him any opinion. I was confused as to why I was being put in the car, half asleep and in pajamas. Did Ickaba believe that we were being exiled? Curious…for now…Namaste.

September 16, 2005: I've returned to reading *The Magic of Shapeshifting* and now understand that the theories of shapeshifting and fairy lore are intertwined. I understand that natural vortexes are present which allow fairies and humans to exist on the same plane of reality. These vortexes can also be artificially created by a human which is a procedure that witches call a ritual.

If humans can create rituals to invoke fairies, then can the fairies invoke humans? Could the fairies dance, chant and consciously manipulate energy in an effort to contact us? In fairy lore humans confess to seeing fairies in a state of dancing and singing. Are humans simply peering into a vortex created by the fairies that are performing their own rituals through dance and song? Is it possible that fairies can perform rituals that create an artificial rip in dimensions that allows the human and the fairy realities to collide?

As I ponder these thoughts I find my mind wondering about me, about my soul or that part of me that travels when I experience a journey. Does my soul leave my human body when I experience myself "shifting" or changing into a wolf? Can my soul actually "leave" my human body without my physical body dying? If it is not my soul traveling, then is it my consciousness? What is consciousness? Is my consciousness traveling back and forth when I meditate flitting from my physical body and its functions, to a journey state, then back to my reality?

Thinking about my physical body...which advice should I follow in searching to heal my own body? I still have back pain and my sinuses are messed up and my asthma is still present. Should I continue to treat my pain and symptoms with traditional medicine? Or should I change to a homeopathic method which re-trains my body on how to react? Could I cure myself simply by eating only healthy, organic foods and avoiding junk foods?

In my heart I understand that the truth lies in the middle and that I need to discover a path that works for me. Perhaps a path that borrows from all these beliefs. I should be responsible and eat healthy. I can use natural methods, such as eucalyptus, to open my sinuses. If I need to alleviate a symptom, then I can rely on modern medications to help boost what my human body is struggling to heal.

Of course there is a fourth mode of treatment. I can ask my guides to assist me through spiritual healing and allow healing energy to flow through me. I realize that this procedure does alleviate all pain but I wonder can this flow of healing energy actually cure a condition.

Asthma is a serious condition. I do not fear an asthma attack as much as respect it. If my chest feels tight I can think about the cause. Is it food related? Is it caused by the environment? I wonder if I could activate healing energy to alleviate the symptoms of an asthma attack as easily as I use an inhaler. Could I activate healing energy and be positive that the condition will correct itself?

I can feel Yellow Dog's presence. I am feeling a tingling; a light headedness that I understand is his energy. I'm sorry

Yellow Dog for not allowing you to step in sooner. I am still used to contemplating life's complexities alone.

YD: *"Good morning Little One. You don't give me enough time to interject. Allow me to answer your questions. Your passion regarding your physical illness, your asthma, this is a good basis to use for an explanation.*

You have neglected to journal about the energetic chords that you have tied to your horse. Your horse has had the heaves for a few months now. When you help this mare, when you give her Reiki energy, you must cut these chords. For your desire to make the horse better is making you ill. You are absorbing some of her pain.

Ask. Ask me to send spirit energy to the horse. I will clean the horse, and yourself, from these ills.

Do not be afraid of love or contact. Just, as you say, be responsible. Cleanse yourself daily, spiritually speaking. Do a visualization of vacuuming of stale energies out of your being. Remember to allow positive, loving energies to flow back in and re-infuse you with healing energies. Go now and feed your animals. Help your horse, cleanse yourself, and then we can discuss the soul/consciousness topic. Namaste."

Still Friday September 16th: Interesting turn of events this morning. I went into the basement to empty the de-humidifier. I noticed that the plug had melted where it was attached to the extension cord. I picked up the cord to examine it more closely. That was when I received an electric jolt. I heard the zzzzzip as I felt the jolt snap through me, up into my head so that I felt my teeth tingling. I dropped the cord immediately and stood there, dazed and surprised. I then unplugged the extension cord from the wall socket and tried to compose myself enough to go outside to feed the horses. My senses slowly recovered from the jolt as I walked down to the barn. Yet my left hand and arm were still buzzing from the zapping even after the horses had finished their grain.

Even though I was zapped just ten minutes before, I knew I had to help my horse Heather. After she was through eating I initiated the Reiki energy, allowing it to flow through my hands. But I noticed that the Native dialect channeled through me differently. Instead of a mono-tone chant it sounded more like a tune. As I sang this song chant I felt compelled to allow my hands to draw little counter clockwise circles over the horse; over the mare's head, her haunches, back and sides.

The pace of these drawings quickened as did my chanting. I sensed the energy building and eventually I felt a release of energy flowing up and out, away from the horse. Then I found myself drawing clockwise circles. I felt the words I was saying were different than before. I heard the English word "balance" as I was channeling this foreign tongue. Then I felt the energy subside. I stood there in the stall and watched my horse quietly walk away.

I drew a bath for myself when I came back into the house, settled into the tub and allowed myself to resume chanting. I closed my eyes and envisioned the counterclockwise circles, the building of energy. Behind my closed eyes I saw a mirror image of myself chanting, drawing the same, yet opposite, circular motions in the air. This image faded as the tempo of the energy grew.

I spoke fewer foreign words for my mouth felt unable to chant in pace with the energy. I felt an upward tornado of released energy. Then I prepared to welcome in the re-balancing energies. I motioned with my hands first but then felt compelled to sit still. I spoke in a foreign tongue rather than a sing-song chant. I felt I was giving thanks and a lovely sense of peace overcame me.

Now that I am at the computer recording all of this I can physically still sense my head cold symptoms. But I also feel strangely recharged. I have a question for you Yellow Dog. "Did you zap me on purpose? Was this supposed accidental electrical jolt a way of spirit increasing my energy channeling ability? If it was, allow me to tell you that I am not pleased. That electrical jolt really hurt!"

YD: *"Oh Little One. It didn't hurt that much and the benefits are great. Yes, the electrical current helped to re-align some of your blocked pathways. Never attempt this yourself in the future for this was an opportunity offered to you. An opportunity that was amiable to your body and life situation. But yes, the psychic energies should flow better for YOU now."*

Q: "Thank you Yellow Dog but I am concerned that this could have been harmful to me. OK, I can feel you. I will stop complaining about the physical pain. Back to a question that I am wondering about, can you please tell me, when I travel outside of my body, is it my consciousness or soul that is traveling."

YD: *"Both. You exist in many dimensions already. You exist on many planes concurrently. Your 'traveling' is simply becoming aware of another consciousness already within you. You never 'leave' your body. You are simply expanding your consciousness into another reality. Bi-location is not unusual. You constantly exist in many dimensions concurrently. What is unusual is being aware, being conscious of bi-locating.*

This is also tied to the shapeshifting you are learning about. You have a self that exists in a more primitive state. This animal side of you is real. You can draw upon it. If it manifests in you too much you may take on some of its characteristics here, in your human earth plane. This trance state is not bad or evil, simply a re-balancing. For if you call upon your animal side too much, if you interfere with your animal world too often

then the invasion will reverse. The animal will boomerang into you. Balance must be achieved.
    Seek the knowledge you wish to know and share. Experiment carefully. For every action does precipitate a reaction. This is why the Wiccan friends you met are cautious of the fairy world. To intrude upon that realm, to touch your fairy self, is to draw power or initiate wishes. You ask that your fairy self surface in your human world.
    All God's creatures, all entities, are entwined. As all cells in the human body function as one human. It takes many souls to form the consciousness of God. You are a miracle of existence. Yet your existence matters in the balance of all. I realize this is a hard concept for you to grasp. In your world time is linear. In mine time is concurrent. Time is overlapping spheres of existence.
    Do not try so hard to understand completely. Just accept that there is more. For the knowledge will unfold with time, linear time of your world, and patience. We are on an interesting path together. Our cultures are so vastly different and our realities even greater in their extremes. But together we will understand. For we are both learning here. You are learning of my greater knowledge. I am learning of your present capabilities and future possibilities to function in my, Yellow Dog's, reality. We will enjoy this adventure together! Namaste."

Still September 16th: It is late evening and I just had an interesting journey with my wolf crystal. I laid a quartz point on each of my chakras with an eighth point in my left hand and my Included Quartz point, the crystal I associate with the spirit of a she-wolf, in my right. Immediately I could feel my right hand becoming a paw. I have been reading about a "full shift" which is the ability to actually physically change into an animal. This idea may seem ridiculous, but then again, so does any new idea before it is accepted as fact. Could I actually change my form into a wolf? I had pondered this scenario in my brain several times over the course of this last month and now that the opportunity was here I declined. I was afraid. I feared the unknown for what if I changed into a wolf and was not able to change back? And as I lay in bed with my crystals on I could feel my hand shift into a paw. This was not a meditation but a sensation. I knew that I should exchange the wolf crystal, the included quartz, with the quartz point that was laying over my solar plexus chakra. Instinctively I knew that this would allow my whole body to shift into that of a wolf. But I also knew that I wasn't ready to experience a full shift and I don't know if I ever will. I was fine with this sensation just in my hand, the sensation of my hand actually being a paw but this was all I was willing to experience. In lieu of the physical shift I elected to use the building energy of the crystals towards the intent of enjoying a journey which I proceeded to do with my being only slightly into another reality, with only my hand shifting into that of a wolf.

    I prepared for my meditation as I usually do and consciously opened each of my chakras. I started at my root and visualized an energy tornado flowing. Then I opened my second chakra, then my third, fourth and fifth but when my attention was focused at my sixth chakra, my third eye which is the center of my forehead, I noticed a change from how I usually felt when I enjoy a meditation. This sensation was as though my existence was being pushed through my third eye. Having noted this difference I opened my seventh chakra and allowed the energy to flow. I began my journey:

    I could sense my she-wolf with me immediately and she was anxious for me to proceed into the journey. I was a wolf playing amongst wolves in the snow. My pack was on a mountain top and the day was beautiful, the sky blue, crisp, calm. We were a flurry of fur. Running together, jumping and tripping each other, enjoying the tumbling in the cool, soft, snow.

I was enjoying the wrestling and could see the snow all around me; a pretty, sparkling snow. My narrow padded feet were falling through the snow's crust. The snow was starting to feel cold. I looked down and discovered that ice had formed between my toes. I burrowed under the snow and curled my furry body into a fetal position. My breath felt warm under the snow. My curled position under the protection of the snow allowed my body to warm. I drifted off to sleep.

Still as a wolf I dreamt of spring. I was a pup following a nursing she-wolf with pendulous swinging teats. I was playing in the sun with my litter mates. The grass was so green and smelled sweet. I was wrestling, running, yipping, nipping, and having a wonderful time! Then we were all tired and laid in a pile. We all rested as one large mound of pups panting in the warm spring sun.

The she-wolf wanted to go. We knew we must obey. We all followed, but not in a straight line. We were bounding, wrestling, running back and forth and around our mother. The she-wolf entered a thicket of dense bushes and I followed with my siblings. It was dark for the foliage blocked most of the sun's rays. There was movement and I could see small birds expertly flying through the cramped quarters.

Then another movement caught my attention. I looked over and instead of more birds I saw an odd creature; a very thin man like being that had a head similar to the insect called a praying mantis. He was brown and thin with strangely large eyes. His appearance was odd but he felt friendly, almost fatherly towards us pups. As I looked at this creature he disappeared and the scene changed.

I started seeing human spirits and I could sense my father-in law's brother. He wanted to know why his eldest son didn't want a college education. Then I saw the local casino, the place where my cousin-in-law was currently employed. I could sense, I could feel, my deceased uncle-in-law's frustration. Then the number of spirits around me increased. I didn't feel that I belonged and I had no further connection with any of these beings. I began drifting and felt a happy weightlessness. It was time for me to leave this spirit place and return to my body. I pulled my energy back in. I opened my eyes and returned to the pen to journal this cool experience before I forgot the details.

What a cool meditation! I am not exactly sure if the praying mantis being was a fairy or an alien and I'm not sure why he appeared in this meditation but I do know that he felt safe. As far as shifting goes, I am perfectly content with traveling in meditation and I know that I don't want to venture into a full shift without another person around. I feel blessed to have this experience although I don't completely understand it. Much to think about…the time is late. Good night and Namaste.

September 19, 2005: I've been enjoying the shapeshifting book written by Greene and have a question Yellow Dog. "If shapeshifters can manifest themselves physically into animal form is it possible to shift into a fairy? Or, because fairies are not from my dimension, is this an obstacle?"

YD: *"Good morning Little One. Yes, if you were genetically predisposed you could call up the inner fairy in you to shift. Most humans, however, are derived from the animal spirit and therefore it is easier to shift, or call upon, the animal within.*

Years ago, when the lore of the fey was commonplace, fairy shifting was popular. Today, without knowledge of the source, such shifting only manifests itself in acute, emotional states.

Intense hatred can manifest as the fey that humans call demonic. Chronic fear can induce worrisome fey. All intense human emotions may precipitate through personality changes imitating fairy shifting.

What you call an adrenalin rush that precipitates 'super human strength'. The human's strong reaction to a tragic event such as witnessing a fallen car on a be-loved child and being able to move this heavy object, the fallen car. This can, in actuality, be a shift into an animal form, a fey or even the strong channeling of a spirit force.

The human adrenal gland does secrete much during any shift or channel/trance. More natural chemicals are exerted if the human's desire is acute, less if the spirit trancing is more intense. Differentiating between shifts and possessions can be tricky. Monitoring the human body's reaction would help to determine which event is transpiring. This monitoring of the human endocrine production would also provide some 'proof' for your western science minded majority. A true physical shift, that being initiated by the human's inner being, the human's soul, would call upon the human's body, the human organism, to react. Here you would notice endocrine levels changing and fluctuating."

"Yellow Dog, I question this, with a true shift wouldn't the body be within itself? Would the body not show any physical signs, no adverse reaction when the soul is taken over? Wouldn't the animal to be shifting into, wouldn't this animal's temperature and heart rate register as what would be normal for the species but the human body being monitored. Would it not stay constant?"

YD: *"Stop Little One. Stop analyzing what I am saying as you are writing. Allow the words to flow. Freely...allow...thank you. The shift does require the body to react. The shift does require the human body to change, to adjust, both externally* and internally. The human body is only a tangible three dimensional vehicle. In a shifted or altered dimension the human body is without form. It is the human mind that forms its circles of reality. Remember the spheres overlapping for every sentient beings reality? This is how fragile reality can be. Changing reality such as shifting is initiated by the shifter. This initiation, this desire to shift, will register as the human body reacts, as the genes alter the matter.

Possession also registers the human body's response. But the soul to self contact is not in control. It is an outside source's possession that is in control. Here the outside source manipulates another's body. This may only manifest itself as mental shifting, a trance experience of a shift. To truly possess and physically shift is to trance and access the human's DNA. This is very dangerous and could result in errors and damage. So many possession shifts are holographic projections of actual physical shifts. The human body did not actually change. Yes, the hologram might contain suggestions of precise animal temperatures, pulses and respirations. But few holograms are programmed to precisely mimic a true physical shift.

I sense this sounds confusing and unbelievable. Rest assured that those of us that guide and protect you are here to prevent manipulation of you. To us humans are not puppets, not play things, but a developing society of souls. We of the higher order do not condone or accept the manipulation of humans for sport.

Venture into the shifting realms with caution. Always call and establish working relationships with trusted guides. Work with your guides. Establish communication. This can be through ancient means such as the use of a pendulum, tarot cards or runes. You may refer to books on astrology or react to the nature signs and refer to books such as Animal Speak. Your *guides are watching. They are trying to help you to find your own niche, your own language.*

Once you have comfort in your choice of language, then use it! Help others to find comfort also! Traditional prayer is a wonderful way to communicate. Silent prayer can function as a form of telepathy. Ask. Fill your soul with divine energy. Open yourself up to answers. We will, in turn, speak back.

I realize it is hard to decipher imagination from divination. Both are true sources. For imagination is not but the inner soul's voice. If imagination is fearful or full of other negative images then first seek out the source of this fear, anger, jealousy, negative energy. Treat and nurture your soul's ills. Be true to YOUR soul and YOUR guides. For, with a healed soul you can truly lead a life of light and love.

Being a cynic, self preservation, this is necessary in a physical world. Yet do not allow doubt and fear to guide you to not opening. Challenge your cynicism. Root out its origin. For then you can find peace. Teach others how to achieve peace within. For with a population of contented souls the community prospers and blossoms.

Teach self empowerment but be patient with the differences in all beings. Do not force a human to be a rabbit or a lion. Teach the vehicle for each human to explore and discover their own soul's abilities and peculiarities. Enjoy the human difference. Be patient of the altered paths. For these variations make the whole population pulse as one.

Experiment with communication. Explore with guidance. Expand with the knowledge of love and goodness. Enjoy your day! Namaste."

September 20, 2005: At development class on Monday some of our group wanted to stop our conversation about the victims of the recent hurricane. They wanted to stop the 'negative thoughts' our conversation was precipitating and instead, to send healing, loving energy to the victims, to release the negative and send out the love.

This does sound pleasant but I wonder if this is really helping? Is releasing negative energies another way of running away from the physical problem? A way of patronizing your soul into thinking that it assisted those in need? Would it not be more responsible to allow the negative feelings to turn into problem solving?

YD: *"Sending love is fine, but getting involved and assuming responsibility is more than fine, it is the real godsend. For humans are here to help each other problem solve. Accept and discuss the negative to create a positive outcome.*

Yes, prayer is good. But don't rely on just prayer as a band-aid to life's problems. Be human-you are not in spirit form yet! Physically help each other. Mentally reach conclusions. For only humans can truly interact on your earth plane. Do not just complain. Find an answer. Allow the negative feelings to give you that push into creating.

Yes, problem solving is also vexing. Allow the healing energies to flow and recharge your soul. And yes, send out love and healing energies to those in need. But do not allow your spiritual love energy wipe out the human need to tangibly help.

We need the cynic's creativity and steadfast support of the true optimist's love energy. Interact with each other; support each other, for it's this cooperation between souls that is the ultimate goal. Souls that share, learn, cooperate, meld together to form the sweetest positive energy. An energy that is both tangible and spiritual.

Do not judge too quickly. Do not try to escape your normal human reactions, your normal human feelings for it is this development of self that is the ultimate goal. Use your human

life to develop your spiritual soul. Enjoy the myriad of human experiences, the various human emotions.
     Learn to harness your inner animal. Allow the animal to guide your passion, your creativity. But remember the pureness of your spiritual soul. Use its positive energies to buffer what you cannot easily endure for we do not intend for you to suffer. But to experience, taste the many flavors of life, and to grow and expand, evolve into the magnificence your soul can achieve. Remember-the journey can be as grand as the goal! Namaste."

September 21, 2005: I was just watching the latest news about hurricane Rita which has strengthened from a category one hurricane to a category three overnight. Watching the swirling energies of the hurricane cloud model on the weather channel's computer screen has set my mind to wondering. Does man have the ability to change a developing natural disaster such as a hurricane with only the use of his energy, his intention, his mind? Could combined people use a common mental power to counteract the swirling clouds of the hurricane? Wouldn't this be much more productive than just praying? Visualization! Could a group of people be effective in establishing positive energy which could alter the swirling winds of the hurricane? Could a human force, the combined will of human desire, have the ability to slow down the winds of the hurricane? Can humans use an invisible force to tame the storm force winds?
     YD: *"Take control! Use your magic to help out Mother Earth. Use your magic to help your fellow man avoid destruction, disaster, and de-materialization. Assume the responsibility in assisting the Mother in caring for her children. Open up to the possibilities! They are, like time itself, endless! Namaste"*
     Thank you Yellow Dog for your insight but this latest hurricane has my mind wondering once more. I used to turn the

television on and watch a natural disaster unfold as a form of entertainment. I never thought I could do anything to help the situation. The image of the weather guy blowing in the wind, the destructive force of the storm, nature at her fiercest, this was more entertaining than a horror flick. Homes flying away, waves destroying the shoreline buildings, why was this so interesting to me?

Could this horrible destruction of property and life somehow make me feel better about myself? Was watching my fellow humans suffering making me feel fortunate in my life situation? I am thankful that I live in an area of the country where tornados, hurricanes, earth quakes, floods are rare or non-existent. Could it be that I felt separate from another's dilemma and thus somehow immune to their pain? As I reflect these questions I know I have grown for I no longer feel privileged when I watch these events unfold. Rather, I feel compassion for the victims and want to send them all healing energy. I wonder why people can't simply alter bad weather. Why doesn't positive healing energy change things? Why don't our guides assist and fix things?

I can sense that spirit guides must face the decision of how much to reveal and educate the human population in re-discovering their natural gifts. There are no short cuts. (I sense Yellow Dog's energy as I continue to write...)

YD: *"You cannot receive a college degree in a semester. You need all those years of general studies and back ground training first. You need a foundation of beliefs and trust. Then you can be assisted in fine tuning and awakening your abilities. You need to be sincere, human, and responsible and then further the course of evolution.*

Yes Little One, it is a daunting task which we have initiated many times over the course of your history. Maybe we will succeed. Maybe we will fail. It is not for me to know, nor you.

Try your best, enlighten all you can. Trust that we, as guides, will buffer the power of those with poor intentions. And enjoy the show, the ride, your life! It is a precious opportunity this living.
   Take each day with a new breath. See each morning in a new light. Marvel at the complexity and miracle of your life supporting planet. Marvel at your own human organism and its glorious ability to develop your own soul. Marvel, accept and enjoy. Namaste."

September 22, 2005: Shortly after I had fallen asleep last night, I had a quick vision. I saw water everywhere, flooding. The buildings were old in architectural style so I believe I was in the recently flooded streets of New Orleans. I woke up with this vision in my mind and a sense of confusion. I knew I was feeling the memories of someone who had recently died. Being tired and irritated at waking up because of a "dead person" I grumpily asked Yellow Dog to help send this spirit to the light. With that settled I rolled over and went right back to sleep.
   Then I woke up again, I knew it was too early to get out of bed. When I looked at the clock it was just after 4 AM. Ugh! I felt irritated at being awakened and as I lay in bed staring at the dark ceiling I started to remember my dream state moments before. This is what I recorded in my dream journal:
   I was in a wide plane that had three groupings of seats with two aisles. In my dream I got off this plane because of engine trouble, or the flight had been delayed, or perhaps cancelled, and now I was boarding a different plane. I felt irritated and unorganized over this inconvenience. Then I questioned if I left my purse on the plane I was on before or did I misplace the purse at the terminal? I sensed the frustration over not having my purse and not remembering where I could have left it. I had to board the new plane late and was still feeling frustrated at

not locating my purse. It was with this sense of frustration that I woke up at 4AM.
   Later, when I was having my tea, I put on the morning news. The news lady shared that an Air Bus had to circle for over three hours to make an emergency landing in LA. Then it arrived in New York City this morning, around 6AM. Could I have, somehow, tapped into the acute feelings of a woman that was on that flight in my 4AM dream this morning? Could I have been sharing her experience about misplacing her purse? Curious.

Still September 22nd: I just gave my first, official Angel Reading to a friend this morning. I fumbled through using the cards and felt awkward at referring to the booklet. I was able to piece together a reading that was appropriate for my friend which left her with an appreciation of the cards. My friend was impressed with the positive pictures in my deck of Angel cards and shared that she had previously thought of tarot cards as "evil". When she left my house she was eager to buy and experiment with a deck of her own. This experience helped me to realize how I have overcome much of my own superstitions and fears which is a path of growth that I am eager to share with others. The question is how to share my new beliefs without sparking suspicion, fear or prejudice. For now, Namaste.

September 26, 2005: I just completed a beneficial self healing/crystal meditation. I started off by allowing any negative energy to escape my being by imagining Archangel Michael putting a vacuum hose into my crown chakra and sucking out the negativity. Then, instead of inviting a healing energy into me, I opted to allow a healing color to envelop my body. I envisioned a can of luminescent green paint pouring over my head and covering my whole body. I could see the glowing green color covering every inch of my skin. I wonder if I allow a paint color to cover me every morning if I would be creating a protective barrier thus sheltering me from unwanted negative energy. I know I have been lax at "protecting myself" when I leave the house in the morning. Maybe I could put colorful hair ties to hold my pony tail and envision the color of the day. Perhaps this way I will consciously be aware of setting out a barrier of protection?

Enough about my protective glove of color, I want to record a cool meditation I just experienced. I placed seven crystals on my chakras and held the eighth in my left hand, my wolf crystal in my right. When I tried to meditate with my wolf crystal on Saturday all I saw was the she-wolf puking. I didn't pursue that meditation and opted to fall asleep. I felt confident that I could establish a positive connection with my wolf tonight but when I started this meditation my she-wolf once again felt different, as though she was sick. I drifted in a meditation state and viewed her slinking around and whimpering. Not knowing what else to do, I once again pulled out of the meditation.

I missed my wolf journeys and couldn't let this go on. I questioned what to do and got the inspiration to try a different crystal. Last year I experimented with many crystals and found a little green stone that I associated with a frog. I pulled my frog crystal out of my night stand and held it in my left hand along with my neutral quartz point. Still holding my wolf crystal in my right hand I immediately felt a healing energy starting. I did not journey but I believe I helped my she-wolf guide to feel better. I know that I physically feel happy and stronger after the meditation. I wonder how the frog crystal could have helped. Now that I am typing this into the computer I can sense Yellow Dog is near with wisdom to share about the spirit of the frog crystal:

YD: *"She can live in the water or on the land feeling both the buoyancy of water as well as the grounding gravity of land. She enjoys baking in the sun, sucking up the warm energy rays. Yet she can cool her form when the air blows across her damp body. She is a being of all elements. Her healing energy is that of transformation and adaptation. She can mutate and shift to accept many energies and morph them into a healthy, useful, energy.*

Embrace and learn to use frog energy. She will help with the bombardment you feel amongst many humans, many spirits, and many energies. Her varied abilities can help you to adapt and mutate these energies causing a metamorphosis into pure, white, healing light. For the energy of frog is the energy of true healing.

Wolf, she is strength. She is maternal love. She is the pack, an existence through cooperation. For these reasons wolf cannot cope with negative or incompatible energies. Wolf requires similar energies to her own so she can function as a larger being, function as a pack.

Little frog, she lives alone. She lays her eggs and leaves them alone. She goes through drastic changes over the course of her life. She breathes under water. She later breathes on dry land. She adapts to all. She is wonderful medicine for those who travel too close to the wolf.

The frog can guard and mutate energies. The frog can help your own cells to go through their own metamorphosis. Help your own cells to adapt to a barrage of foreign energies. Spend time with frog. Learn her ways. She will teach you medicine that is very ancient. She travels back to the evolution of the human body.

When humans and frog were on similar paths both were in a warm, pre-historic sea. Both learning of existence yet humans looked for more. By doing so they sacrificed much. Humans sacrificed their ability to adapt to the environment. Human's sacrificed their ability to tolerate change.

Frog is secure in her body. Secure in her changing environment. She has much to teach. She has much to share. She spreads out her green healing energy as slimy esoteric ectoplasm over your human form. Coating you in love and energy and allowing your inner human frog energy to combine with your Angelic soul. Intertwined, mixing and learning how to function into a new being.

This is a metamorphosis into a being that can now walk on an energy diverse land. A change into a being that may be exposed to foreign energies and has the ability to adapt to that which previously could cause harm. Change your worries to courage. Do not have empathy or pity for another's ills. Instead, enlighten others to their own, natural healing abilities.

The wolf, she would isolate herself when faced with adversity. In your over populated world you cannot afford yourself the luxury of isolation. As a frog that is able to exist in a crowded pond you must learn to adapt. The challenges are great but you will learn. Learn, teach others and enjoy the journey! Namaste."

September 28, 2005: After taking my bath I felt compelled to sit down at my computer and write down a request.

Q: "The ability of the human body to support my soul is flawed. I am unable to fully understand the emotions. Unable to fully access and, more importantly, retain memories. I know the answers but am unable to fully explain why. Help me learn how to access these memories. Help me to develop these abilities. Help me to articulate so I can share my findings with others."

YD: *"The different dimensions, the different realms, are indeed difficult to transverse while within a three dimensional* body such as yours. While in dream sleep you may experience a form of astral travel, a form of soul education.

Your soul does retain what it has learned. Your inner being, your psyche, does retain much of this information also. It is when you become aware of your human body. It is when you start functioning within the limitations of your three dimensional cells, your three dimensional human brain, that communication becomes flawed.

We do 'tweak' your human DNA. Fine tune your human body. I know this appears invasive. We only work this way with those who desire to communicate with us. We are not here to invade your privacy, invade your life. We are here to assist you as you live out your human existence.

This is your chosen path. If you chose not to work with us this is fine. If you want to rely on the signs of tarot cards to receive answers and the magic of herbal spells to ask for help, this is fine also. We are here to help. We are not here to 'scare the pants' off of you. If you are not ready to experience clairaudience we understand. You are ready now so we are opening that door...Namaste."

September 30, 2005: I've been using color a lot this past year in my dress. I don't consciously pick out the day's color but rather just know what color I need. I usually rely on pink for a horse show. Turquoise or purple feels right when I go to psychic class. Brown or green feels right if I go to a Wiccan class. I wonder if I subconsciously incorporate colors to protect or enhance my intended experiences for that day.

YD: *"Yes Little One, color is an important tool. Color calls upon certain spirits, certain powers and certain abilities. Our veil on this side can be difficult to penetrate. By using color you help us to better understand how to assist you. Better understand how you are feeling physically or emotionally.*

You can achieve the same effect by wearing jewelry or mixing herbal magic. You have created your own path, started your own form of communication. What started as a fashion statement has developed into a helpful tool for us.

The 'paint can' meditation is just an affirmation, another way of us assisting you in your daily tasks. For it is not our intention to rob you of your earthly experiences. We simply want to assist and protect. We want to make your chosen path of enlightening others easier for you to achieve.

Thank you for understanding this color code. Keep using what you 'feel' you need. For it is your emotions that we understand and need to support the most. Namaste-Yellow Dog & Hidden Deer."

~ CHAPTER 5 ~

HEALING WITH HIDDEN DEER - INTO OCTOBER 2005

September 30, 2005: I have agreed to practice Reiki on a friend today who is also an energy worker and was more than a little nervous about channeling this healing to her. This would be the first person, other than my Reiki teacher, that I have used Reiki energy on that understood energy work. My mind whirled with self doubt as to whether my friend would be judgmental as to my abilities.

Last year I learned that when I send distant healing, I sometimes receive psychic impressions of the person I am working on. I never asked my friend if she would want me to send her distant healing the day before our scheduled appointment. Without her formal approval I hesitated as to whether or not this was proper and decided that my friend's "higher self" would accept or deny the energy. It was with this mindset that I settled into my evening meditation last night. I used the Reiki distance symbol I learned in my Reiki II training and hoped to receive some insight that would prepare me for today. I sensed the energy pulsing through my hands and knew I was with my friend, I knew distant healing was happening, but the only impression I received in my mind's eye was the vision of a black hole. I wondered if my healer friend had some sort of protective bubble around her that could be blocking my energy and preventing me from peering into her aura. I accepted that I wasn't to receive any psychic insight last night and quickly fell to sleep.

This morning I woke up thinking about the promised healing session and instantly regretted having made this appointment. What if nothing happened? What if I sensed something totally different than what my friend would feel during the healing? What if!!!! I opted against my friend's privacy and once again I initiated the distant Reiki with the hope of glimpsing into my friend's aura. This time I did receive impressions:

I saw a rainbow of colors; sparkling, dancing, splashes of colors. My friend was bathed in a beam of bright, Angelic light and appeared further inundated with dancing fairy lights of green, yellow, orange, blue, red and purple, mostly purple. The only thing that was odd was that her legs appeared brown. Then I saw an image of her bare feet in the sand. She was walking in the sand. The sand was bathing her feet, massaging her feet, radiating its retained warmth into her feet. Her feet then turned reptilian, or maybe into bird feet.

What this meant I truly don't know. Before I leave today I am curious if Yellow Dog has any wisdom to share with me about the upcoming healing.

YD: *"Don't be nervous Little One. We are with you, plus many others. Feel their presence, feel their power. Just allow, allow their energy to flow, allow the healing to transpire. You do not need to think, just let us perform. We will do what is best as always... Love & Namaste."*

I was still apprehensive as I drove to my friend's business. Once at her office I waited in the adjoining room trying in vain to busy myself with a magazine. I put the magazine down and allowed my mind to wander, to remember the first time I met my Native American healing guide. I was in a church service when the medium on the podium told me that I had an Indian Maiden willing to work with me as a healer guide. I was surprised because I already had a healer spirit guide, a Druid who I called Red. Later that day a mentor through my church explained that sometimes our energy changes and new guides step in. I was not sure of this change, but stayed open to the idea and meditated that evening. While in this meditation I traveled on a canoe and floated downstream through overhanging trees. The woods were dense and finally the canoe hit land. I got out of the canoe and walked towards a fire barely visible through the dense foliage. As I approached the light I could make out the form of a small woman with long black braids and light colored buckskin clothes, then I'd fall asleep. I fell asleep every time I meditated with the intention of meeting this new guide. I knew that something was happening, that I was learning from her, but I never received any tangible information into my consciousness. Not knowing what else to call this maiden I called her Hidden Deer, because she was like a deer in the woods, barely visible but always there. With time I developed the ability to chant while healing and the energy that came out of my hands seemed stronger and more beneficial to those I worked on. I was startled out of my memories by the voice of my friend; she was through with her last client and ready for me to work on her.

    I peered past my friend into the treatment room where the massage table was already prepared for me to work and like a scared rabbit; I followed her into the room. My friend crawled up onto the table and laid face up with her eyes closed, her face smiling and her body totally relaxed and waiting. I placed my hands above the area of her shoulders and began chanting quietly to myself as Hidden Deer greeted the four elements. My hands would initiate a Reiki symbol then would morph into other movements, an outward sweeping movement repeated three times in each of the four directions; sometimes a circular spiral clockwise, sometimes counter clockwise.

    I asked my friend if she wanted to hear Hidden Deer's language, she did, so I spoke out loud. At first I was self conscious not to get too loud, not to let anyone in the business next door hear the "crazy woman" chanting through the walls. Hidden Deer sensed my need for discretion and her words flowed out low and even. She did not loudly evoke any spirits but opted to calmly chant her blessing with an even, methodic voice.

    I could feel the energy opening into my friend's elbow, then to her right hand. I knew the energy was flowing because I could feel the same sensation through the palm of my hands as I passed them over my friend's body. I closed my eyes; this helped me to concentrate on the feeling through my palms easier. Then I would open my eyes briefly as I moved my hands to another spot lest I accidently poke my friend. In an out of sensations I worked with Hidden Deer. We then worked on my friend's left hand and established an even energy flow there as well. I felt Hidden Deer work the energy through the fourth, third, second and first chakras. I could speak English if I felt any specific peculiarities and share my insight with my friend lying on the table which was handy because when I was working over the heart chakra I saw a mountain lion beneath my closed eyes. I then felt the presence of this mountain lion, it was as though I was the large cat, I experienced a brief shift into a mountain lion then the sensation was gone. I opened my eyes and saw that my hands were over my friend's body and shared the reality I was experiencing. To my surprise my friend readily agreed that a mountain lion was in the massage room with us. I'm not sure why the lion's energy was emanating out of my friend's heart chakra but I was now curious. When I worked over the next chakra I looked for signs of animal energy. I didn't feel any animals at her sacral chakra but I definitely felt snakes at her root.

    It took awhile to establish a consistent energy flow over my friend's left leg and my hands stayed still above her right leg even longer. As I worked and my hands moved I could hear

Hidden Deer mumble and chant. I could also sense Hidden Deer's thoughts such as: "We need to work on this a little longer." Or "The energy flow is not right yet." Hidden Deer then asked me to tell my friend that there were deer mice present that are going to carry energy out of my friend's feet. I could see the little rodents behind my closed eyes and feel them around my feet. I felt safe but a little freaked out by the sensation. Then Hidden Deer wanted me to ask my friend if it was ok with her to leave some mice in this treatment room so these mice could finish moving the negative energies out of the soles of her feet after our healing session ended. My friend agreed. Time was getting late and my friend felt the need to flip onto her stomach.

As she was positioning herself on her belly on top of the massage table, I had time to think about the healing session I had channeled thus far. My friend was experiencing the same sensations and impressions that I was. And Hidden Deer's voice was coming through so clearly one moment and the next I could easily switch to English…this was pretty cool! I felt as though I was participating in a conscious meditation or journey. I noticed that my friend was settled comfortably on her stomach and knew that it was time to get back to work. I placed my hands above my friend's prone body and allowed Hidden Deer to resume her healing.

Little energy work was required on the upper chakras because my friend's crown, third eye and throat were sufficiently open. My hands stopped over the heart chakra, Hidden Deer chanted, then I immediately felt the back of my friend's heart chakra open and a plethora of many different species of animals flew into my friend through this open chakra. While the animal energies entered my friend my right hand stayed quiet above her crown chakra. I felt a strong angelic energy flowing freely through my friend's crown as the animals entered her heart. Energy seemed to be exchanging through my hands between my friend's crown and heart chakras as well. Hidden Deer then chanted over my friend's solar plexus, sacral and root chakras which burst open to allow for another invasion of flying animal energies. I then worked on both knees at once, one hand over each knee. Hidden Deer chanted and my hands began moving, they swept the energy down to my friend's feet.

I walked to the foot of the table and stood at my friend's feet, closed my eyes and chanted Hidden Deer's words. Behind my closed eyes I saw animal feet emerged from my friend's soles. My eyes flew open as I thought how weird this was then I regained my composure and allowed the healing to continue. I stood there, my hands positioned above the soles of my friend's feet and watched as the animal feet came out. Hooves, paws and bird feet, the energy flew out while Hidden Deer chanted in my mind and out of my mouth. The energy became less and I channeled Hidden Deer's prayers as my hands moved in a sweeping motion over my friend's body. I then felt the energy subside and knew that Hidden Deer was done. The healing was finished.

My friend and I talked as she lay on the table, absorbing the last remnants of sensations. As we were sharing perspectives I noticed that I felt slightly "stoned" and a little shaky. My friend noticed my unsteadiness and shared that this was normal and that I would soon feel more "grounded." We left the treatment room and my friend shared a new healing technique with me that she learned at a recent workshop where she places her feet on the client and gently moves their body. I wonder if this was why Hidden Deer spent so much time on my friend's feet. Could Hidden Deer have opened up the energies to work out of my friend's feet to better aid my friend in implementing her new healing technique? Yellow Dog, do you have any wisdom to share regarding my friend's healing?

YD: *"Hello Little One. The healing was very beneficial, very good. Your friend works well within her upper body and calls upon the angels with ease. We believe she could benefit if the animals, if the earth energies, can channel through her with as much ease. Hidden Deer performed an ancient ceremony, a ceremony of the animal dancers. She called upon those that were, the animals of our core, and the animals of our inner existence. She called upon them to recognize your friend. She called upon them to enter your friend. She called upon them to become familiar with your friend. And it is Hidden Deer's hope that these Animal Spirits, those that have met your friend, will channel through her when needed.*

Your friend does much good with her clients. She helps many to heal. She helps many to understand. It is our hope that the animals that have flowed so freely through your friend's heart can now utilize all of her chakras. It is our hope that the energies of Mother Earth can balance your friend and her clients; balance the yin and the yang, balance the male and the female, balance Heaven and Earth, Father and Mother.

You have felt these energies, called upon them naturally for you have chosen to walk with the animals. It is now time for your friend to also walk with the Animals. She is wise. She will use this new found energy ability with wisdom. She will share this new strength with others. This is a good and necessary step.

Go, enlighten others of their abilities. Enlighten others of the abilities of the Angels as well as the earth and her animals. Enjoy your new path. Thank-you for accepting these possibilities. Namaste."

October 2, 2005: After service today I was approached by the lady who had channeled healing to me. She shared that while the energy was coursing out of her hands she experienced a very beautiful, very royal, feeling. She saw, in her inner eye, a white light around me. I was dressed in a white flowing robe, wearing a crown, and as I was being healed all these white doves were entering my aura. This woman shared that the whole healing was very peaceful and although she admits not being sure of the symbolism of this experience she felt that I must be from royal descent. I was not sure what to make of the images this woman was sharing with me and felt unsure how to react to the possibility that someone would think that I could be, somehow, from royalty. But I did enjoy the energy of today's healing. As I am typing this into the computer I am trying to resist asking but I have to know... Yellow Dog, any insight as to the healing I received at church today?

YD: *"Hello Little One. The Goddess energy was around you, streaming from the Heaven above. They are eager to mix with your natural ability to ground with the earth. They are mixing the two, the Heaven and Earth. This is through a beautiful feminine Roman type ritual. A ritual of the doves, a ritual of Paramedeus, Parametheus, (I struggle with the spelling of this name) the Goddess of flight, the Goddess of love and beauty.*

You were dressed as you did in the past, so many eons ago; dressed for the ritual of fusion and dressed for the mixture of energies. Your energy like the dove; from earth yet of sky, an animal of earth, of flesh and blood, but as light as a feather, as white as purity, god like in its movements, abilities, clean clear whiteness.

Keep learning. Learn of the forces available to you. Learn of the diversity that can exist; the diversity of believing in more than one possibility, the goodness of the heavenly, loving energy, the reality of the inner animal, the earth, the life sustaining force of the mother. For your peoples, all people vary greatly in their abilities and beliefs. They vary greatly in the energies that their bodies can accept. For where some rely on love, others need the tangibility of the earth. Keep learning and share you discoveries. Love and Namaste, Yellow Dog."

Before I forget I want to record that I saw a brief glimpse of a spirit this morning. I put the dogs out and was using the upstairs toilet. As I was leaving the bathroom I heard a noise that sounded like a kid bounding up the stairs, a few stairs at a time. I looked towards the noise and saw a brief form of a male, in a white t-shirt? Thinking the form was my son I wondered why he was up so early. But when I went to his bedroom to check on him I found he was lying in his bed, asleep. This was when I realized I saw spirit. I smiled as I walked back to my own bedroom to share my experience with my husband. As I recanted the experience with Greg I realized that I wasn't afraid and that seeing spirit elicited an emotion of curiosity rather than fear…Cool!

Later this morning I went to my development class and shared my experience about seeing the form of a young man upstairs with a friend who asked why I didn't question the spirit and ask what he wanted. I never thought about interacting with the spirit. I was so surprised to surmise that I actually saw spirit that it never occurred to me to talk to him!

Still October 3rd: I finished reading Rosalyn Greene's book *The Magic of Shapeshifting* last week which offered a unique perspective into the world of shifting and shifters. Greene's ultimate goal was the physical shift, the ability to transform your human body into that of a specific species of animal. Her book outlined the history and lore associated with "were beasts" citing the legendary werewolf as the most commonly understood account of a physical shift. Greene teased my mind by proposing that, possibly, a person could shift into more than just one species, more than just a wolf, a process she called poly-shifting. All of this makes sense because I have delved into these sensations through my past meditations where I have journeyed with a wolf, or a frog, or a horse. But then I started to read about how obsessive some people can become about shifting.

Greene shared information about "furries", a subculture of people who transformed themselves within the confines of a costume to create the illusion of being an animal. On page 225 Greene explains that many furries "feel that they have been 'mis-incarnated.' They feel that they are animals trapped in human bodies. The furry movement has many similarities with transgenderism, except that it relates to species instead of gender identity." I personally accept meditating in the confines of my bedroom to see if I can change my physical form into a wolf. But the idea of me getting on my hands and knees while dressing and acting like a wolf seems, well, strange. I enjoyed reading *The Magic of Shapeshifting* yet I needed another author's viewpoint about shapeshifting.

I found some answers in Yasmine Galenorn's book, *Totem Magic,* which approached the more spiritual aspect of shifting. Not only did Galernorn explain how to search for your animal totem but her book also shared a belief that different species of animals can be within a person which Galernorn called her totem. A third author, Ted Andrews, wrote in his book *Animal Speak,* about a belief that each of the seven major chakras harbors a different animal energy. Andrews throws in an eighth animal at the foot chakra as well. Three authors, three experts, three different viewpoints, I am confused and wonder exactly how many animal totems do I possess? What is the difference between an "Animal Spirit Guide", a "Power Animal" and an "Animal Totem"? Yellow Dog, can you please explain?

"Animal Guides are similar to spirit guides. They exist separate from you. They choose to visit with you and inspire or educate you. They are the essence of multiple-animal

intelligence. They are the combined forces of evolved animal spirits, combined into an enlightened soul.

The human soul can resonate singly from other humans. Yet the human soul does rely on other animal souls to exist. The animal souls 'take a back seat' and agree to watch, exist, learn from the human soul within the human body. Then the animal soul may combine with another animal soul or two to become an Animal Guide. Or an animal soul may choose to evolve into a human form.

The human needs the animal souls for they are closer to Mother Earth. The animal souls function within the five senses. The animal souls allow the human body to exist on the earth plane. For the soul of the human is not of this earth. The human soul is a transplant, an experiment, a way of growing, cultivating, maturing souls.

When the human species is mature it may choose to lose its grip on the three dimensional plane. At this time it will no longer need the Animal Totems to exist. Humans will not even need their three dimensional body to exist. For at this time humans will exist as pure energy. The human species has the ability to evolve past its cellular restraints. But while in cellular form, while in a form bound to mother earth, the human species is intertwined with all of earth's creatures.

I am not sure of the expression 'Power Animal'. I assume it is either the Animal Guide or the Animal Totem. I know not of a third way in which the animal spirit can function without its animal body."

"Thank you Yellow Dog. I don't really understand you but I appreciate the wisdom. Namaste."

October 4, 2005: I described the animal healing I channeled to my friend last week to a "development class" friend today. After class we agreed to experiment and see if I could sense animals in her chakras like I did during the healing of September 30th. My friend lay on her back on the elevated church stage in the front of our deserted church and I stood on the lower level, enjoying the convenience of this makeshift treatment table. I felt compelled to start working over her heart. I barely traced the Reiki symbols when Hidden Deer's energy eagerly started to flow. I allowed Hidden Deer to chant and talk through me.

I felt many animals stream into my friend's heart, solar plexus, and sacral chakras. I sensed some blocked energy at my friend's root chakra and heard Hidden Deer chant as my body gestured to free up the energy. Then I sensed a swoosh, a change in the intensity of the energy and knew that there was a release. Through my hands I could feel the energy flow down the legs, past the knees, to the feet and out the soles.

I walked to my friend's feet and this was where I sensed a difference from the other woman I channeled the healing to on the 30th. On the 30th I sensed forest creatures and today I saw water creatures around my friend with webbed feet emerging out of the souls of her feet. After working on the feet I found myself gesturing above my friend's body. My fingers were moving and I knew a gentle shower of rain energy was being sprinkled onto my friend. Hidden Deer gestured, chanted, commented and I sensed that the rain turned to a cooling light snow. I watched in my mind's eye as the snow covered my friend's body and encrusted her into a safe cocoon. Then I sensed that Hidden Deer was closing the healing. I felt my hands performing a few more sweeping gestures coupled with prayers of good wishes and then the healing was finished.

My friend got up slowly, smiling. I asked her if she was comfortable with the water energies to which she replied that she was. This healing was similar to my other friend's healing, but different. As I am typing this into my computer and reflecting upon today's healing I find myself intrigued at Hidden Deer's ability to speak through me, gesture through me and heal through me. My development class friend commented on how peaceful Hidden Deer's words were and how soothing her energies were. She told me that she thought I was using 'trance channeling' when I performed the healing. I thought that trance required the person channeling to be asleep and that spirit would take over the body. I am only in a partial trance, for I am fully aware of Hidden Deer. I am aware that she is speaking and gesturing through me and I am even starting to understand the meaning of her methods. I am definitely channeling Hidden Deer's healing energies. This I can feel through my hands.

The friend I did the healing on Sept. 30th called Hidden Deer's healing/channeling a form of Animal Medicine and felt Hidden Deer was using Shamanic energies through me. Hidden Deer was calling upon the animal energies through my hands. But on my development class friend today I definitely felt a different energy, a water-energy, not just earth and animal energy. I don't quite understand how to define Hidden Deer's ability to move energy, her ability to heal through my hands. Do you have any suggestions Yellow Dog?

YD: *"Good evening Little One...Hidden Deer is a great priestess, a solitary shaman that has achieved great skills in harnessing the energies of the earth as well as the universe. She is eager to help. She is eager to enlighten. Feel blessed that she has chosen you to use as a vessel. Her intents are pure, her powers great. What to call her abilities in your modern day culture? This is a good question.*

I would not confuse or scare potential clients with complex names or titles. Just label your abilities as psychic healing. Explain to clients your ability to chant and channel. Allow the client to decide if he/she would be comfortable with hearing Hidden Deer. If they are not comfortable, then quietly chant to yourself. Use your discretion. You have the intelligence and the abilities to decide. Namaste & good night."

October 5, 2005: I awoke around 4:30 AM because the dachshund was whining. Begrudgingly I took her downstairs and let her out then returned to bed. I started to experience vivid, obtuse dreams after I fell back asleep. Memories of a past horse show or was I receiving visions of a horse show yet to be experienced? In and out of dream state and consciousness I floated. Tired and sensing that I wasn't destined to fall into a deep sleep I rolled over to peak at my clock which revealed a time of 5:28AM. It was too early to get out of bed to start my day so I grabbed my two large healing crystals from my night stand with the intention of giving myself a self healing.

I asked for any negative energies trapped in my body to leave. I visualized a golden sword cutting any energetic chords that may be in my aura, tapping into me and draining my energy. I then asked for the positive energy to enter my body and fill me with health plus shield me from any negative energies that I may come across today. I sensed being covered in two different colors; first a green was poured over me, then a metallic gold. I was told that the gold layer's purpose was to deter any golden energy sucking chords from attaching to me.

As I progressed through the stages of my healing I sensed my sinuses pulsing and an energy shifting in my head. My awareness was no longer within this meditation for I was actually feeling physical sensations of something touching me. I've experienced this sensation before and I knew that an unseen entity, a spirit was performing either a healing or a psychic adjustment to my third eye chakra. I started to experience a bliss-like state; floating, happy and free of pain. Inside my closed eyelids I saw an eye. I recognized it as the eye of a cat…with a red reflection…I drifted into another dream…

...I am at a church type meeting where a group of people are discussing matters. I disagree with a man's opinions and purposely get up from my chair to choose a chair next to him. I must have been offended by whatever he said or implied for I confront him in front of the group. I challenge this man to express his opinion directly to me. I can feel the man's nervousness and I know that I am right. As I verbally berate this poor man I can sense the power in me. Then I notice the reaction of those in the meeting and try to calm the cat within me. It has been a long time since I've had an emotional outburst in a social setting. I am surprised and embarrassed that this cat anger has slipped out during the meeting. The church or group leader pulls me aside to discuss my inappropriate behavior.

I wake up out of this meditation/dream with a sense of embarrassment over not being able to control my anger. But this was only a meditation, a dream state that allowed the emotion to surface. I noticed that I was still holding my crystals. It was still early so I replaced my crystals to their spot on the night stand, rolled over and returned to sleep.

(As I am editing my manuscript the date is December 15, 2008 and I am fascinated by the synchronicity of this "dream" and an actual event I lived through in March of 2008. I am now the President of my church and there was a major disagreement amongst some of the members. I had called a meeting and sensed similar feelings as those described in the aforementioned dream. But I was wiser and able to control, or dissipate, the feeling of unjustness that surfaced. In my present reality the conflict was resolved without any arguing. I wonder if spirit was somehow coaching my emotions through a dream state practice of an event that would happen more than two years in the future.)

Back to 2005...I am still in bed after the dream of conflict and once again I started to dream: *I'm talking to a different friend that I rarely see because she lives out of state from me. She is explaining how she is sad and frustrated. She feels she has little in common with her spouse and is complaining about her desire to change their retirement situation. I am listening intently because this friend seldom confides in me. I was interested in helping her with her dilemma and was listening to her words as she explained her situation. I could hear her voice so clearly.*

Then I wake up. I wake up to actually hearing my friend's voice in my ear in my right ear! The dream stopped but her words continued for a second or two more. I actually heard her speaking in my right ear! Weird!

I understand that spirit has been "tweaking" my ability to hear in the metaphysical realm, fine tuning my ability to be clairaudient. And this morning I heard words and was able to recognize my friend's voice as clear as if she was sitting next to me speaking. I am pleased and excited to become more clairaudient because I fear that some of my Yellow Dog discussions may be my own opinion, my own imagination writing the words. If I could hear spirit this may be a more definite line between what is imagined and what is spirit.

Yesterday afternoon, after psychic development class, I allowed a friend to do a "magnified healing" on me. I didn't feel my friend would do harm nor did I believe that I would be healed. I allowed him to perform the brief ritual and didn't sense any tangible changes. I wonder if yesterday's magnified healing could have been the reason for my sensations this morning.

YD: *"Good morning Little One. I was wondering when you would ask for my assistance through your contemplations....Yes the magnified healing did help adjust your hearing abilities, as did the meditation during Tuesday's yoga class. You are on your way Little One. We are pleased that you are progressing so rapidly. We are pleased that you have learned not to fear the unknown. You have a natural tendency to mistrust. You have a natural tendency to defend. We are pleased that you are willing to be "tweaked" so you may better understand us.*

We understand how difficult it is to overcome your inner animal. We respect and honor the beings that make you...you! We respect and honor the soul of your soul. We respect and honor the life on earth you have forged. We do not want to interfere with your human life.

We have a need to be heard. We honor you for allowing the adjustments necessary to your body; adjustments that free your body from the third dimension. Adjustments that allow you to hear what your human DNA previously did not allow you to hear. Remember to consult us if you feel confused by this new ability. We do not intend on making your life uncomfortable.

We are eager to work through you. We are eager to work with you. We, however, do not want to rob you of a comfort level you need in order to exist. Communicate with us if we cause you pain. Communicate with us if you are having a hard time differentiating between realities. We are here to help you as much as you are here to help us. Together we can accomplish much good."

Q: "Thanks Yellow Dog. Can you please answer one shamanic question for me? Yasmine Galenorn in her book *Totem Magic* described an Elk Spirit which she considered a protector Animal Spirit. Galenorn shared through her book that she leaves out a basket of apples for the Elk in her home and even replaces the apples when "they get mushy." The author explained that no human or animal on our plane of existence were allowed to disturb this basket because the apples were intended for the Elk to consume in his dimension. I have a hard time understanding this. If the apples are "getting mushy" in our dimension wouldn't they be spoiling where the Elk exists as well?"

YD: *"A good point Little One. Many items, objects, even creature and beings, cross exist. To a human you function in your own three dimensional world. To an elk spirit he exists on a different plane, a different dimension. The elk eats and exists in his plane just like a three dimensional elk exists in your reality.*

The apples you offer have energy. Positive intent or the offering of love is imbued within this basket of apples. Whenever the apples are exchanged the human is recharging the basket with positive intent. The author is infusing the basket with love and respect for the elk. It is this that the elk feeds on; the symbol of the perishable apples, the act of replacing the offering and the constant reminder to acknowledge and send positive energies to the elk. This is the true purpose of the apples.

I know you are asking this in reference to your Brownie friend Ickaba. Do not feel the need to leave him butter or similar offerings. Journey, meditate, and in this state give him the treat. While meditating, acknowledge and send appreciation or love to all of those entities you wish to remain in contact with.

If you need an idol, if you need a tangible symbol to acknowledge spirit, then do so. If you look at a crystal, name the crystal, use the crystal with the intent of meeting and journeying with a spirit animal, then do so. This is a method that seems to work for you.

We do not set the rules. It is you humans that get all caught up in herbs, spells, candles and magic. We need to understand. We are patient. We will learn a pattern of intent through pagan rituals. But we believe you humans can evolve psychically. We believe humans can learn to cross the veil of realities. We

believe that you humans can adjust your human bodies and enable yourself to tap into your own senses for communicating with us. This is our goal with you.
  We are honored that you go the extra yard to understand and learn. But it is our hope that you will develop your mediumship to the point where you will understand our intent and we yours so do whatever you feel compelled and comfortable performing. As long as you keep your intent pure of heart we will learn to understand your meanings. Namaste."

October 8, 2005: I had a neat meditation this morning. I started out using my two big crystals, but my chakras felt stagnant. I put away my two large crystals and switched to using my quartz crystal points along with the wolf crystal. My little quartz points helped me to achieve an upper body flow of energy that was very pleasant. Then I started to journey:
  I felt my she-wolf guide. I too was a wolf. I greeted her and we stepped into a tunnel of underbrush. We moved quickly, purposefully. We briefly went into a big, open, green field. Then she guided me into the Petrified Forest.
  This place was a desolate, colorless place. No vegetation, just old bones of trees that once were. The landscape reminded me of the post apocalyptic scenes I've seen in science fiction movies. The earth belched smoke out of would be ponds. There was ash on the ground, on the dead vegetation, in the air. The place felt cold even though smoke was visible, thus implying warmth. I don't like this place. I followed a boar in a journey to this place once before. Now wolf beckoned me to follow.
  We traveled to a small pool of water where I saw a few thin, mangy looking antelope. Then I noticed a thin, raggedy haired, dark colored horse. Instantly I knew that this horse was very wise and prophetic. I then sensed myself changing. I began

traveling to a place where I was no longer with the wolf and I was flying, looking down on a horse show arena.

I recognized this place, a Fairground that I show through. I saw the activity of a horse show in progress and then noticed my daughter in a class riding my mare Ginger. My daughter hasn't loped Ginger during a horse show during my time yet but in this journey/dream she was loping the mare. The pair looked good! My daughter was wearing a teal and pink outfit. I strained my sight to try and locate myself in this setting and noticed that I was wearing the colors of lime green and pink. I was riding a palomino horse, a horse that I've never seen before...

...I heard household noises and was jostled out of the meditation. Damn! I stilled myself in an effort to return to the meditation, to return to the scene at the horse show. But I couldn't attain that blissful state. Regretfully I accepted that it was time for me to finish and that the old horse at the pool had shown me what I was intended to see. I pulled back to my body, thanked the wolf and woke up and started my day. Now that I am typing this into the computer I am curious as to the significance of this journey. "Yellow Dog, am I seeing prophecy?"

"Hello Little One...Yes, the old horse, the wise one of the ancients, has chosen you to be enlightened. The ancient horse has chosen you to learn and share the secrets of the ancients. The ancient horse has seen much; much suffering, much misery, and much unnecessary waste.

Do not repeat the devastation of this world. Learn the wisdom from the ancients. Learn so you are not destined to repeat the suffering. Draw upon the talents of the ancient ones. The wolf will help you. Experiment, taste and learn what is available.

We, too, will learn what it is that you are able to understand, what you are able to access. The place of the ancients is devastated. Their world has been used up. Enjoy your world. Enjoy its lushness. Enjoy its ability to harbor and nurture life. For life is a gift. Balance of life is a delicate dance.

Earth took many beings much time to create. Earth has many, many layers of existence. By traveling into an altered state and by traveling into another layer, another layer of dimension and time, you may access what is to be, what can be.

Those that exist in the Petrified Forest, those that have lived long, long ago and those that have lived so long ago that their world is all used up. They know how to travel. They know how to travel to the lushness of other worlds. They know how to transcend time and dimensions.

The old horse understands your noble cause. The old horse wants to assist you in achieving enlightenment. The old horse wants to help you enlighten others. Turn to the horse if you feel the need. The respect is there. The introductions have been made.

Your future is what you choose it to be. The scene you saw is very likely to come true. Think of the wish embedded in your heart. Stay on the path of your inner desire. You will achieve the happiness that you seek. Goodnight and Namaste!"

October 10, 2005: I did a really dumb thing while feeding the horses this morning. I had just put hay in the stalls and stooped under the closed upper stall Dutch door when BAM. I was sitting on the stall floor. I didn't stoop low enough! My head wasn't bleeding and no bruise or lump swelled on top of my head but my neck was killing me! When I got back into the house I began filling the bath with hot water seasoned with bath salts. I disrobed and settled into the filling waters with the intention of allowing a healing energy to fill my throbbing neck.

The hot water felt wonderful around my back as I lay back against the cool porcelain side wall of my claw foot tub. I closed my eyes and sensed a peacefulness, a buzzing of energy and I knew that Hidden Deer was near. My lips chanted softly as Hidden Deer greeted the elements in front of my heart chakra, my hands danced in elliptical sweeping movements not unlike a Hawaiian folk dancer. I followed the dance in my mind, imagining my hands gesturing gently across my mid-back, the back of my heart chakra. Lazily, I relaxed in the tub of hot water and drew movements in the air by my neck, my right and left shoulder and the top of my head. I felt high, enveloped in the warm bath waters and the growing energy field forming around me, through me and in me. The bath was adequately filled so I turned off the water. Since the children had the day off from school I didn't feel comfortable voicing my chant without the droning of the water faucet. I saw my rose quartz healing-wand sitting on the window sill and decided to give myself a distant Reiki treatment.

I've used this wand before when sending friend's distant healing. I'd hold the wand between my hands, picture the Reiki symbols in my mind and allow my mind to wander with the energy I sensed pulsing through my palms. Sometimes I would receive images, sometimes I felt like I was out of body, actually floating in the room where the person I was sending the distant healing was located in. I wondered if I could see my own healing. With nothing better to do I decided to experiment while enjoying this morning's bath.

At first I had a hard time floating to the ceiling and viewing myself. I only saw brief glances. I saw a form kneeling or squatting in the bath water next to me which must have been Hidden Deer. I was surprised at how she looked, a human form with angel like wings coming out of her back. Flying around Hidden Deer and I were several worried little one inch fairies. I could hear their little voices exclaiming "oh" and sighing "oh no" as they busily worked outside my heart and throat chakras. I saw myself as a rainbow of swirling colors with the exception of a hole of colorlessness where the little fairies were busily working by my neck. I also sensed Yellow Dog outside the bath tub with other beings. My bathroom was filled with company…Weird!

I longed to receive more glimpses into this alternate reality but the healing energy that was working on my body also clouded my mind. Eventually the healing energy faded and I knew it was time to get out of the tub. While getting dressed I felt my arm adjust and smiled as I knew my body was recovering. My mind wandered into the upcoming day and I wondered how I was going to accomplish the chores I had planned on doing. As I was brushing my hair I silently made affirmations as to how I would proceed today:

"I will honor my body and busy myself with light work, such as typing into the computer. I will honor my body and not lift anything too heavy today. I will honor my body and find time to meditate and self heal today. I will not allow anger over this accident or fear that I have hurt myself with this bang of my head to overcome me. I will allow the loving healing energies to help me. I will fight off my instinctual urge to use aggression."

As I listened to these affirmations, these thoughts in mind, I knew that these weren't my true feelings and I started to wonder. Could I learn to remain open to only *loving* energies? Could I learn to retard the natural animal instincts within me such as my impulse to swear in anger that I might have messed up my back? Could I harness my anxiety that this injury could escalate and my health would, once again, fail? Are the emotions of fear, anxiety, and anger natural negative energies a way of my physical body to call for help? Could any of the lower, animal-like, negative energies be beneficial to me and my existence?

I have spoken to people that believe all negative energies are bad and that man should only feel love. They believe if all men felt only love then the whole world would only feel love. Then the whole world would exist in peace. This reasoning sounds so idyllic, but is this a rational, realistic goal? To not protect myself, to not fear, hate, feel anger, jealousy, or related emotions. To blind myself to the existence of negative emotions, would this ultimately open me up to destruction by other less enlightened humans? Would I be turning myself into a doe exposing her neck to any predator that feels hungry? If our natural animal instincts to survive were suppressed could the human race survive? Or would all of humanity be plummeted into the evil created by a few power hungry, negative energy feeding, humans? I wonder if Yellow Dog could have any opinions regarding the necessity of negative energies.

"Yellow Dog, are the Angels being unrealistic in their efforts to de-animalize the human mind? Are the Angels 'setting up' those humans that have faith for destruction? Are the Angels exposing the neck of those believers who follow and live only in love?"

I just stopped typing to make a cup of green tea. Often the tea bag holds the answer to my question. This tea bag read *"Be proud of who you are."* Not receiving clarification from my tea bag wisdom my mind reeled with possibilities.

"Yellow Dog, are you saying that my path; the path of reason and the path of speculation. That by traveling this path, I will be a guardian for those who do not choose to be exposed to negative energies and will be responsible to assist those who choose to live their lives only in the light of love? If this is the path of my destiny I naturally recoil. I recoil at the thought of being responsible for those who wish to remain blind. I recoil to the thought of fighting battles that others refuse to accept. I recoil at the thought of having to decide what is right or what is wrong. I do not want this responsibility."

YD: *"Little One accept, accept the diversity of others. This is the marvelous feature of the human race. For where one has the ability to live only in love, where this love-filled individual can assist many to find peace and happiness, there are many others who are like you, others whose natural ability is to live in the reality of all emotions.*

You will balance out those who live in the love. You are in the middle for there are humans who choose to live only with negative energies. There are those humans who choose to live without love. Is this wrong? No. For this is their choice.

Do not see the world only from your eyes. The world is full of a complex balance of energies. Just like the human body needs different cells to perform different functions, so the world needs different energies to fulfill different opportunities for the evolvement of souls.

Do not be overly critical of someone who has the loving innocence of the doe. They have chosen this path. This is their destiny. They would not be happy accepting the tiger, just as you would not be happy living with the doe.

You humans are varied. Your destinies are varied. Seek out harmony and happiness for your own life. Live your life with happiness and with a purpose while causing no harm to others. This is the ultimate task at hand.

For the divine to direct such a diverse species, for the divine to give instructions, and for the divine to outline a spiritual path, this is an impossibility. For a path that might be suitable for you; a path that would coincide with a human that is comfortable with the spirit of tiger, horse, peacock and dove.

This path, this guidance from the divine, would be entirely different than the path chosen for another human.
   Teach. Teach others about their inner animals. Draw up a model that many can understand. You understand that not all humans can easily experience your world. Accept that only a percentage of humans are willing to walk your path. Only a percentage of humans can heal as you have healed. Only a percentage of humans have the abilities of the tiger. Recognize that this small percentage will benefit 1000 fold by your channeled wisdom. For if you help just a handful, or even one person, to overcome depression. If you enlighten one person as to the abilities locked within them. Then you are a success as a teacher.
   Try to stop categorizing. Finish developing your techniques. Expose your Reiki abilities to others. Teach about the other side. You can modify what you have learned. You can tweak your techniques slightly to accommodate others. But your abilities will not be accepted to all. Your abilities are not meant for all to experience. Those that need the healing will come. Those that need the enlightening will listen. Travel your path with honor and pride, for this is your destiny. Namaste."
   Q: "One more question please. About me channeling Reiki...Can I safely work on people in my home?"
   YD: "*You don't want me to answer.* (I can feel myself listening. I want to know the answer before I type it. I realize what I am doing. Let go, let go...I can feel Yellow Dog's energy again.) *The home is not the ideal place to practice shamanism. You may release spirit into your home. You may infect your home. It is best to travel to another's place. If you must use your home then set up a triad of stones and allow Hidden Deer to smudge the area afterward. Do not worry. You will not harm yourself or your family. You will learn. You will experience.*

You will enlighten. We are ready to assist. We are eager to enjoy this drama that will unfold."

Thank you Yellow Dog and Namaste... *"Namaste"*

~ CHAPTER 6 ~

DIGESTING THE POSSIBILITY - LATE OCTOBER 2005

October 13, 2005: I have been trying to get to the metaphysical shop a few towns over and every time I seem to have the opportunity, parameters change and I am unable to free up the time. This afternoon, finally, I drove there. I wanted to purchase the new Wiccan calendar for next year that lists the Pagan holidays, the moon phases and the color of the day. I thought it would be interesting to see if my personal experiences coincide to what the calendar had calculated as relevant. The shop owner told me; "The calendars were late in arriving this year. I had just put them out this morning." Was this synchronicity or what!

I feel more at ease at this shop and its patrons of practicing witches. I feel that the witches I bump into while at this store also accept me. I enjoy the store owner's vast knowledge and while I was there today, I bought three more books. One was a large paperback book called *Faeries* by Brian Froud and Alan Lee. I am excited about learning from these new books and understanding other's viewpoints. I have many things to do today around my home...for now...Namaste.

October 16, 2005: Was reading my new *Faeries* book about the lore involving fairy islands and how people that traveled there could not return to our plane of existence. What intrigued me about these stories was the description of islands that disappeared and reappeared out of the sea and a land that was only visible from under the sea. These beliefs actually made sense to me if using the model of multi-dimensional thinking. If the realm of the fairies was an altered dimension and if this dimension becomes visible to our human eye when light was refracted and light was refracted through water, whether it was water in the air, such as in rain droplets (when rainbows are visible), or the water of the sea, then could a fairy realm under the sea be visible to the human eye? Could the human eye be seeing, through refraction, a different dimension of reality?

    YD: *"Traveling into and staying in an altered state and living amongst the faerie in the faerie realm. This can be detrimental to the human body. The human DNA cannot withstand the altering. The faerie realm's time is different than yours. What appears as days to us in the faerie realm is actually years in your three dimensional world.*

    Crossing realms without magic can be harmful to the body. We should not experiment with bodily dimensional travel. Better to allow the consciousness to travel. Better to allow, explore alternate realms without the human body. Better to journey with the mind or learn to shapeshift into a body adaptable to the alternate realms. The physics of these realities are complex. There is truth to the lore."

    Interesting insight Yellow Dog! Thank you and Namaste.

October 17, 2005: I woke up with the need to write in my dream journal: *"The number seven, if you should reach this number during a meditation or in a dream state you will experience pure bliss. Some think of the symbol as the hangman's stand. But it is actually the holder of life, the support of the life force, the symbol of the soul.*

    Feel at ease when you see this symbol. Run to it, stay with it. For it is indeed lucky. It will provide protection. It is a buoy, a beacon of safety while you are immersed in a dimension of uncertainty. Use this symbol as a friend. Find it and wait. For we will find you and help you return to the dimension for which you have originated.

The child's game of drawing the hanging man. This evolved from the use of the symbol. It developed from man's fear of not being seen by us. It developed from man's fear of being 'stuck' in a separate realm or dimension. It developed from man's emotion of waiting, of hanging around or hanging there while waiting for us to arrive.

Do not fear that we will not assist. Allow the thought processes to flow and we will understand. Communicate and we will always come to your aid. We are eager to enlighten others. Please instill a commitment of cooperation in yourself too for together we will accomplish great things. Together we will unravel many mysteries. Together we will open the doors to other realms, other worlds, other possibilities.

Thank you for opening your door, your consciousness, to us. Make us part of your daily ritual and we will teach you. Little by little we will feed you information, information about crossing the realms. Listen, Learn and Enjoy!"

I then drew a picture of three smiling faces, each with a headband and a single feather. I am not sure the true meaning of this channel, but it was interesting. Thanks & Namaste.

October 19, 2005: Yesterday I went to see a third friend who agreed to let me practice my trance/channeling Reiki on him. I'm still unsure what to call my work with Hidden Deer and was a little anxious and nervous about working on my friend. What if Hidden Deer's energy didn't channel through me? My nervous energy was put to ease when I arrived at my friend's place for we sat and talked first. Not only did this allow my mind to delve into my friend's stories but I was able to relax. He shared with me his recent vacation with friends, a sort of UFO search. Ever since he has returned home he has felt "off", which could be a sadness over not fulfilling expectations of UFO sightings or was his energy somehow affected by the vacation? I listened to his vacation but did not understand his curiosity with extraterrestrials. I try to avoid the thought of aliens, not seek them out! I've read about alien abduction cases and the thought of seeking out alien contact scares me. Our conversation changed into town politics and the environment but I was there to do energy work and the time was getting late. So our talking ended and my friend put on CD of crystal bowl music and laid on his treatment table, face down. It was time for Hidden Deer and me to go to work.

    The healing started out fairly normal. We worked on balancing his heart chakra that was wide open, with a throat chakra that was almost closed. Then I allowed my hands to scan his body and was surprised to find that, except for the heart chakra, my friend's chakras were low or closed. The energy poured out of my hands and I felt the low chakras exchanging energy with his heart chakra and other times I could sense energy pulsing through my body as a chakra was recharged from an outside source. His seven chakras were feeling balanced and I had moved to work on his feet when his office phone rang. I sat in a chair, trying to ground myself, while my friend talked. I've never felt energy flowing so strongly through my body before. My hands were aching as I sensed this healing needed to be done, the energy was eager to finish its balancing. The phone call was over and my friend returned to the treatment table. This time he laid on his back while Hidden Deer and I went to work over his third eye. While placing my hands over my friend's face I sensed a difference in the energy, it felt softer, kinder…or was it gentler?

    I became aware of the singing crystal bowl melody that was playing and my voice reacted. Instead of chanting, my voice, or should I say it, Hidden Deer's voice, was mimicking the different solitary tones and pitches of the crystal bowl music. The energy that was emanating out of my hands had a singular music note feel to it too. Such a strange energy, it was as if I was feeling the notes as I was toning them with my voice. I never felt this before. I closed my eyes to tap into the sensation, to explore what it was, and then I saw them. Little toddler sized light blue people were standing next to me working on my friend's supine body. Aliens, this strange melodic energy was from the Aliens!

After the initial shock I was curious. I felt completely safe and trusted in my healing guides so I closed my eyes and watched what the aliens were doing. Then I shared my visions with my friend for I was seeing aliens pulling golden chords from my friend's forehead, his third eye. Then I felt compelled to place one of my hands above my friend's forehead and my other hand slipped underneath his head supporting the opposite side of his third eye, the sixth chakra. They, the little blue aliens, worked on my friend's ears, pulling golden cords out of his ears. Then I looked up and saw that these golden rods streamed from his ears and his sixth chakra, up, up, up and out to the outer perimeter of my friend's aura. Weird!

The energy once again changed and Hidden Deer resumed her normal chanting as she worked on the crown, heart, solar plexus and the rest of the chakras. The energy coming from my hands felt like the normal earth, animal energies I was accustomed to feeling. I knew that Hidden Deer was sealing my friend in a protective shell of Earth energy located approximately a foot away from his physical body. Then my hands stretched further away from my friend and I watched as a second shield, an outer golden matrix of chords located around four feet away from his physical body, formed. I could see the grid of gold lines and although I understood the intent of this matrix, I couldn't interpret its meaning. I could still see the golden rods reaching out of my friend's third eye and his ears. These rods passed through the earth energy shell, up to the outer matrix of golden cords so that my friend's ears and third eye were connected to this outer golden grid. I knew the healing was finished.

    I looked at the clock and was surprised to see that forty minutes had passed. My friend confessed to feeling a little light headed and very, very relaxed. His smile was infectious. I was pleased that Hidden Deer and I were instrumental in precipitating relief from the melancholy he had felt since returning from his trip. Before leaving his office we scheduled another healing session for the following week. I left his building feeling satisfied and wanting to share this sense of peace. So I did not return home as was my earlier intention and instead stopped to visit the friend that I've channeled the animal healing to before. With the success of today's healing fresh in my mind I wanted to see if she had any free time this week for me to practice "energy work" on her. I was surprised when I walked into her office to see her at the front desk for usually she would be working on a client. When I inquired about the time for a practice Reiki session, my friend smiled for she just had an unexpected cancellation in her own schedule only moments before I walked in the door. Coincidence turned into opportunity and I followed her into her treatment room prepared to channel another healing.

    This healing was entirely different from the others that I had experienced. I didn't sense animals, I didn't sense aliens, no this time I sensed...mud. Hidden Deer drew mud up through my friend's feet. My friend confirmed what I was sensing and shared that she could feel the mud go up to her neck. Hidden Deer then gestured around her head and I watched behind my closed eyes as Hidden Deer placed energetic straws in my friend's nostrils. She then worked around the crown and encased my friend entirely in the mud. I understood what was happening and explained: "The mud was drawing, like a poultice, pulling the negative energies out."

Then Hidden Deer's gestured by allowing my fingers to wriggle with sweeping hand movements above my friend. She was calling in a gentle rain. The energy water was washing away the mud and allowing the diluted mud to rinse away the negative energy. The rain then turned to a light snow which covered my friend and incased her in a beautiful glass like ice. The ice then burst and sparkling ice crystals were floating in her aura, refracting white light into many colors. My friend had her rainbow of colors back in her aura. Pretty cool Hidden Deer!

I then saw a sword in my friend's left hand. It was a short fat dagger of a sword and a small shield was in her right hand. I knew my friend was right handed and wondered why the sword would be held in her left hand. Hidden Deer explained that this was the method of fighting with these tools; *"The shield was for knocking your opponent off balance. You could then stab with the blade. It is natural to keep the shield in your dominate hand for the brunt of the force would be the shield. The stab didn't require arm accuracy. It was a swift guess of an attack."* I don't know why I would be able to share knowledge of ancient combat. I suppose I was channeling wisdom from a greater source. This was a strange and insightful healing. I wonder if all the healings with Hidden Deer were going to vary so much? For now...Namaste.

October 20, 2005: Fairies....I had contact with the little elf like beings this morning. My story begins with a dream that I awakened to today. *I was talking with a pleasant, clean young man. He was a travel agent and I felt a sense of guilt over seeking out this new travel agent. But I wanted another opinion about the spring trip Greg and I were planning to visit Stonehenge. I asked the travel agent about England, he gave me* *some brochures and we talked. When I asked him about traveling to Ireland he smiled a big knowing smile and said; "Ireland, yes Ireland is right for you."*

Then the scene changed and I was walking home. I was in a familiar city town that I've traveled to in dream before but can't remember being at this place in my conscious state. The scene changed once more in my dream and this time I was at the campus of the University I graduated from. I was by the old graduate housing buildings walking my dachshund, Lily. I could hear footsteps and knew that someone was following me in the dark. It had rained and the streets were reflective of the dim street lights. I tried to see behind me but the fog and the reflective lights...I couldn't see well. I wanted to get away from there so I picked up Lily and started to walk very fast. I heard footsteps following me and the faster I walked, the faster this being walked. Closer, closer, he grabbed me! I woke up.

I opened my eyes and it was still dark in my bedroom. As I lay in bed and my heart slowed to a normal pattern my consciousness surfaced. I knew I just had a "bad" dream, just a dream. My body was relaxing, it was too early to get up, I started to fall back to sleep. I felt a cat walking on my feet, my legs. I looked, there was no cat. I felt for Lily. She was asleep on my other side. I felt the light stepping on my body; a soft cat like walking up to my thighs. Sleepily I reached for Lily. She was lying on the opposite side of my body from the walking sensations. My mind started to register the obvious, the dog was not moving, there was no cat in the room so what was walking on me? I bolted to consciousness with this realization!

I lay in my dark bedroom calming myself and contemplated on what I should do. I knew Yellow Dog was near and I knew I was well protected. Curious I asked Yellow Dog what invisible being was walking on me. Immediately I felt Yellow Dog reassure me to be brave. I closed my eyes and could see lights under my closed lids, as if someone turned a bright light on in our dark bedroom. I picked up my dream notebook from my bed stand and started to converse as I asked; "Who are you?"

A: *"We want to help. We want to enlighten the humans also."*

Q: "What kind of beings are you?"

A: *"We are the 'Say-a-nors'. We travel a foot. We are small compared to your form. We can heal you humans. We are small yet very powerful. We travel with the mice. Mice are like our horses. 'Neigh-o-beigh', this is my name. I am the leader of my small clan. We can help your nose."*

YD: *"Care...take-care".*

Q: (I interpreted Yellow Dog's statement as a warning to be careful with the fairies' intent or abilities.) "Are you familiar with the frailty of the human condition? Are you familiar with the incompatibilities of our two species?"

A: "*I have worked with humans before. I know of your limitations."*

I hear a high pitched noise in my ears. Now my ears feel as though they want to pop.

Q: "Are you trying to use my ears? Are you trying to tune my ears so you can speak directly to me?"

A:"*Yes".*

YD: "*It's ok*"

Q: (I am seeing the fairy in my mind's eye.) "I see you now. Your facial features, your nose, ears and hands, they are larger than ours? You have a pointed hat. Your shirt is folded and tied shut. Your pants are held up with a draw string. Do you use buttons or zippers on any of your garments?"

A: *"No. It is hard to use our long slender fingers."*

Q: "Oh"..."I would like to hear you. Perhaps my ears will adjust".

A: *"Perhaps, you never know."*

Q: "Was it you that I felt walking on my legs earlier?"
A: "*Yes, we wanted you to wake up. We wanted you to meet us.*"
Q: "What are we to do together?"
A: "*I do not prophesize. I am here because we sensed you had a need for us. We are curious about you as you are about us.*"
Q: "How many are amongst you?"
A: "*Five of us have made this journey tonight, the morning to be.*"
Q: "Is it difficult for you to cross the realms?"
A: "*No, we know the herbs.*"
Q: "Are you just curious about us humans?"
A: "*Curious but concerned about our earth in our realm. Our interest lies in the environment of earth. Your guide has enlightened you as to our deteriorating world because of human ignorance. If you enlighten the humans we can all survive.*"
Q: "We endanger so many species out of our greed and ignorance. This is so sad."
A: "*Yes, we see the destruction. Years ago we had many species too. Some have perished. This is the way of time. Do not fret for their spirits evolve. Get together your questions. We will return again. Fair well and a good morning day!*"

When I finally returned to sleep I slept so deeply that I overslept. Later, while feeding the horses and cleaning the barn this morning, my mind wondered about the fairy beings that visited me last night. I was thinking if I could, somehow, invite them to the evening circle planned for tomorrow night. How does one invite or transport invisible fairies? Do they just materialize or would I have to physically transport them? Should I bring along a cat carrier sized purse that appears empty, but actually holds five small dwarf-like fairies? My pondering about fairy transportation led to a reality sooner than I had expected.

I drove to my 9AM yoga practice this morning and all was proceeding as usual; the regulars filled the room, our yoga mats lay on the floor and we flowed through a routine following our instructor. When I practice yoga I know many of the poses so I frequently find myself closing my eyes, relaxing and breathing into the pose. This morning I was following the group, flowing from the cobra pose into the down dog pose. I closed my eyes and breathed as I enjoyed the stretch on my calves and back. That was when I saw a group of little dwarfs playfully trying to contort into yoga poses.

The vision startled me out of my moving meditation and I struggled to follow the instructor who was assuming the next pose. Then I would settle, I would breath, stretch, close my eyes and there they were again, standing on their heads or wrapping their arms around their torsos. I spent most of today's class with a stupid smile on my face as images of these little fellows curiously trying to bend into contorted yoga poses while breathing with exaggeration flashed behind my closed eyes. They were so cute and sincere in their sense of play. At least now I know they can transport themselves wherever they want to go. If they want to come to the circle tomorrow night that my development class friends are holding then I guess I'll see them there.

I set up a time to meet another friend to practice energy work on after class. We visited briefly and I explained about the Reiki energy before I worked on her. I am starting to feel more comfortable in practicing energy work on others. Today I noticed that my voice sounded different, or rather the words seemed more Asian or oriental in sound, when I worked on this woman. The energy flowing through my hands was strong and I sensed a sea serpent type dragon by her, as well as snakes. As on my other three friends before, I felt the energy move and I felt blockages being opened. My friend shared that she felt better after the "treatment". These positive reactions have inspired me to practice on more people. I am curious about the change in sound when I worked today but I don't have time to meditate and talk with Yellow Dog. For now…Namaste!

October 21, 2005: I just came home from a home circle where a group of my fellow development class students sat to practice our mediumship. The man who organized this circle, who I'll refer to as Joseph, was eccentric and somewhat childlike but most of all he was a very talented medium so our small group accepted him as the leader. Joseph started out the evening by leading the six of us through a group meditation. Then his voice encouraged us to journey and share what we were experiencing and immediately one woman in the circle was sharing the grief over losing her son. I knew that this was not something from her current life and while I listened as she shared her impressions I could feel her need, her pain and I desperately wanted to help her. I didn't speak but listened as other people in our group took turns, sharing their experience. Then I heard Joseph instruct us to leave these "past lives" and ask our "guide", our "gate keeper" or our "control" for a message.

Yellow Dog shared with me; *"Experience your own journey Little One. Don't put energy into the journeys of others but use the energy of the circle to discover your own truths."* Then I felt a strange energy envelope me.

I could sense the fairies of yesterday around me but I also sensed that I was in two realities. I could sense small fairies around the left side of my body but to my right the fairies appeared close to my size. In my mind's eye I would look to my left were the fairies were the size of dolls and then to my right where the fairies were the size of six year old children. What a weird and wonderful sensation! I was quite entertained for some time last night and I hated to stop the meditation, my participation in this group circle of friends.

Now that I am at home journaling my experiences into the computer, Yellow Dog can you please explain why you told me not to help my friend during the circle and also explain this feeling of two realities that I experienced.

YD: *"Hello Little One. You are so sensitive. You feel others more acutely than the average human. This is a blessing and a curse. In order to develop psychically you must learn to filter out other's thoughts and emotions. You must learn how to tap into the energy of the collective. You must not allow yourself to get pulled into another human's reality.*

Yes, there is a time and place to show compassion. But you must learn how to function in alternate planes. You must learn how to work with us. You must learn not to be side tracked by the needs of the other humans in your circle. This is a cross that you can learn to discard. But you must practice. Practice during your circles in class. Practice hearing only us on the other side. Practice feeling only us. You do so well when channeling healing with Hidden Deer. Now you must develop your mental energies too.

As far as the fairies and the alternate dimensions. You experienced the small, dwarf like faerie on your left side while your right side was in the Faerie dimension. Here the Fairy was full sized. This is the way of other planes. What appears to occur at a fast pace, or appears in an altered smaller scale, are just the bending of time and space. This is just how the human mind perceives crossing into other dimensions.

You did well. You experienced what few have; existing with one foot in a dimension, one foot out. The fairy from your bedroom helped you to experience this inter-dimensional feeling. Thank Neigh-o-beigh. He is a wise old elf. He and his clan have strong knowledge to share. Please consult me if you are unsure. For I have existed in human form. I understand the ways of the human body. I am here to help you in your journey for knowledge.

You are progressing. Do not give up. For, like in your yoga practice, it is the things you aren't comfortable doing when you first experience them. These are the tasks that you will master and learn to enjoy. Life is a wonderful journey. Breathe, see, hear, taste, smell, feel, the moments pass so quickly before the body is gone.

Blessings and Namaste...Yellow Dog."

October 24, 2005: Sadly, my daughter has outgrown Ginger; my pony sized half Arabian mare. We've spent the fall searching for a new horse and settled on a palomino half Arabian gelding. The process took a few weeks of riding and soul searching but I finally committed, purchased and trailered my daughter's new horse home yesterday. He was nervous when I first placed him in the stall of my horse barn. I watched him walking circles and reasoned that if he was eating some hay he would "settle in" so I grabbed a flake of hay and threw it over the stall door where he could eat it. The flying hay must have startled the gelding for he kicked out with one back leg. I saw a violent, lightning-fast, kick of his hind leg and heard the stall wall resound from the impact. I jumped back at the fierceness of his kick in surprise!

I didn't think twice about yesterday's event until I woke up this morning because I relived the memory of seeing the palomino kick in my dream. I felt the violence of the kick was aimed towards me. I woke up with a jump confused and feeling my heart beating in my chest. Curious as to why this aggressive memory resurfaced and purposefully startled me into an awake state I started to journal:

Q: "Yellow Dog what is the significance of the recurrence of this vivid memory?"

YD: *"It is a trust issue. Trust in this horse and he will trust you."*

I closed my eyes and saw falling little shards of light being pulled together. The light came together as if pulled by a magnet. I asked Yellow Dog the significance of this symbol of the broken pieces forming a common shape?

YD: *"Like attracts like. With positive attitude you will continue to form a positive outcome for it is the mixing of the energies that leads to true greatness. Allow these powers to blend. Enjoy the mixture of the new whole. Revel in its being, vibrations, existence. Then you will truly understand what it is you are searching for. You will see the truth, your true heart's desire."*

It was still early so I put my pen down and rolled over to fall back asleep. Then I heard in my left ear the phrase whispered: *"Do what you love."* Obediently I wrote this down and once again tried to return to sleep but one more bit of wisdom needed to be recorded; *"Don't go through the paces to please anyone but yourself. You don't need to support anyone but yourself. Enjoy, live, prosper in the healing light of love and peace...Namaste."*

Still October 24th: Today was interesting at my Monday morning development class. This Sunday is scheduled to be a "Student's Day" service so instead of our usual development class we practiced going up on stage and talking into the microphone while facing the large grouping of chairs that would hold the congregation. Our teacher looked in my eyes when he asked who wanted to go first and I knew I was elected. I was assigned to do the invocation, the blessing, and my teacher encouraged me to channel Hidden Deer's native tongue. I was unsure if I would be able to channel a native tongue while standing in front of people but as I walked onto the podium I knew Hidden Deer was ready because I could feel my palms pulsating.

    I looked at the dozen of my classmates sparsely populating the congregation's chairs as I settled behind the microphone. I felt a little conspicuous pretending it was a Sunday service but I acquiesced and introduced myself and explained how I perceived Hidden Deer. Then I closed my eyes and allowed her to speak. I heard Hidden Deer's proud, secure voice as I felt my hands greet the four elements. I explained that she was greeting the elements. I then heard Hidden Deer talk proudly and felt her make three circles with my right hand. I then explained she was sending blessings to all of you. I allowed Hidden Deer to talk in her tongue and gesture with my hands and I explained that my hand movements were part of the blessing. She said a few more short sentences then I interpreted that she was done.

    I opened my eyes and saw the shocked look on some of the faces of my classmates while others were smiling broadly. I looked down and extended my left hand in an effort to ground myself. Wow...I was shaking from all the energy! I heard my teacher ask if I was alright. Still feeling light headed and trembling I took a few deep breaths and shared that I was ok and just needed a minute to come back. I returned to my seat and our teacher used my demonstration as a chance to educate the rest of our class. He asked if anyone noticed anything unusual about me while I was channeling. Someone interjected; "Besides the fact that she was speaking Indian?" The class laughed. Another spoke up; "She gestured with her hands." Our teacher seemed pleased. Yes, when I was allowing Hidden Deer to use my body my hand was always gesturing. Now that I think of it...my classmates were right for my hands always move when I speak in tongue.

My participation in today's practice was over and I enjoyed watching the rest of my classmates taking their turns going up onto the podium. Some practiced their part for Sunday's service and other students just used this opportunity to share an impromptu experience. I was surprised at how relaxed everyone was and how natural and honest the stories were. The mediumship was not spectacular but the demeanor of my fellow budding student workers was so relaxed. I, and for that matter, many of my fellow students, could see spirit over the faces of the students when they talked up on the stage. Our teacher explained that this was called transfiguration and we were all surprised to be able to experience the light transposing of multiple faces that developed with more detail as each student took a turn on the podium. I saw a blurry face overlaying the face of one student talking from the podium while the next student had an overshadow that looked like a nun. Another female student's face was changing from an Asian man to the face of a hooded monk back to the Asian man when she stood on the podium and I also noticed a distinct orange or pink glow around her. Even our teacher went up to the podium to do an impromptu speech and his appearance changed into an older, heavy man with multiple chins. As I watched the confidence of the students and the strong presence of spirit around them I started to wonder. Did Hidden Deer do more than bless the students? Did Hidden Deer actually do some energy manipulations that helped the students become more psychic and less nervous of performing? I will never know, but it sure was a curious shift in confidence in us all. For now…Namaste.

October 25, 2005: I woke up this morning hearing strange words. Phonetically I recorded in my journal; *"Ah ma na mah nen"*. Then I became aware of a presence around me. In my mind I could see a strange looking being. Squat, bent legs, all knees and feet, I couldn't make out a head or torso. I had that sense that someone wanted to contact me so I grabbed my pen and wrote:

"Beings may make you fearful because of their appearance. Truth being they are harmless. Understand the unknown can be frightening. Be truthful but not overbearing and enlightening without frightening your clients."

I awoke remembering a vivid image of a small Native American girl. Like from a "Save the Children" commercial she was in a rundown town of some sort, standing along a street, alone and appeared very poor. Or was I sensing her loneliness, was she waiting for the return of her parents? I don't know the meaning of this image but I felt compelled to record the experience.

October 26, 2005: I went to a healing class held through my Spiritualist church last night and although much of the information was review for me I was disturbed when our teacher shared that not all Healing Guides were permanent. The wonderful soft spoken teacher shared a story of her first Healing Guide, an Asian spirit who was very philosophical and had a wonderful view of life. But our teacher shared that her energy changed and this guide left her and was replaced by a trio of three early nineteenth century doctor guides; one was a family doctor, one was a surgeon and one was a psychiatrist. These three guides worked through our teacher when she healed during service for many years and then it was time for them to leave as well. A new and final guide stepped in who has been using a stronger energy and working through her now for years.

I worried because I don't want to lose Hidden Deer as my healing guide! Perhaps because I have had Reiki training I was assigned a more permanent healer guide? I don't want to have to factor in a replacement of my healer spirit guide when I consider working for money. What if I and my clients are used to Hidden Deer's abilities? If I build up a clientele that enjoyed Hidden Deer's chanting, her spoken words, her gestures, would my practice suffer if I had a change in spirit healers?

YD: *"Don't worry Little One...When you were attuned with the energy you were assigned a permanent healer guide. Part of your Reiki Master attunement was the solicitation of your relationship. You and Hidden Deer vibrate to the same energies. The two of you are as one. This is why you are able to speak with her voice and so easily switch back to your own. Do not worry. Hidden Deer, like I, is here to stay. Namaste."*

Thank you Yellow Dog for the reassurance...Namaste!

October 31, 2005: Yesterday, Hidden Deer and I did the invocation during our "Student's Day" service. Much like we practiced in class on Monday she did a wonderful job! She spoke clearly and with authority while I allowed her to gesture with my hands. Hidden Deer would pause, I would interpret in English, and then Hidden Deer would speak again. She called in the four elements, blessed the congregation while honoring the elements, allowed the energies of the elements to shower in on the people and she allowed the energies to bless the people. She closed the prayer by thanking them for their understanding. At least this was what I recall of her invocation. I stood back when she was through, grounded myself with a few deep breaths and returned to my seat.

I spoke with a fellow classmate this morning during my development class and was surprised when he told me that I caused a little controversy yesterday. Some people were entertained by me speaking in tongues while others were offended by the extremity and felt I was "showing off" and was not respecting the sanctity of the service. I felt offended, saddened and confused by my friend's observations. I meant no malice and thought I was participating in an acceptable manner. On the bright side I have become more visible to my fellow church members for Hidden Deer's speech has led me to become more believable as a medium with "gifts."

During class today a fellow student said she saw me as having very ancient Native American knowledge. She felt I had the blood of the Hopi Indian. I have felt, perhaps, my mother's side of the family had some Navajo but I could never know for sure because my mother was orphaned at an early age. The subject of Native Americans came up in my development class before and my teacher felt my connection to the Native Americans was through my guide. But numerous other people have mistaken me for having Native American blood when they meet me. I wonder if my guides could be influencing my outward appearance.

I usually wear my hair in a long ponytail braid. My hair has been down past my shoulder blades since I was twelve years old but since I started to do energy work it has grown down to my butt. I was given the message during service a few weeks back that I should consider donating my hair. I've heard the same comment from others in a short period of time so I devoted one of my evening meditations to the question of whether or not I should cut my hair. During this meditation I saw an image of a stalk of corn and I understood. I felt that my hair was like the corn. It would grow back. So on October 17th, which was a full moon, I had a friend who was a breast cancer survivor cut fourteen inches off my hair and I saved the hair for donation. When I was at church yesterday one of the mediums in our congregation was surprised I actually had my hair cut. She told me that she heard my guide say that my long hair was part of my heritage and that I should not cut my hair. I was pleased that she cared enough to share this belated information and felt gratified that I am fitting into the family of my church.

Another medium from church over heard me tell of my intent of donating the hair to the cancer society and she looked at me and said; "Thank you." I gave her a questionable look for which she explained; "The little girl that will get the wig made out of your hair. She says thank you."

This life is getting to be a wonderfully strange one. I understood and was grateful for that medium's comment. I have to remember to get the proper address for "Wigs for Kids" because my amputated pony tail is still sitting in an envelope, waiting to be mailed.

After service yesterday I shared a potluck lunch and waited to participate in yet another circle that was to be led by Joseph. I filled my paper plate full of food and looked for an empty chair and saw two next to a lonely looking white haired lady. After I started to talk to her I discovered that there was a reason why she was eating alone. This woman was strange. I don't know why I was drawn to sit next to this seemingly hopelessly unsociable woman who complained about her physical pains. I tried to commiserate through the sharing of my own story of an accident that took me years to mend from. Instead of looking towards the possibility of healing her body this woman changed the subject and complained about her loneliness after her husband's death. I suggested that she could join a social outlet such as an exercise class or a flower club to which the lady responded by saying she enjoyed her solitude. Lastly she complained about the upkeep of her property. I suggested downscaling into a smaller home with less land. The woman snapped back that she would never sell the home that she lived in for thirty years! At that point I got up to get some dessert and sat to eat my brownie in the company of my fellow development class students. I thought that would be the last time I would interact with the white haired lady but I was wrong because she chose to stay for the psychic circle after lunch.

We pulled our chairs away from the tables and formed a large circle in the middle of the church basement floor. Joseph directed who should sit where and when he was pleased with the "energy" he led us through a pleasant meditation. Then a chair was placed in the middle of the circle. Joseph coached different people to sit in the chair in the middle of the circle while the rest of the circle would "read" the person or give psychic impressions. Some of these impressions would be in the form of channeled wisdom while others would relay past events and some students preferred to share spirit messages. We were having fun until the white haired woman took the chair.

A woman that sits in development class with me was seated to my left and I could feel the energy go from this woman to the white haired woman sitting in the middle which felt like a buzzing in the air. The white haired woman started complaining about how hard it was to live without her husband. Those of us in the circle tried to gently nudge her towards positive thinking in an effort to keep the energy of the circle going but the woman in the middle simply wanted to complain to an audience. When sharing the story of her dead husband she stated "I will carry the pain of his death into my next life." That statement broke the mood of the circle and my fellow prospective mediums grew into an awkward silence. Then the classmate sitting to my left started to channel. She was in a trance and in a strange voice she said: "BLAH, BLAH, BLAH..." I heard one person gasp and noticed a smile being forced from Joseph's face. But the lady in the middle had no control and shot out of her chair amidst cursing. The sudden outburst caused my friend to snap out of her channel in a state of temporary confusion over the sound of the metal chair almost thrown down against the cement floor coupled with the cursing. I was surprised that the white haired lady returned to her chair in the circle while still cursing and complaining under her breath. At this time Joseph took control of the circle and led us through a closing prayer. Our circle was closed.

But the crazy white haired woman wasn't finished. I was standing in the kitchen helping to put the leftovers into the refrigerator when the white haired lady stormed into the kitchen. She verbally attacked my poor class mate by ranting; "We don't know what it was like to lose someone we love." My friend was visibly mystified as to how to react to this lunatic as was I for we've both lost siblings. In the Spiritualist's opinion death is not an end but a transition. Yes, we miss touching someone in the flesh but they are not gone. They're simply existing in another dimension of reality. I tried to offer some insight to this woman but she had enough and seeing that no one was offering any sympathy or conflict the white haired woman left the church.

Now that I am recording this into the computer I am surprised at how unruffled I behaved yesterday. I didn't feel anger at the injustice unfolding in front of me when my poor friend was being accused. I just felt pity for the shortsightedness of this white haired woman. I felt pity regarding how she hides behind her shield of tragedy as well as her inability to move onward to enjoy this wonderful life we have the opportunity to live through. I am still at a loss as to how she could be helped. I supposed it is her burden as much as her responsibility to help herself. Self empowerment, the white haired woman has to want to blossom before she can...Namaste.

~ CHAPTER 7 ~

CONVERSATIONS WITH YELLOW DOG - NOVEMBER 2005

November 2, 2005: I mailed my hair donation out this morning. I called the American Cancer Society on the telephone to get an address and the woman at the ACS was very helpful and gave me the *Wigs for Kids* website. When I logged on to the website I couldn't stop crying. I'm not sure why the outpouring of emotion. It was not a grief cry but more of a "this is a beautiful thing" cry. Even as I am typing this I am crying, the emotion is so strong, as though a being of pure love is here with me. I need to step away from the computer and gather my thoughts...

There, I feel "normal" again. I'm not quite sure what exactly was attached to this hair donation thing but I no longer sense it. To change the subject I had an interesting telephone chat with a horse friend this morning. She was asking me about a mutual friend's horse and I knew the answers to her questions. I sensed this horse's frustrations without even going to my bathtub sanctuary to meditate first. I was surprised at how easily I understood her horse's thoughts today. I realize I have the ability to channel animal's thoughts but I am unsure as to whether the channeling will happen when I NEED it to happen. I don't always "feel" a sensation when I am channeling information like I can "feel" the healing energy traveling through my hands. I wonder why I was able to read my friend's horse so easily today. Maybe I am developing as a Pet Psychic.

After I hung up the phone I started to question my abilities. Could I have heard information about this horse through a previous conversation with this woman? But I reasoned that I have a hard time recalling what was said to me a few hours ago.

Was I really channeling information about this little mare or was I recovering information stored, somewhere, in my own memory? I never met this horse before, this a fact. But in my mind I envisioned her "clear as day". Yellow Dog, Can you please explain?

YD: *"Your mediumship is more developed than you would like to admit. What are we doing right now? You are typing my response. This is mediumship. You are 'plugged in' to the other side. You hear us. You know the answers because you sense us. You are especially developed in your ability to sense the animal's feelings.*

I know this is a mystery to you. How do you know how to tap into the vibrations of the black and white pinto? It is your friend on the phone. It is her guides that are helping you. Through your friend's interest, her concern over the well being of this horse, this is how you can 'tune in' to the mare.

Remember Little One, we are all interconnected. All of the life forces on Earth are intertwined. When you start believing this, then the logic will follow. Discard your previous beliefs. Open up to new realities. Open up to the realities of your life force; the reality of your soul. Then you will be better off accepting the new boundaries of your existence here as Suzy Graf."

Q: "Yellow Dog...How do I go about marketing myself? Is it correct for me to be selling these services? Am I at risk if I bring people into my home for Reiki or Angel Readings? Do you have any direction to offer? Please remember that I want to enjoy raising my children. I also want the time to continue with writing this book."

YD: *"Yes Little One, I am fully aware of your life's circumstances. You must do what you enjoy doing. Do not perform Angel Readings at parties if you do not enjoy this. Do perform Angel Readings for people who are afraid of the* unknown. For these, cards are a wonderful gateway for acceptance.

Trust! Trust that we will help pave a path for you to walk into opportunities that suddenly appear. If a friend wants to hire you to teach riding, then accept. Instruct horseback riding by your own rules. You do not have to ride unruly horses. You do not have to ride a student's horse at all. Use your talents. Use your psychic abilities. You will acquire a following. You will acquire a respect for your abilities. Practice and the rest will fall into place."

Q: "How much should I charge?"

YD: *"Go where you feel most deserving. Do not undercut your talents. Do not be overly boastful and charge too much. The 'going rate' is fair. Charge what you would pay. This way you will attract people much like yourself. Be cautious on charging too little for this will set a precedent that will be hard to change in a short period of time. You can give a friend a special rate. Let it be known what the rate usually is. This way new clients will be charged the fee you feel comfortable in receiving.*

Start teaching, the rest will fall into place. Trust. Trust us and we will provide. You are on your way. The future is bright. You have left the past behind. You have learned well from the lessons. Continue to learn. Continue to evolve. We will be behind you. We will assist you in your new endeavors.

Do not abandon the psychic healing. Allow yourself to channel Hidden Deer. Allow yourself to be a vehicle for convincing. Hidden Deer will be with you for a long time. She enjoys working through you. She too is eager for more practice. You are a good match. Do not worry about any change in healer guides. Develop and enjoy what you do naturally. Namaste!"

November 4, 2005: Yesterday I ate lunch in front of the television. Even though the documentary on TV was interesting when my meal was finished I decided to close my eyes for a minute. I wanted to watch the program unfolding yet I was tired. Finally I was asleep when "Bam"! A very real vision of a horse kick behind my closed eyes woke me up. My body felt frightened, the same feeling I felt when I was first startled by the violence when my daughter's new horse kicked out in his stall last week but this time the horse's leg was grey in color. My mind tried to reason why I received this image. Was it my grey mare, Heather's, leg I saw? Are my horses trying to tell me something? Am I having a vision of a future event? Are the fairies messing with me? I asked the last question because the only time I have had a similar event in the past year was when the flower fairies squashed me like a bug during a deep sleep. That dream event also woke me with a bodily sense, of fear.

Q: "Yellow Dog, can you enlighten me?"

YD: *"Good morning Little One. You need to be careful about the teas you are drinking. They have caffeine that does affect you. The dream was the fairies. They were messing with you. They thought you wanted to watch the TV show. They were sad that you were missing the best part. They woke you up the best way they knew how.*

The horse kick is not a vision of a future event. Do not worry. I do realize prophetic visions and what you just experienced do feel similar. Rest assured that this was a repeating memory loop. This is how you would know that this dream event was created by the fairies. Also listen. You can sense the laughing. They do love a good joke so. I will speak with them.

Go ahead and enjoy the new horse. Use normal caution and good sense. Rest assured that the animal is not vicious. Rest assured that he is eager to learn. He is eager to become the show horse you want him to be. Enjoy this beautiful Sunny Day! Namaste!"

Still November 4th: This evening I worked on the same friend that I had sensed the small blue aliens being around before. Similar to our first session, I visited briefly with my friend before I started the healing with Hidden Deer. The topic revolved around the UFO that my friend thought he saw in the evening sky the other night which he described as a bright light in the sky that changed colors in a way that was atypical for a satellite. The excitement in his face as he described the prospect that the lights in the sky he saw was, indeed a UFO was infectious. I wasn't convinced but I enjoyed the possibility of wondering.

It was with this discussion held in my mind that I began to work on my friend. His energy was very different from last time I went to his office to channel healing to him. His chakras were no longer closed but instead permeated energy. This energy felt different from the Earth or Angel energy I was used to feeling. This energy pulsated like low sound waves under water. Hidden Deer chanted through me quietly and I had my eyes closed. Then I saw them; small metallic silver/blue people. I counted three of them standing off to one side of the room. I remember chuckling to myself that only moments before my friend was excited about seeing a light in the sky that might me a UFO and here I was in his office looking at three actual aliens!

I told him about our visitors and channeled Hidden Deer's, or someone's, interpretation of why the aliens were in the room with us. I explained that these aliens were watching us from another dimension and were simply peering into ours to observe this healing. Then I sensed a concern over the weak energy in my friend's legs. This was when I realized that I knew the alien's thoughts. I interpreted that the alien's did not understand how humans use their feet and legs because in their world beings use their feet differently and healing energy is freer to travel through the feet.

I also received information about bones...bones of birds? The alien has bones like birds? Are our bones lighter than theirs? Or are our bones heavier? I didn't understand the full intent of what the aliens were trying to tell me and channeled this confusion over interpretation to my friend. As I am talking to my friend and interpreting the aliens I am not understanding or thinking but simply saying the words. I don't worry about the believability of the situation nor the absurdity that I am interpreting the thoughts of aliens that are observing us through another dimension. My friend appears unfazed by the bizarre scenario unfolding in front of us for he jokes about how he should learn T'ai Chi Massage so that he can learn to heal through his feet!

I moved to work on my friend's head; his forehead/third eye, his ears and the top of his head or his crown. I noticed that the energy coming through his crown was not the Angel or Spirit energy that I sense in Spiritual healing. This energy was foreign to me, undulating and very soothing. I then felt compelled to return to my friend's feet. I sensed that the aliens were somehow working through me and were discussing with Hidden Deer how to treat the low energy in my friend's legs and feet. Hidden Deer thought that a psychic mud pack would draw out the stale energies and stimulate a fresh energy but the aliens wanted a more technical solution. My hands moved and I could feel a block of energy around my friend's feet where they placed a pair of silver mechanical boots. I could sense my friend's frustration at not feeling the presences around him when I was channeling what little I could understand.

I returned to my friend's head and allowed energy to travel into his third eye. I talked and lead him through a brief journey.

Somehow the aliens were instrumental in this. I could hear them discussing where to lead him in this journey; "A red sandy landscape? No. Water? No. Outer space? Yes! Outer space!" Finally, they all agreed. I began to channel the guided journey. I coached my friend to bring his consciousness to his head and to feel his feet far, far away so that he felt he was 20 feet tall. Then I channeled that he was leaving his body, up to the ceiling, out of the building, up into the atmosphere and into outer space. We shot through the atmosphere quicker than I've experienced before. I was concerned that I might not be in control of the situation and heard myself reassure my friend about our ability to return. He did not seem concerned but lay on his back with a bliss-like smile on his face.

We were in the weightless abyss, floating. I've been in this "place without time" before and understood that the scene would soon be changing, an event would be unfolding. I also somehow understood that the purpose of this event was not for me. We waited for my friend to get an image. He started to journey and shared that he saw an Asian man. He was in his early 30's. He was in a factory, like an old "sweat shop". Yet the man was alone, playing a violin. He acknowledged my friend at the moment they made eye contact. The Asian man stopped playing his violin then the image was gone. We returned to the office, our reality, our time.

I went back to channeling healing and closed the healing session for tonight. My hands were motioning and I thought Hidden Deer was sealing my friend in a protective egg but something was different about this protective energy egg. It felt like a thick gelatinous substance. Hidden Deer had covered my friend in goo! Then a bright light shone through and the substance melted away from his body and pulled the negative energies out of his body and melted into the Earth. The healing was finished.

Before I left my friend's office we visited and discussed the bizarre healing and the journey my friend had just experienced. Who was the Asian guy in my friend's meditation? Was he part of my friend's past life or maybe a man existing in another dimension? Or did we accidently drop in on a guy playing the violin on the other side of the Earth? We joked about the Asian man's perspective in regards to this event. What if this man was enjoying playing his violin in the solitude of his industrial studio apartment and the "ghost of my friend" stepped in to look at him. What was reality? We can only guess.

And what about these aliens that my friend calls "star people"? My friend seemed touched that they were so close to him. I am still stunned by the bizarreness of all of this. I accept dead people as normal. Then I learned how to accept fairies. Now I need to drop my prejudice against aliens too? Do they exist in different planes or realities, just like Spirits, Angels and the Fey? I left my friend's office with more questions than answers.

November 5, 2005: Early Saturday morning I awoke and wrote the following in my dream diary: *"Thick atmosphere sort of like the water. Bathes in energies, energy all around, this is how we live. This is how we are comforted. Like whale noises we speak. We hear yet feel the vibrations of speech. This is normal for us.* (To experience this as a human you must) *take a bath. Sit in the bath to meditate. Use the water to feel the sound. This will help you to understand. Feel the sound through your skin. Not just through the bird bones of your ear. Take time to do a small meditation daily. We will enlighten. We are always near.*

Listen to the sound of water. Listen with your body. Hear with your skin. Then you may begin to understand. Thick, viscous air is normal forces. Your water is the closest to our environment. Our water and air are one. Our atmosphere supports our way of communication. Our speech here is like your speech under water; buffled/marbled. Do not despair. Together we will form a path."

November 6, 2005: My husband woke me up this morning by saying in an agitated voice; "Sue, I've just been scanned by aliens!" I usually stir out of slumber slowly but the urgency of his voice brought me to full consciousness. I sat up in bed and listened to him explain the strange and vivid dream he just had.

We were on the street where Greg's business and my church were located. (This is a reality because the church I now belong to is located up the hill around eight buildings away from Greg's store.) *I was with my church friends, walking and conversing in the distance while Greg was at the bottom of the street looking up at us. Then Greg started to fly which felt like a swimming motion through the air. He flew back to our house and then settled back into our bedroom, back in the bed with me beside him. Then, in the distance, from the corner of our bedroom, he could see a bull, a grey black bull. The bull trotted towards him, coming from the far right which is the location of our bathroom, towards Greg's left. The animal had a loose jointed, ambling gate. The bull was of a slighter build than our traditional modern day bulls and moved gracefully, with purpose.*

Then Greg felt an earthquake feeling and he was stirred to consciousness feeling this sensation of being suspended in jiggling jello. Greg woke up and saw a red orange light beaming into our room from our bathroom. Greg explained that the light was touching his body and causing the jiggling sensation. He watched the light move from his feet, towards his head and then back to his feet then the light disappeared. Greg explained that this felt as if he was "scanned" like a piece of paper in a photo copy machine. Greg knew he was being scanned by aliens and he woke up with this strange knowledge.

While Greg was being "scanned by the aliens" I was holding my two large crystals and envisioning the Archangels removing the pain from my right shoulder. Or at least I was trying to relax my shoulder muscles but I couldn't achieve a meditative state of healing for I knew that more than the Angels were in our room. I peered behind my closed eyes and saw the figure of a man who wore a tan camel hair trench coat and I also sensed a woman figure but couldn't see her clearly. I assumed that these spirits followed me home from the restaurant I was at last night. I didn't want to be bothered with these spirits so I placed myself in a bubble of energy and hoped they would go away. It was early, I was tired, my shoulder hurt and I wanted to feel better! I tried to remain calm and not allow my frustration to turn to anger. Then I briefly thought the bedroom was brightening. I opened my eyes to see if the sun was shining through our windows but the room was still dark. I rationalized that the wayward spirits must be causing the lights behind my closed eyes or maybe the fairies where here. I was still trying to achieve an energy flow when Greg pulled me out of my meditation to share his story about the aliens. I sensed no "aliens" in the room. Not that I would know what aliens felt like anyway.

One more observation was that during the time that Greg was being "scanned" and I was trying to initiate a self healing our dachshund had scampered towards the foot of the bed. This was unusual for Lily because she usually buries herself under the warmth of our bed linens. When Greg started to talk to me I noticed that Lily was out of the covers sitting by my feet, waiting. Was she sensing entities in our room? What was going on with Greg? Was I feeling the presence of these "alien" beings also? Was this light that I saw behind my closed eyes the same light which had "scanned" Greg? Was Greg developing the ability to tap into other dimensions or was Greg just being drawn into my energy field when I initiated my own self healing?

Greg and I discussed all of these possibilities over breakfast this morning. Was the bull Greg saw in his dream a spirit animal, a sort of protector or was the bull a sign that the stock market was improving? Were the aliens simply checking Greg out just because he was accessible or were these aliens associated with the healing I did Friday night?

It is now almost 9PM on Sunday evening as I type this into the computer and I think I understand why Greg felt the aliens this morning. Could they want me to give the message I received on Saturday morning to my friend I channeled healing to on Friday? I will get in touch with my friend tomorrow and relay this channeled message to him. I feel a little overwhelmed with the information I am receiving and am channeling. I do trust Hidden Deer, her healing and wisdom. I am just mystified at how this is all unfolding. I will journal any new developments. Goodnight and Namaste.

November 8, 2005: It is early Tuesday morning and once again I felt the presence of these aliens in my room. I allowed myself to write: "*Good morning, we are trying to understand, trying to experience life in your reality. It is so different, so open, and so lonely.* (In our world) *we can always feel each other no matter how far away* (we are from each other). *In your air we need to actually be by the aura* (of another) *to feel. Then this can be too much. For the other entity has no preparation to our approach. I stay then in the outer bands of the aura. Then I can better acclimate to interactions with other humans.*

*Enjoy the clarity of sight, especially the colors! For in our world colors are distorted and muted. This is why we (*have overly developed the ability to) *hear and feel so much. We depend on our eyes less. Human skin, our skin (*while) *in this world, is so unprotected, so bombarded by the elements. You can feel the Sun so easily. You can feel the wind. You feel cold and hot. We are bathed in a liquid atmosphere of comfort. We are sheltered from the environment. We function with other beings as a whole.*

On your planet you can experience the wildness of Earth. You can feel the gravitational pulls. You can see the changes. You can experience so much! It is a lonelier journey for you cannot easily share with others like we can. Do not despair. Enjoy the planet. Learn, experience, this is the purpose."

I inserted the words in parentheses while re-writing this channel into the computer because I knew the intent of what I wrote and felt that my words make the alien's thoughts more legible. I am not quite sure who this message was intended for. I gave my friend the first message yesterday and will share this one with my friend as well, but, somehow, this message seems like it was for me. Could this treatise of two worlds be for my benefit? Strange...for now...Namaste.

November 9, 2005: I'm off on another apparent tangent to my learning. I have been wondering how mythical creatures, such as the unicorn, could fit into the unrealities that I have been experiencing and purchased and just finished reading an interesting little pocket book called *A Natural History Dragons and Unicorns* written by Paul and Karin Johnsgard, which was first published in 1982. The authors divided the book into two parts. The first half dealt with dragons, their habitats and habits, and the dragon's dealings with man through lore. The second half outlined the different varieties of unicorns, their biology, interactions and legends.

Both varieties of species were treated with the utmost believability in this book. The authors blame the Christian religion and our modern government for not publically acknowledging the existence of unicorns or dragons. Of course my mind questions this logic. Why wouldn't National Geographic produce a documentary on the dragon or the unicorn if they existed? Why wouldn't the cheap weekly newspapers, or half hour "entertainment" early evening news magazines, do a dragon expose? Why wouldn't our National Zoo proudly display a unicorn? I enjoyed the authors viewpoints; their information about animal evolution and animal lore. But I think the authors were missing an obvious link to the existence of these beasts.

I now believe in the reality of inter-dimensions. I believe these altered worlds support fairies and aliens. I even support the idea that rare beasts, such the dragon or unicorn could exist in these altered planes of reality. Why isn't this explanation obvious to the authors? I find it curious that authors who can expand their realities to believe in mythical beasts stay confined to just our current three dimensional reality of existence. For now…Namaste.

November 10th and 11th of 2005: I've spent this past Thursday and Friday at the Equine Affaire in Massachusetts which was a four day event for horse enthusiasts. On Thursday evening my daughter and I made plans to meet friends at a restaurant. The traffic was horrible and we had tickets to an evening performance so we made a last minute change in our plans and decided to eat at a fast food restaurant close to our hotel. As we opened our foil wrapped meal I scanned the small dining room of booths and was surprised that besides my daughter and me only two other people were in the dining room. It was dinner time so either this restaurant served horrible food or everyone was in a hurry to get home and were not concerned with stopping off to eat. The "musac" hummed in the background while my daughter and I talked in a low voice. It was strange to be sharing such a large dining room with only another pair of men.

I was half way through eating my French fries when the pair of gentlemen that shared this too quiet of a space with us walked by our booth on their way out, then hesitated by our booth. I noticed that this pair looked out of our time period for the older man wore blue jean coveralls and had an Amish type beard while the younger man, perhaps his teenage son, was clean shaven, dressed in conservative blue jeans and collared shirt and stood behind the bearded man smiling silently. The pleasant, weathered, old man started talking to us and shared a story about his work horse. I thought it was strange that he knew we were in town to attend the horse event and not just local people grabbing a quick dinner. The old man was friendly and in no hurry to leave. He told us that he was from New Jersey and was at the Equine Affaire to see the Shire draft horses. He explained that his son accompanied him on this trip and they have to take the ferry to get home. I asked him if he knew an acquaintance of mine that owned a Shire horse and was active in the exhibition this weekend. He said he didn't know her which I found strange because horse people that own a breed that are somewhat rare, such as Shires, usually all know each other, or at least, of each other .

Then the old man went on to explain how he takes the second traffic circle when traveling to the convention arena from the road where the restaurant we were seated in was located. I thought it was odd that this stranger would lapse into sharing directions with us and I pointed out that traffic was not a problem now. The man reiterated the importance of avoiding traffic by taking the second traffic circle. Not willing to argue about traffic when the rush hour was obviously over, I politely allowed the man to explain his directions. While the old man was talking I looked behind him to see his silent, smiling son and wondered if the young man could talk. The old man was through with his directions and looked at my thirteen year old daughter and said; "It is a good thing your daughter rides the horses. The horse teaches a child many things, many lessons and girls that are involved with horses stay out of trouble." And with that wisdom the pair left the building.

That next morning my daughter and I left our hotel room and drove our SUV past that same restaurant on the way to the convention center. Just a few miles down the road the traffic in the right lane slowed to a stop. Remembering the old man's words from the evening before, I flicked on my left turn signal, entered the left lane and continued past the blocked exit. At the next traffic circle I exited the main road, turned down a side road and probably drove a few extra miles but I never slowed due to traffic for there were few cars on the "detour" that the old man had told me about. When I saw the fairgrounds approaching I smiled as I realized that I was to enter the "Exposition" from the opposite direction. I took an easy right into the entrance as I noticed the long line of cars in front of me waiting to take a left turn into the fairgrounds. As I parked the SUV, my daughter asked the question I was thinking; "Was that old man a real human or was he some sort of spirit or earth angel?" I guess we'll never know for sure. But later that day I asked about the ferry to New Jersey when I told the story to my friends and no one I had talked to knew of a ferry that was still running that this man could be taking to New Jersey. Weird!

Later that same day my daughter and I were looking at the jewelry displayed at one of the booths at the exposition. I stopped by a vender who sold beautiful silver jewelry with turquoise stones and was impressed to look at a bracelet. The

Native American looking man in the booth showed me the jewelry and told me that the piece was made by the Zuni. Zuni! This was the second time I've heard of these Native American people this week. Just this past Tuesday a woman from yoga class was describing the Zuni fetishes her husband collected and I learned that the Zuni people were from the same area that I feel somehow drawn to, the Southwestern area of the United States. I wonder if Hidden Deer, or is it something else in me, or around me, that is connected with the Navajo, or is it the Hopi or the Zuni?

I did purchased the bracelet for my daughter and talked briefly with the salesman. He was a native Navajo and when he told me that he spoke the Navajo language I immediately felt light headed. I could sense Hidden Deer and knew that she wanted to speak but there were so many people around the convention hall and my daughter was next to me. I decided to leave his booth to go and get lunch and to return later when the area was less crowded.

As I walked amongst the food vendors I discovered that I couldn't concentrate on buying my lunch for I was occupied with Hidden Deer's strong presence pressing into my consciousness. I wished I could channel Hidden Deer's Native tongue to this Navajo man and solve the riddle of her language. But I knew that the time was not right and I intended on returning to this vendor later in the day when he wasn't so busy. But this Friday was the Veteran's Day holiday and the exposition hall was over crowded with patrons. I walked by the booth a few times over the course of the afternoon and there were always potential customers jockeying for position around his booth. I wished I could find this man alone so I could talk to him in confidence but the opportunity never arouse. I suppose the mystery as to why I was feeling so excited when I was around the Southwestern jewelry would have to remain unsolved.

I did have some time to watch the clinicians demonstrate how to work horses at liberty in an arena. I watched Clint Anderson and Gwai Ni Pony Boy work a loose horse with just a lariat. I also watched a man work a mule with a stick. All three men could get the horse to turn and behave with their eyes, voice and the extension of their hand in the form of the rope or stick. Then I started to understand that these men weren't using any psychic or magical power over the horses. They were extending their own energy out and touching the horse, they were energy workers, simply bouncing energy, their outer auras, off of the horses! I wonder how I could explain this concept to the average horse owner without appearing like a new age lunatic. How do I share my questions, my insights to other people without frightening them? Maybe with time I will formulate a clear solution. For now...Namaste.

November 13, 2005: I went to a daylong workshop called "*the 13 phase unity merkaba lightbody activation*" yesterday. Well, I activated my "merkaba lightbody" and I've felt like shit ever since! I developed my period while I was taking the workshop and now my body still feels achy; my lower back aches as does my old shoulder injury and my spine. What really sucks is this headache. I realize that I opened my third eye chakra, the energy center in my forehead during the workshop and I especially felt a strong energy flow through my crown chakra yesterday. I learned yesterday that the "lightbody" was formed by moving my energy centers, or chakras, within my physical form. To explain this concept with a model, envision how electrons spin around the nucleus of an atom and understand that our body is not still but constantly vibrating just as atoms are always spinning. Yesterday I was coached on how to visualize chakras that I previously thought of as stationary as moving, vibrating energy centers. Even the chakras that were pictorialized as above my head and below my feet were invited to move and vibrate into my personal body space. My new reality is not one of seven linear chakras but rather thirteen chakras looping or vibrating within and out of my body. I feel so strange now that I am home and I'm unsure if I should continue using this concept of a "13 phase unity merkaba." The woman that taught the class yesterday told us that we could take more classes and learn more about this concept further. I wonder if I should pursue working with my lightbody or is this squashing of chakras into my body causing my acute menstrual symptoms. I sense Yellow Dog near.

YD: *"Good morning Little One. We are saddened by your discomfort. Light work is one of joy not one of frustration and physical pain. We are surprised at your physical body's inability to adapt. I have no great wisdom, no fool proof insight, as to how to remedy this situation. Rest, rest today and let your body recharge. Perhaps you are simply beyond being tired and simply over stimulated. With rest you can clear your head. With rest you can rejuvenate your body. Then you can assess more clearly how to proceed with this new found skill."*

Q: "Yellow Dog, I need to know, were you once on Earth?"

YD: *"Yes Little One, I lived on Lemuria, many, many years ago."*

Q: "Did you practice a group meditation similar to what I experienced yesterday."

YD: *"Yes, this was a common, even daily, practice for me and my peoples. We advanced beyond speech. This caused a major rift in our society. We had the peoples that could manifest themselves in altered realities. The peoples like me that could communicate through thought. We also had the people that choose not to advance into other realities. These people simply enjoyed existing on the Earth plane. They enjoyed feeling the Earth's bounty. They were not comfortable suspended without the body of the animal. I believe this is the struggle you are having.*

Feel assured that you will not lose the ability to shapeshift. You will be able to travel to and from this new altered state you learned. Do you not have the ability to journey to the Other World? Can you feel the presence of the Other World? Feel the sense of floating, the sense of bodilessness? Then you learned how to meditate and travel to the Upper World. Here too, you learned to become comfortable with the floating, nothingness, the feeling of being out of body. You now accept shapeshifting and stepping into the altered realm of the faerie?"

Q: "Yes, Yellow Dog, but these are quiet, still travels. I feel motion sickness now. This spinning is affecting my physical body."

YD: *"Little One, I believe it is the invading chakras from above that are disorienting you so much. Take the time to re-introduce these chakras into your body proper. Take the time to feel their presence. Play with moving these chakras in and out of your body. You will find your comfort zone when and if you can accept the upper and lower chakras into your body space. This will be the time to begin again. This will be the time to reactivate the merkaba."*

Q: "What about my little merkaba crystal? (My Reiki teacher had given me a gift of a little merkaba shaped crystal last May. The stone is a three dimensional representation of the Star of David.) Perhaps it can help initiate a more quieting shift? Perhaps I can rely on the little stone to support me?"

YD: *"And here lies another of you innate problems. You do not rely on others in the group. You are uncomfortable drawing upon others' energies. You tap into universal energy through your own source only. Do not despair. You will develop your OWN technique. This is your true path."*

Q: "Yellow Dog do you have any wisdom to share that will allow me to clear my mind and still the achiness in my body?"

YD: *"Take a bath. Invite Hidden Deer in. She will realign your energies."*

Q: "Thanks."

YD: *"You're welcome and Namaste."*

Q: "Namaste."

Before I take my bath I want to journal the experiences of yesterday. Before yesterday's workshop I was enjoying soaking in a morning bath and decided to use the time for a brief meditation. I opened and aligned my seven chakras and allowed a self healing as I sensed Hidden Deer chanting. In my mind's eye I saw the color silver flowing into the top of my head or my crown chakra and the color coated my skin. Then I sensed the color gold coursing up through my root chakra, up into the base of my spine and out over my skin where the silver mixed with the gold. I thought the two metallic colors where unusual and unique but I then sensed my heart chakra opening and the color pink came out of my heart. I was intrigued by such an unusual scenario for I am used to colors being poured over me like a can of paint, I was eager to visualize more. I stilled myself and saw a spider web and then saw a figure of myself. I was attached to a silk string of the spider, my head and feet were slumped and my back was rounded. Then I saw spider webs spilling out of the crown of my head and my root chakra too. Some sort of grid or matrix was being shaken or discarded out of my body. I didn't understand the purpose of this meditation but I dressed accordingly for the day.

When I arrived at the workshop on Saturday there were illustrations in the workbook I was handed. I looked at a color picture of the 13 chakras of the body and discovered that the two chakras that were below my feet were called; the "earth star" which was platinum silver in color, and the "heart center/earth" which was gold. The book also illustrated the four chakras above my head and the first three were multi-color with the fourth was white/gold. What are the odds that I would choose gold and silver in my morning's meditation only to later learn that the new chakras in my aura are gold and/or silver? But the coincidence gets stranger for this workbook altered some of the colors traditionally associated with the seven major chakras and I was surprised to learn that the heart chakra was pink and not the emerald green that I have previously learned.

   I don't understand the symbology of the web being discarded out of my root and crown. Was Hidden Deer trying to tell me I need to clean out more cob webs? I need to open up my chakras more? (As I am writing this into the computer, one year later, I have learned that the spider web I saw in my meditation was actually a torus of energy that runs into the body of the human, an energy field that would go through my root and crown chakras, through my pranic tube, and encircle the body in an energetic, magnetic, bubble of energy. Was I being introduced to the concept of the human magnetic field months before I actually learned it? And now that I think of it...I saw this same torus or matrix while doing the alien healing on my friend on 10/19/05. Also, when considering the symbol of myself being pulled by a single string emanating from my heart. I wonder if this spider string coming out of my heart could be a representation of the heart chakra connection that binds all "light workers?" Curious!)

   Back to yesterday's workshop… we followed a CD produced by Paul Hubbert, the creator of this workshop, as our teacher played her "crystal bowl" and simultaneously sang a strange melody, which was called voice toning. I listened to the voice toning, the meditation, and learned how to envision myself spinning. I felt like a human gyroscope; listening to the tones around me and not sensing reality. The feeling was not animal and did not feel of Earth. When listening to the voice toning and spinning my chakras I felt enveloped in a mathematic, computer, mechanical type of existence. The feeling was free and light but I missed my animal body and my peripheral senses.

In order to compensate for the dizzying spinning we were taught how to stabilize this spinning sphere of light and energy by bringing in a hula hoop of pink out of our root chakra. Like the rings of the planet Saturn this pink energy band extended beyond the hologram of light around my physical body thus stabilizing my spinning energies. The theory was that by keeping this pink hula hoop horizontal I could maintain a sense that my head was up and my feet were down thus keeping me oriented upright. I tried following the instructions but I still felt a little motion sickness.

The last meditation I was led through at the workshop on Saturday was memorable. I achieved the suspended spinning light body state then I could see myself mirrored, over and over again. I could see all around me as though I was a sphere and in the distance I saw a tunnel but I couldn't maintain my concentration, I couldn't pass through the tunnel or communicate with those beyond it. I was frustrated at this obstacle and curious about how I normally perceive the Otherworld. So I pushed energy out of my third eye and immediately sensed a fairy near which surprised me because I didn't sense him sooner. This made me even more aware that this new energy of the merkaba I was practicing with was so different that my normal senses of what existed around me were off.

I peered through my third eye and saw a gnome-like being not unlike the ones that followed me to yoga class last week. He was neatly dressed with his coat buttoned and his hat centered and he was lying supine next to me apparently concentrating on achieving the same energy work as the rest of the group of humans in my dimension enjoying the workshop. His demeanor was respectful and serious compared to the usual jovial fairies I've come to know. I got the sense that this one gnome was chosen to attend this workshop. This was an honor and I was touched by this little being's determination and respect. I smiled when I noticed him and allowed my imagination to float into the voice toning that was engulfing me. I lost time and was surprised when the sound ceased and our teacher called us back.

    I left the workshop feeling out of balance and was exhausted by the time I got home on Saturday evening. As I type this into the computer on Sunday night I've had the time to digest yesterday's experiences. During crystal meditations in my room this past year I have felt this atom-like spinning, this gyroscope sensation, but during the crystal initiated spinning I have done in the darkness of my own bedroom I never lost my peripheral sense of things. Or at least I wasn't aware of not sensing the three dimensional reality around me. Yesterday I felt so vulnerable. Was this because I was initiating the experience with my sense of hearing as I listened to the toning of the crystal bowl and not by holding a crystal in my hand and feeling its vibrations? During this workshop the spinning was activated by sound through the use of the crystal bowl, the methodical speech of the CD and the vocal toning voices. All of these auditory cues caused my ears to feel blocked by this overwhelming sense of noise that did not allow me to hear anything else. I could not hear distant, approaching noises, only the rhythmic whew, whew, whew of the bowl combined with the varying pitches of voice toning. I don't fully understand why this was so unsettling to my psyche. It must be the level of comfort I have inside my human body, that innate need to defend myself. Must I always feel compelled to somehow sense my physical body to be comfortable?

When meditating in the quietness of my darkened room I have my ears and my eyes as a failsafe. If the room was brightened I could pull out of the meditation. If there was a loud noise I likewise could pull out of the meditation. During yesterday's workshop I was blind and deaf. The lights were on so there were no contrasting shades to trigger my sense of sight. The noise of the bowl, the voice toning, the CD, this permeated through me like a white noise of nothingness. It would take an extremely loud noise to pull me out of meditation for my sense of feeling my surroundings was muted by the steady vibration of the crystal bowl. My self-preservation was wary.

I realize I should count on my guides and should entrust myself to the highest and brightest good but I am a human animal. I enjoy my human body's ability to sense the approach of other energies and the ability to sense other people being around me. I do not enjoy being blinded by the possibility of approaching energies that are not my own. I suppose this is a challenge I must sort out before I pursue any further tone induced meditations. I am confident I will come to a comfortable solution. Must go out now, until later...Namaste.

Still November 13th: At first I was irritated at having to leave the house when Joseph invited me to an impromptu psychic circle tonight. When I talked to him on the phone just before dinner I whined that I was tired after such a busy few days but Joseph, as usual, was persistent that I join the group. In retrospect I am happy that I pulled myself out of the house tonight. When I arrived at my friend's home I was surprised at how mild the temperature was for November in New England. The group that had gathered agreed that we should take advantage of the fifty five degree temperature and we decided to meditate outside on the deck by the uncovered hot tub. I shared a quilt a friend and the five of us sat in displaced kitchen chairs that formed a circle on the deck next to the hot tub that belched a gentle chlorinated mist around our feet. As Joseph began to lead us through a guided meditation, I looked up at the sky and noticed that the moon was nearly full and the sparse grey black clouds only occasionally dimmed the moon's light. The air was still and I had a sense of magic as we opened the energy of our circle. Joseph led us out of our bodies. We traveled up, up above the clouds, up into space, in the stars, then past the stars and into a peaceful place void of light. I floated in this abyss, the blackness of nothingness, not sensing my body, free of pain and with no earthly body sensations.

It was here that Joseph prompted us to travel into a past life. Immediately I was in another place and another time. *I sensed myself walking, chest high, in a field of grass. I was cautious, hunting? I looked down and saw my own chest and felt my tight muscles. I was a young man and could feel the grass scrape against my bare chest as I walked. Or was it water? Was I in water? Yes, I was chest deep in the water and I had a log by my chest. I was floating down the stream, hiding behind the log.* As I was reliving this experience out loud I heard Joseph ask if I was with anyone. I answered that I sensed I was with another from our circle.

A heard the voice of one of my friends volunteer his presence with me. As he took over the experience he shared that he was hunting, hunting another man. He needed to kill another man. We needed to kill this man. *That was when I saw him, a figure of a Native American man standing on the shore. His back was to us and I wanted to hide. Or I wanted to keep floating on down the stream. My friend wanted to kill the man.* He said the man needed to be killed.

I heard Joseph ask for my name. I answered in Hidden Deer's tongue and stumbled with the English eventually forming the words; "Two Feathers That Fly." Then I heard Joseph ask my friend for his name. He hesitated and then said his name was Dave. My mind acknowledged that Dave was a strange name for an Indian but I was too deep into this journey to really absorb the absurdity of the name. At that point a woman in our circle joined our story and offered that the man on the river's shore was a sacrifice and had chosen to expose himself. She said; "He had volunteered for his people to be the one to be killed."

I didn't like this experience and was feeling unpleasant. I wished Dave would call off this hunt. I wished I could keep floating down the river. Then an animal screamed in the distance. The noise was repeated a second, then a third time. We all came out of the meditation for the animal scream was real.

One of the men in our group defined the cry as that of a raccoon. The home owner commented that the animal was crying a sort of death cry. The moon pulled behind a cloud and the area around us grew darker. I could no longer see the faces of my friends clearly. Joseph took the darkened sky as a sign. Collectively we all resumed the meditation. But the Indian journey was finished and another man in our group started to speak. He was with Merlin the Magician. He had crystals and explained how he would grind up the crystals but they retained their powers, their memories. This crystal powder can then be used on people. The memories of the crystal would be given to the people the powder touches. My friend channeled all of this in great detail. Then he was quiet.

His journey complete another person spoke. This man was in Ireland. He was about to board a ship. He only gave us his last name. He was blunt, rude as he described his despair over running from something, someone with something to hide. The group then shifted out of this unpleasant journey and grew silent. Joseph broke the silence with a booming voice of authority. He said he was the Oracle. He spoke to me. He told me that once I was a (or the) Phoenix. Then he spoke to others in the group sharing his wisdom.

The wind seemed to work with us. When we shifted from one scene to another, from one person's past life to another's journey, the wind blew and the moon beams shone through the clouds. It was such a magical feeling, as if the elements were participating with the five of us. It was if the Earth, Wind, Air and Fire were actors in our play of experiences that night.

When we finally closed the circle I became aware at how cold it was and how cold we were. Someone checked their watch...we have been in this meditation for almost two hours! No wonder we were so cold! We all filed inside the house and while we warmed up we shared impressions of our experiences. Joseph smiled and asked; "What the hell kind of Indian name is Dave?" We all laughed at the obvious absurdity then switched to teasing another man about his "expertise" with crystal powder. The time was late and there was a comfortable camaraderie amongst all of us. It was a fun and interesting night. For now...Namaste.

November 15, 2005: Hidden Deer and I worked on my friend that believed in UFOs tonight and once again the experience was interesting. I started working on my friend as he lay on his belly with my hands positioned over the back of his solar plexus chakra. Immediately I felt a vortex opening whose energy formed into a very large oak tree shape. I watched behind my closed eyes as the tree's large branches reached up and away from my friend's body, into his outer aura. The image of a tree then turned into a fiber optic lamp with thin hair like fibers of white that were peppered with a hint of color at its outer end. Behind my closed eyes I could sense the arms of the fiber optic lamp flowing and undulating and this movement allowed the image to morph into a line of as many as twelve small blue flames. The flames lined up in a single file down my friend's spine and I watched the blue of the flames grow in concentrated brightness as if a dozen old "Bunsen burners" adjusted their propane fuel. These small blue individual pockets of lights then joined and formed a blue tunnel.

My perspective changed and the tunnel traveled away from me and towards the walls of the room, yet, somehow, this was beyond the confines of any room. Two figures emerged from the tunnel. Aliens! There were two Aliens standing on the opposite side of my friend's body facing me! They ignored me as though I wasn't in the room and went to work on my friend's back.

I had my hands suspended above my friend and was chanting while all of this materialized. My chanting ceased and I temporarily froze at the bizarreness of what I was experiencing. I was a little freaked out because two Aliens were at an arm's length away from me. Yes, I've seen aliens around this man before but they always felt further away. Or was it that they seemed smaller or perhaps in another dimension? I'm not sure what the difference was but this time these aliens were large, bigger than me.

I breathed in an effort to regain my composure and announced to my friend that the Aliens were here. At this point I felt compelled to move and stand at my friend's feet. With the distance between me and the two beings established I placed my hands on his feet and chanted ever so quietly while the two Aliens went to work at his head. I could feel energy coming out, information emptying out of the soles of the feet. I sensed symbols of mathematic equations and some sort of hieroglyphs spilling out of his feet. I looked at my friend's head. I could see the Aliens through my closed eyes. One alien appeared to have the head of a praying mantis which was barely visible under the hood of a robe. This robed being was working with a device shaped like a pyramid on my friend's head while the other being appeared to be assisting. Time passed, I chanted, energy flowed and finally I could sense the energy lessening. I peeked at the aliens through my closed eyes and noticed that they seemed to be finished because both beings stepped back and were looking at me, apparently waiting.

Hidden Deer and I scanned the energy over my friend's body through the palm of my hands. The field around his head was huge! I knew it was time for my friend to flip over. I told him this and returned to his feet while the Aliens went back to work on his head. Again the images spilled out of the bottom of the soles of my friend's feet and when I felt the energy finally subside I knew the procedure was finished.

One of the aliens, the one in the robe, left. I kept my friend apprised of my impressions as I was receiving them. I shared that I sensed that the robed being was a special being and questioned if he was some sort of specialized cosmic surgeon. I shared that my friend on the table and I should feel honored by his presence. I use the word "he" to describe this robed alien, but I found myself explaining to my friend that these beings were androgynous. The second alien that was still in the room stepped away from the table and positioned himself behind me to watch with an energy of patience, love and protection. I told my friend that one being was still here and that I felt the being that stayed behind was a sort of "guardian angel" for him. I'm not sure how my friend reacted to this information for he appeared overloaded from the abundant energy that was pulsing through him.

Hidden Deer and I ran my hands over my friend's outer aura. She chanted as we smoothed out the energies and I checked to see if my friend's energy was adequately balanced. It felt as though his being existed inside a large energetic sphere, like the bubble that Glendila floated around in from the famous movie *The Wizard of Oz*. But instead of being the "Good witch of the North" who glowed a soft pink my friend lying on the table was glowing in an orb of yellow.

I stepped back, out of my friend's inner aura, and allowed Hidden Deer to chant. I talked with my left hand extended which moved in a rhythmic song of its own. I interpreted private messages for my friend as I first said them in Hidden Deer's tongue. Then I felt a sensation. The Alien had taken my right hand and lovingly squeezed my hand ever so lightly. Then my hand was released. The Guardian Alien approved and was pleased? The healing was done.

As I am typing this into my computer, I wonder. Why did I sense the aliens the same size as me during this latest healing? Why, when I worked on my friend previously I sensed the aliens were more child-sized? I feel that this may be a dimensional related question. Could it be that when aliens are in a slight dimensional shift they appear smaller? When an alien is functioning fully in my earth dimension they are the same scale, or size, as I am? "Yellow Dog, am I correct in my altered dimension size differential observations?"

YD: *"Hello Little One. Yes, you are correct in your hypothesis. I am proud of your observations and progress. I am especially proud of your ability to accept and not feel threatened by the unknown. You did well when confronted with these gentle, yet strange to you, beings. You will continue to grow and expand your knowledge. Enjoy, journal, share. Your path is a joyous and fruitful one. Namaste."*

November 16, 2005: I wrote in my dream journal last night one word, "Delphi". Is this the name of the alien's that exist in the water like environment which are the protector species of alien that watched over my friend? No time to question Yellow Dog now but I wanted to record this interesting insight.

November 17, 2005: I was hoping to spend the day without the need to leave my property but I ended up agreeing to practice energy work on a girl friend. It was a very unusual healing. Hidden Deer worked on the center of my friend's body and once again I sensed a vortex was opening up. Through my closed eyes I received impressions and shared them with my friend in between my chanting. The vortex opened up and we traveled out of our bodies, up past the clouds, up past the stars and back into the black abyss of floating nothingness. My friend whose body was on the table and I were sensing the black abyss together as if we were both out of body. I explained to her that I have visited this place before and this was where I have traveled into past life experiences. As I was wondering what we were to do together in the abyss I experienced us returning into our bodies and a lower vortex opened up. This time we traveled to that primal place that I was told is the Petrified Forest. It was a place of warm bubbling mud, an ancient time, a place before time this was the place where I have experienced prophecy. We lingered in the Petrified Forest briefly then once again we were back in our present time and bodies. The energies were shifting and I felt my friend was being covered in gold. A gold basket weave pattern covered her legs which was a tight covering like a mermaid suit across her legs.

    Recognizing these as ancient Egyptian bindings I channeled knowledge of Egyptian lore. I spoke knowledge about traveling from pyramid to pyramid, about how each building was a school of learning or a school of thought of mystical preparation. My friend and I discussed and channeled our impressions and knowledge. I sensed the energy change in my hands as my impressions and mind wandered with these shifts. With time the energy subsided and the healing was done as quickly as it was opened. But I wonder if this was a healing or some sort of lesson?

Now that I am home I wonder…was Hidden Deer showing my friend and me how to use energy? Were we in a classroom of cosmic knowledge? I am now recognizing that I have the ability to travel to past and future events as well as being able to share this with another. I am curious to try this technique with more people. Until later…good night and Namaste.

November 21, 2005: I've come to the conclusion that my energy has changed. At first I blamed this variation on hormones. Then I felt the cause was psychic exhaustion because I had an unusually busy week; out of town during last Thursday and Friday, the lightbody/merkaba workshop on Saturday, Sunday night's circle, channeled the alien healing on Tuesday, another healing on Thursday and then I attended a horse banquet on Saturday night. I've been busy and haven't had time, alone, to meditate. Could this be the reason why my energy feels so different or did the lightbody/merkaba workshop somehow change me?

I think my energy has changed for today at psychic development class I was led through a meditation where I was directed to search for a mythical animal and a tree which usually would not have been challenging or very interesting but today my meditation had a duality to it. I had the sensation of coexisting in two realities at once. I would experience the phoenix in an oak tree which felt like fire energy then I'd flip to an unfamiliar bird with an unfamiliar energy by an unfamiliar tree. At first I didn't understand what I was sensing, and then I understood that the energy pulsing through me was that of water and I was a tall bird...a stork! I was a stork and I could feel myself eating little fat, fancy bred, bulgy eyed, gold fish. I flipped back to being a phoenix and feeling the heat of the sun, then back to the stork consuming fish. I asked Yellow Dog why I was eating the fish as a stork when the phoenix wasn't eating anything. He said it was for the energy that I needed. I wasn't sure of the tree that was by me as the stork. I sensed the oak tree and the phoenix then the oak morphed into a tree that looked as though it belonged in an old Louisiana bayou with knotty, exposed roots and with its branches tinseled with Spanish moss that hung low over the nearby water. I was wondering what kind of tree it was and heard the word Sycamore tree inside my mind. I've never flipped between two images in a meditation before and thought nothing of this until later.

This evening I drifted off to sleep while watching TV and when I awoke I was in dual planes of realities. Was I dreaming in two dimensions at once? At first I was confused as to where I was for the psychedelic image of swirling energy was still in my mind. I remember knowing that the energy of my familiar fire was mixed with the unfamiliar energy of water. I was told this was a yin and yang, a duality of powers and a duality of possibilities. These elements mix but like water and oil doesn't combine. "Yellow Dog...Can you explain what is happening to me?"

YD: *"Oh Little One. You are growing. You are developing your abilities. You are discovering new possibilities, new realities and new talents. Enjoy the path. Your energies will balance. Your body will adapt. Your destiny is unfolding. Be patient. The outcome will open. The new reality will establish itself. You will enjoy the fruits of this labor. Your family will profit too. This is a wondrous thing. Do not worry. Keep trusting in us. We will open the doors. Namaste."*

November 22, 2006: I was thinking about the Phoenix and researched "facts" about this mythical bird through the book; *Magickal Mystical Creatures* by D. J. Conway. And on page 65 in the section about the Phoenix I read; "*A similar mythological Egyptian bird was the Bennu, a heron-like bird. The Bennu was born in a spice-lined nest in a sycamore tree.*" These two sentences were the only mention of a heron-like Phoenix in Conway's 245 page book. I have read this book before. Could my mind have remembered these two sentences and scrambled them out of my brain during last Monday's meditation? I saw a stork and knew it was associated with the Phoenix and didn't make the "heron-like" bird connection until I just looked up Phoenix in Conway's book. If I was remembering Conway's book then why didn't I call the bird a "heron" in Monday's meditation and what about the knowing the word "sycamore" tree? I first experienced seeing a large old tree by the water and then I heard the word sycamore. Could my mind work backwards in a meditation? Could I see the image then know the word if I am recalling a word from something I read months before?

According to the internet the "*sycamore tree which grows in Egypt is actually a type of fig tree that naturally grows in the rich soil along rivers.*" This information was not in Conway's book. How did I know, or see in my mind's eye, a tree by a waterway THEN hear the word Sycamore? I don't think my mind was regurgitating facts that I read in Conway's book. For some reason I was receiving lore of the Phoenix from two cultures at once. Perhaps this was two lives of my own overlapping. Coincidentally on page 65 & 66 of *Magickal, Mystical Creatures* reads; "*The ancient Mysteries used the sign of the Phoenix to symbolize the immortality of the human soul...accepted initiates were referred to as Phoenixes, or those who had been 'born again'.*" I researched this further on the internet and it turns out that the Phoenix has many links to reincarnation. I'm not sure what all this means...will need to sleep on it. For now...Namaste.

November 28, 2005: I went to a friend's house to participate in yet another circle last night. After a pot luck dinner we settled into the basement family room and eight of us were led by Joseph into the familiar meditation towards the astral abyss. We then were each prompted to travel to our own "past life". I found myself explaining that I was a woman called Serena. I was in the Norse woods, in the mid 1400's and was gleaning the bodies of the dead. I made my living by harvesting the valuables off dead bodies after a battle. I lived alone because my husband was forced into the wars and my children were slain during a raid. As I was re-living this existence my heart was hard. I thought that I lived a good life alone and did well as a harvester of possessions. Joseph was curious and brought me towards the end of my life. I shared that I died a quick death during a raid. I then went on to explain my joy at meeting my family on the other side. This experience was very strong because I actually could feel such a light sense of happiness and love after Serena had died. I felt I was reliving a memory but was this really MY past life memory? Could I possibly have a multitude of past lives? Or am I simply traveling through time and breaking into a time barrier and intruding upon the life a woman existing there?

YD: *"Good morning Little One. Yes, those were your past lives. You have lived many, many times. You enjoy the human experience. You enjoy the feelings of the human form. You are a reborn again and again and again addict. You do enjoy the earth experience as is your right as a living soul.*

Go forth and enlighten others. Enlighten them as to the true gift living as a human form can be. Enlighten them as to appreciating the good and the bad. Enlighten them to the precious gift this human body is. Allow others to see that they are in control of their own destiny. Allow others to see that it is themselves that chose how to live their own lives. Allow them to see and understand that they should be cherishing every moment...Namaste."

November 29, 2005: This morning Greg woke up to another strange dream: *He was alone in a large gravel parking lot of a field. Then he saw movement off towards the perimeter of this field. A common looking, brown colored horse was there. At first glance Greg thought this animal was a mule. Then, upon closer study, he realized the animal was an older, drab looking horse. Greg shared that nothing about this horse was outstanding or flashy.*

Greg then realized that he was in a large bubble. He was standing in this field protected in this large bubble. The horse was circling the field from far away then the horse approached and came closer to Greg. As the horse was approaching my husband when he stood alone within the bubble of protection Greg admitted that he was a little fearful of what was about to happen. But he remained still and allowed the horse to nuzzle the bubble. The horse was not biting or attacking the bubble but quietly exploring the enclosure. The horse was using its lips as fingers to touch and feel Greg's outer aura, Greg's presence, Greg's being. Then Greg woke up.

I don't interpret dreams and Greg seldom has dreams. What intrigues me about Greg's story is the old drab horse because I've seen this horse in that ancient bubbling place that I call the Petrified Forest and some of my psychic friends have commented seeing an "old, ugly, mangy" horse around me. I wonder who is this ancient old horse and what sort of relationship does he share with me?

YD: *"I was wondering when we would discuss this matter. The old horse is you; a mirror of your past, a mirror of what you once were, a symbol of your being. Follow this inner being. Follow the force from within; the instincts from your being, the soul from within you. For this is part of you. This is part of your essence; the knowledge of your knowledge, the light of your light, the inner guidance from within. Allow the idea to grow. Allow the thoughts to blossom. Allow and, with time, you will understand. Namaste."*

"Thanks Yellow Dog...I don't understand but appreciate your input...Namaste."

December 27, 2005: A quick journal entry written during the night; *"The thinner the veil between the two realities becomes, the more visitors I seem to have waiting to communicate...for now...Namaste."*

~ CHAPTER 8 ~

ALIENS...THE DELPHI - DECEMBER 2005

December 10, 2005: My computer has crashed with some sort of computer virus. I am frustrated because I had entered much of last year's journal entries into the computer and neglected to save it on a back up disc. I fear that information was lost. Yes, I have my original notes hand written in journals but I'm heartbroken over this apparent waste of time I spent typing, typing and typing. Now I need to go back to journaling on paper and I hope to transcribe my thoughts into the computer at a later date, when it is repaired.

I've been watching a program dealing with a child visiting a mall Santa Claus on the television. These images stirred my own memories of my childhood and my imagination started to wander and I needed to journal this wisdom down about the stages of life:

*"The first is the **Wonder of Development**; the true Disneyland of life, the human animal growing through the life experience.*

*The second stage is the **Stage of Enlightenment**; a space of remembering through experiences, an understanding of the development of spirituality.*

*The third stage is of **Wisdom and the Sharing of knowledge**. In this last phase of life you may need to assist those struggling through their second phase of life. But you are also entitled to enjoy watching the youth, those blossoming through their early years as well."*

I'm not sure why I was thinking of this but the wisdom is interesting...for now...Namaste.

December 12, 2005: I spent yesterday, Sunday, away from the house. I went to church, did Christmas shopping, and then went to a restaurant for dinner. I wasn't home for more than twelve hours, which was unusual for me. Being away from home that long offered me no time to get grounded in my own surroundings during the course of the day. Last night I went to bed tired, physically, spiritually and mentally. As usual Greg lay next to me in bed with Lily, the dachshund, in her usual position sandwiched in between us. I held my two large crystals in my hands in an effort to meditate into a sense of peace and bliss.

Lily was just spayed on Friday and was still wearing an Elizabethan collar to bed and she shuffled to get comfortable with this large cone of plastic that protruded around her neck like a blossoming flower. Greg and I also spent time placing Lily in a spot where her plastic collar wouldn't be sticking into us. With Lily settled and Greg happy I found myself trying to find room for my hands to stay relaxed in corpse pose while I held my crystals. Resigning myself to the fact that there was not enough room in the bed I put the crystals back on their night stand and tried another method to experience an energy flow and relaxation.

I initiated the 13 phase unity merkaba activation I learned last month. I put my hands on my lap and envisioned myself in a rotating sphere. I was spinning faster, faster and then started to fall asleep. I was drifting in and out and achieved a wonderful healing energy flow, and then I saw the lights. I've learned to casually accept lights appearing behind my closed eyes as a normal association with achieving a state of bliss. I watched the lights that appeared behind my closed eyes and I was floating, floating off to sleep, floating off into another dimension, floating off in a meditative state of comfort, love and peace when Greg sat up in our bed with a start and said; "Sue, the aliens are back!"

Greg's announcement jostled me back to full consciousness. I sighed at having lost my meditation but was curious as to what Greg was feeling. I listened as Greg told me he just felt "scanned" again. He explained that he was almost asleep when he saw a bright light behind HIS closed eyes that "woke him up". When he stirred towards consciousness he felt an undulating energy in his body. It was as thought he was rotating; his feet going to the right, his head to the left. Greg was fully awake now and a little frightened by this unnatural experience.

I calmly explained to him that I was in the middle of activating the Merkaba energy field and that I probably accidently included him in my meditation. With the dog touching the two of us this probably drew Greg into my attempt at inter-dimension travel. I only half believed this explanation myself and was surprised that I blurted out these words for I wasn't looking to travel inter-dimensionally. I just wanted to achieve a relaxed balance state in my body.

The next morning, when I was fully awake, Greg and I talked about what he experienced the night before. The poor guy was up for a good hour or so last night. He was afraid to return to sleep and to be awakened by the same strange floating sensations. "Yellow Dog can you please explain who, what and why Greg got pulled into an alternate reality last night? How can I help him be less afraid of experiencing the same feeling again?"

YD: *"It is unfortunate that Greg was unaware of what was happening. We have become used to your acceptance. We forgot he is still afraid of the unknown. For this we are sorry.*

We were trying to re-align his being. We were trying to tune him into the frequencies that you too experience. We now understand that this is not his wish for now. Rest assured that he is well protected. No harm will come to him.

Tell him he is always in control of his human form, his consciousness, his destiny. Teach him to say "no" and "stop" when he feels sensations that are unsettling or unpleasant. Then we will abide. We do not wish to cause fear or anxiety. We do not want to cause sadness.

Allow him to find his own path. Support and re-assure his uneasiness. We will assist you in your creativity. We are with you both, with your whole family unit always. We cause no harm. We only wish to enlighten.

Be patient. Time will deaden his anxieties. Remember your own concern over similar experiences? He will acclimate, accept and then enjoy the experiences. With exposure and time it will proceed on a positive and happy path."

Q: "By using the merkaba that I learned about in class, the light body activation, did this precipitate Greg's experience?" I sense an energy different then Yellow Dog. Less human for that feeling of love is missing. I allow them to answer my question.

Answer: *"No, you were tired. We were allowing, assisting you in cellular repair. We sensed his nasal distress. We decided to help him also."*

Q: "Who are you?"

Answer: *"We are the Delphi. We are what you call 'ET's'. We want only to enlighten."*

Q: "Yellow Dog, is this ok for me? Are the Delphi safe for me to be working with?"

YD: *"Yes Little One. Communication with such beings is natural for us on the other side also. Ancients have drawn and learned much from many types of entities. The human 'Ascended Masters' achieved the same knowledge, the same communications, through these beings.*

Allow your light body to advance. Be patient with Greg. He will learn to accept. He will re-learn not to fear the unknown. We need for him to understand for he is a part of you. You need Greg's strength. We will re-assure him of his position in your life.

Be patient with the Delphi. They are trying to understand human relationships and jealousies. Mammalian tendencies are foreign to them for they are more reptilian in nature. They want, they take, they process. They don't want to cause fear. They want peace and understanding."

Q: "Are the Delphi trapped inter-dimensionally? Are they in a type of Faerie Realm?"

YD: *"No. They travel at will. The dimensional shift is a way of cloaking their existence. Rest assured that your husband is NOT an experiment. The Delphi are wise. They know much. Their intent is pure."*

Delphi: *"Enlighten and educate so the human race may advance beyond their physical state. I sense your doubts, your mammalian habit of self preservation over my words. Draw upon your sense of trust. Trust in me. Trust in our wisdom. Trust in yourself and your own intuition. Namaste."*

Later, that same day, I was watching a television program that retold the story of Joseph and the coat of many colors. The program documented that around 1800 BCE Joseph was betrayed by his brothers and was sold into slavery only to later become a powerful and happy man while living in Egypt. Joseph was happy because of the pleasant existence he lived in Egypt AS WELL AS the awareness of overcoming the tragedy of his early adulthood. To this Joseph said: *"Before you can have a whole heart it must be broken"*.

This statement resonated in me. I wonder if I needed to live through the physical pain of a damaged back and shoulder plus the psychological pain of resolving the conflicts with my mother-in-law in order for me to learn to be happy. Is it possible that in order for me to experience the true realm of love and spirituality I first needed to experience these feelings of loss and rejection? Was that difficult time in my life all part of a plan for my enlightenment? No time for discussions with Yellow Dog. For now...Namaste.

December 13, 2005: I woke up before daylight with the lights beaming behind my closed eyes. I grappled for my pen and paper in my dark bedroom and wrote in my journal: *"All this silliness, silliness about how to pray to God and how to worship God. Don't humans realize? There is one God, the same God.*
Technique is individual. Procedure should be a choice. Worship from the soul. Not as a form of culture. Not as a way of display. Worship from within. Find the altar of your soul. Find the inner light of love. Then share with others. Join your lights and let the flame of eternal love flow.
This is how to worship God.
Worship is not a competition. It is not a race or a battle. There are no losers. All who want to bathe in the light of God's love, these participants are the winners. Share your insight. Share your technique. Share the knowledge that God is always around, always loving, caring.
Enjoy his embrace of love and comfort. Enjoy the light."

December 18, 2005: I've been reading a new novel about a Native American called *When the Legends Die* by Hal Borland. Borland writes about how the native characters would sing about the hunt before actually hunting deer. Was this "song" raising spirit? Was this song similar to Hidden Deer's chants when I channel her healing energies?

The more I read and learn about Native cultures the more I realize that what I used to observe as absurd superstitions are actually effective spiritual tools. The uses of chants or songs are not meaningless rituals but a way of communicating whether with Spirit Animals of other realms, with mother Earth or with Spirit hunting guides. I have come to realize that the list of possible uses for song could be endless.

YD: *"Yes, Little One. My people had a closeness to the Earth, a closeness to that which is unseen. We could beseech the Mother for assistance. We did not care to know exactly who was helping us. We simply accepted that we were helped. We simply accepted that this is the way things are, the things that we have no control over.*

We pray for help. The assistance comes. This is the way it was and should be. We were one with the Earth. We existed as part of the Earth. We respected and honored her bounty. She re-paid us with love, comfort and the means to survive, the means to sustain our physical bodies.

The path of the 'Natives' is a path of peace and harmony. Those that didn't fight perished. This is how we transgressed. This is how our societies became separated. This is how our peoples functioned as separate parts rather than parts of one whole.

We now watch the people evolve over many generations. We watch the infusion of intellect. We pray for the insightfulness that will allow the harmony and will allow people to once again function as one; one with the Earth, one with each other and one with all that is around.

Then the true lessons would be learned. When the state of oneness has been achieved the knowledge would have been shared. All will be truly enlightened. But all must be prepared to accept the path of one. Man has to stop the judgments. Man has to stop the competition. Love, peace and oneness must prevail.

Start with trusting in the Earth. Start with trusting in those that are not seen. Start with the hope in the knowledge that the path has been laid. The people are walking the path and the beginning of oneness is at hand. Namaste."

December 19, 2005: I went to development class this morning and was approached by a student medium who shared messages with the congregation yesterday. He asked me how "good" his readings were yesterday and wanted to know how well they were received by the congregation. I tried to be polite over this uncommon request and recanted what I could remember about the reading he gave me. Not appeased by my response the man walked up to another classmate and asked her how accurate his reading was on Sunday. I don't understand why he was so persistent in asking about his "performance." Doesn't the man remember what he said and how he worked yesterday?

YD: *"Your friend's asking is not due just to his ego. It is more of a curiosity. For when he is channeling he is not fully aware of what it is that he is saying. He is not fully aware of his performance. This is the reason for his persistent questioning. For his perception of your reality is clouded when he channels."*

December 20, 2005: I woke up at 1:40 this morning and sighed when I saw the time. I rolled over in an effort to fall back asleep. The lights were bright behind my closed eyes but I ignored them…then I woke up again…I fell back asleep and then woke up again…the clock read 2:52. Damn! I grabbed my pen and paper and wrote down: *"Umabala-the guardian with the sword, or is it a spear? The Nubian from the tribe of the cheetah sent to serve and sent to protect. Unakoot-will defend. Can run like the wind. Stab like the fangs. Very strong protector."* As I am typing this into the computer I remember how the spirit that shared this with me appeared. He was a tall, elegant, black man dressed in a simple loin cloth. I understood that he was sent here to help me and I silently welcomed this Nubian warrior before I was finally able to drift back into my dreams.

Before I got out of bed this morning I questioned Yellow Dog as to why I was traveling so much in my dreams now. I shared that I don't seem to get enough rest and feel tired when I wake up. When will I return to a peaceful, restful, dream state?

YD: *"Little One, be patient. We are adjusting. You will adjust to the changes. You will feel better tomorrow. Namaste."*

Not the insightful answer I was hoping for. For now…Namaste.

December 22, 2005: I feel better today, more balanced or perhaps simply better rested. I've also become aware that I chose what color I am going to wear for the day as a reflection of my mood. Or maybe I am choosing the color because of my guides, or intuition. Whatever the reason I feel compelled to wear specific colors and I've been especially drawn to bright colors enhanced by rhinestones, much to the chagrin of my conservative thirteen year old daughter. I wonder if there is a purpose for my color selection of the day.

YD: *"Good morning Little One. The connection is weak. I will try to accommodate…The prism enhanced colors lend a three dimensional signal for your body. When you envision the color or colors for the day and when you draw protective colors up from the Earth and down from the Heavens this is a way of communicating with us from the other side. As I have told you before our connection is sometimes vague. Any assistance you can lend us will be helpful. Colors are significant. Colors are a refraction of light. This refraction is easily sensed from our side, from our dimension of existence.*

If you need to heal, if you are a healer, wear the sacred color of Red. We will help draw the comforting energy of the Earth up. We will assist. The Earth, her energies, her vibrations, will be enhanced when the red is called upon.

The multi colors you chose yesterday. These are a sign of socialization, a sign of celebration. Good cheer is sent. A healing energy of joy is shared. Those that can solve medical issues are not called upon. Those that can assist with wisdom are not asked to assist.

Of course we will modify and step in should the situation warrant. The colors simply help amplify our abilities. The colors also alert us as to what kind of assistance you require that day.

Yesterday you did not cloak yourself in a protective coating of color. You have been very diligent about consciously drawing in a color from above, a color from below and mixing the two. You have been slow in awakening. You have not been devoting the time to preparing for the day.

Yes, you have discovered the chant. By chanting you can also alert us to your intent, your mood. Hidden Deer lends her words to your song or verse. By allowing her to step into you, Hidden Deer can sense your body, its moods, its needs and wants.

Hidden Deer's chants and words alert us to what is needed. She may call in the elements herself. Or she may sing the song of the ancients, a song that will alert us to a specific problem or need. Make the time to meditate about the colors. Or allow Hidden Deer to sing her song. These are two ways in which you can protect yourself from stale energies.

Now, as to why you and your friend felt the pressure yesterday at her place of business. (I channeled some private wisdom to share with a friend and sense this wisdom was not coming from Yellow Dog. I hesitated from my writing and used the computer's spell check. I frequently do this as I automatic write for all those red underlined words become irritating. But the spirit sharing wisdom with me became irritated with me as I write...) *Please stop interrupting me to use the spell check...you can do that later..."*

Q: "Who are you? You do not feel like Yellow Dog?"

Answer: *"This is not important...the lesson learned is what you need to know."*

YD: *"Little One...I am here. Please be patient with the wisdom of this man. He is one which assists the friend you questioned me about earlier. He had the insight of your friend. Trust that his knowledge is pure."*

I asked this new entity to please continue and as he shared insight regarding my friend I started to feel a mixture of many different energies trying to write through me. Not being able to focus on just one energy I stopped typing and mentally asked them to come in one at a time. I paused by the computer and waited. I sensed that these beings that were trying to communicate to me were arguing. Not able to clearly understand what was going on I stilled myself in an effort to sense Yellow Dog. I can sense Yellow Dog close, as thought he has placed himself between me and these beings and is somehow blocking them from communicating with me.

I'm sitting by the computer, waiting to channel type and can feel the energy change; inside my head I can hear Hidden Deer's song. I fall into a semi-trance state as I listen to this repetitive sing-chant song. At the same time I can sense the color lilac and can actually feel this light purple color through my skin. I can also sense the smell of lilacs and my hand moves in a circular motion as I draw spiral of lilac color down around me. At the same time I can feel the smells.

Then the color changes and I watch as the red is drawn up from the Earth into my being. I can feel the warmth of an orange red color as it swirls upward inside me, swirls upward and mixes with the lilac. The color lilac is warmed and the new color has a metallic sheen. I understand that any communication with the other side is finished for now. I am unsure what had just transpired. But for now...Namaste.

December 24, 2005: I was stirred from sleep early this morning by my husband's coughing and as I lie in bed, struggling between sleep and awake, and I became aware of a "fast forward movie" playing behind my closed eyes. I've had this experience in the past where I see images behind my closed eyes that appear so quickly that I can't comprehend what they are. I've asked my teacher at development class what to do to understand the images and she had suggested telling spirit to slow them down. I stilled myself and asked spirit to slow down but the moving shapes still buzzed by too fast for my mind to comprehend. I was only able to process an occasional, brief, symbol or form. I've accepted that I can't understand the meaning of this stream of images so I usually resign myself to lying in bed and watching as the scenes fly by.

This morning's images were different than what I have been experiencing, off and on, over the past year. This morning's images were playing through my mind, behind my closed eyes, in multiple screens. It was as if I was watching a picture in a picture television with three different scenes playing out at once. As I was first stirring towards consciousness I was, at first, confused as to where I was and what was going on. When I realized what was happening I drifted back to sleep while being entertained as if I was watching the three different movies screens all simultaneously being shown at high speed. I accepted that I couldn't slow any of them down nor understand what they meant. The cadence of the flashing lights were soothing, comforting...I fell asleep.

Now that I am typing this experience into the computer I am reminded of the healing I channeled to a friend last Tuesday evening. This time I saw three beings, a large knowledgeable center being was performing the procedure with two smaller beings assisting. Later, during this same healing, I sensed Hidden Deer working over my friend's third eye. Here I sensed something very odd. Instead of one vortex where the chakra, or energy center, was located I sensed four separate little tornados, four separate vortexes spinning out of my friend's third eye. This was when I channeled to my friend; "Each vortex would be downloading separate information over the course of the next few weeks."

I wonder...could the three movies playing in my mind actually be three separate "downloads"? If I am being downloaded when I sleep with information from Aliens, Spirits, Angels, Fairies or whomever, when will I become aware of this information? What is its purpose? Why must I receive three channels at once? I hesitate at the computer and try to channel a response but I sense no energy, no answer from Yellow Dog. I suppose I am to wallow through this mystery on my own...for now...Namaste.

December 26, 2005: I was thinking about how the main character in Hal Borland's novel *When the Legends Die* was Ute and the Ute's reservation was located in Arizona. I still feel I have some connection with the Native Americans from the Arizona area. In my dreams and meditations I have seen the snowy Mountains, felt the thinness of the mountain air and marveled at the crispness of the areas beauty with a longing view of the desert from the Mountain's height. Are these "dreams" simply thoughts from Hidden Deer? Are they memories of an ancestor of mine? Are these memories from one of my own past lives? I don't know the exact answer but I know that there is an Arizona connection to something within me.

I talked with my dad today and learned that my nephew became engaged to be married yesterday. The wedding date was not officially announced but my extended family was planning on using this upcoming wedding as a family reunion. I smiled when I learned that the location of this event was to be in Phoenix, Arizona!

I wonder what the significance is that just last Thursday Arizona was the topic of conversation during my evening yoga/meditation class. Marie asked the question of where you would travel if you could plan a weeklong vacation just for yourself. One of the ladies said "Sedona, Arizona". The woman went on to explain the feeling she had while standing in one of the vortexes and shared that it was unlike anything she has ever experienced before. I've never heard of Sedona before nor do I know what vortexes are, but I wonder how far Sedona is located from where my nephew lives. For now...Namaste.

Still December 26th: It is now 10:15 PM. I have been dreaming about a fox over the past few nights and decided to go to my darkened bedroom and experience a meditation with my fox crystal. I was surprised that the clock on my night stand told me the meditation lasted for almost fifteen minutes because I sensed this experience lasted less than one minute.

I placed a quartz point on each of my seven chakras and held an eighth stone in my left hand. In my right hand I held a piece of included selenite that I associate with the energy of a fox. I stilled myself and started to journey. *Immediately I saw Fox. We stepped into the green field. Then the fox began to follow his tail. Around and around he circled. Then the grass fell away, the ground fell away, and we both dropped down. Down we dropped until we settled into a primordial ancient place. A place of early earth, a place before time, this was the place I call the Petrified Forest. This was where I saw the old, thin, dark horse. This was a place where I have experienced prophecy.*

At the same time I was experiencing this journey I felt a strange energy pulsing through my body. It felt as though my right leg was asleep but I understood that this sensation was the product of an energy. A deep, deep, pulsing energy vibrated into my leg. Having identified the physical sensation my attention returned to the journey.

I was at the primordial pools and could see that something was in the water. They were vaguely visible as humanoid forms existing under the water. They were immersed in the bubbling pools, the amniotic fluids of pre-life. Suddenly I found myself swimming in these pools of warm salty water. I looked over and saw that fox was next to me, happily paddling around in the pool. I became aware of the aliens and heard them say; "We are the Delphi." Then I felt a strange, deep, low pulsing. This feeling was so deep, so foreign, but strangely comforting, strangely euphoric in its frequency that I felt comforted.

The energy was much deeper then what exists in my root chakra. It was drawing me down, down into the earth, into the past, the past before the past. The Delphi were there. The Delphi are here. Before man's time, before the earth, they live in the primordial soup. They witnessed the beginning of time. Then it is time for fox and I to leave.

These energies are too deep, too slow for my human body. I must return to my own time and space. The fox takes me back up to the greenness of the other world. Then we come back into my plane of existence, back into my bedroom, my bed, with my crystals.

I am awake now but long to return to the deep, deep comfort of the beginning. I know I must journal this before I forget. But I would rather just savor the feeling. I can still feel the buzz. This is not a "high" but a deep, deep, dizzying low. I want to sleep now. My body is so, so relaxed. I can barely feel my legs. My eyelids are heavy. My hand writes the memory onto the paper with speed, in a hurry not to forget. In a hurry to return to a blissful sleep. Namaste and thank you Fox. I fell asleep.

My husband came to bed late. The Patriots won their football game and the time was after 12AM. Shortly after Greg came to bed and he finally settled into sleep he was jolted awake. He once again began to complain about feeling energies. I tuned him out and rolled over. I've grown tired of listening to Greg discover that he undulates. I was tired and knew that he was safe. I fell back asleep.

The next morning, when the sun was up and we were both fully awake, Greg shared what happened to him the night before. Greg started to fall asleep when he felt the undulating energy. But instead of feeling his whole body effected, the sensation was isolated to his sinuses and nose. Being a clairvoyant in denial he explained that he could also see this energy. He explained to me that he could see a sort of ectoplasm coming out of his nose and he knew that this was the same energy he could feel moving in his sinuses.

I asked Greg why he had his eyes open. He confessed that he was afraid that he was having a reaction to the anti-biotic prescribed to fight his sinus infection/bronchitis. He wasn't sure if his mind or if his body was dangerously malfunctioning. He kept his eyes open to stay awake and stay awake he did, until after 2AM! He first waited for the energy to subside, then he had to wait for his body to acclimate to the peace of the sensation being passed and finally he was able to allow his body to relax and invite sleep.

I guess I was not of much support in my semi-sleep state. When Greg first tried to wake me up I mumbled something about saying the Lord's Prayer if he felt threatened by Aliens again. Now that we are fully conscious and it is morning the ability to reason this out seems obvious. Greg's frantic reaction last night now appears funny but at the time Greg felt the incident to be anything but humorous.

I wonder why Greg was experiencing "healing energy." Was it my earlier journey with the Fox? Did I invite Greg's healing? Or was Greg experiencing a side effect of being on this sinus medication? Thank goodness this was the fifth and final day of his treatment. Let's hope he has no further complications tonight. Hopefully I'll be able to assist him with compassion next time he tries to wake me up during a deep sleep.

Talking with Greg this morning reminded me of a strange frightening dream that woke me up last night. I can't recall anything about the dream other than the feeling of being frightened and waking up. When I woke up I lay in my dark bedroom and I sensed a being next to me. I was half asleep when I opened my eyes and saw a small face smiling back at me. I'm not sure if this was a Delphi or Ickaba. My first instinct was to close my eyes for I felt fear. Then I started to wake more fully and realized I really wanted to see this spirit, this faerie or alien. I re-opened my eyes and the figure was gone.

I reached for my pen and Journal in an effort to record my impressions and then question Yellow Dog for answers. I wrote in my journal my impressions: "I try to sleep. My whole body undulates. My ears are buzzing like the sound of the submersible well pump echoing through the bedroom walls. My left arm buzzes. It feels as though it is undulating. Yellow Dog, can you explain?"

YD: *"Do not fear Little One. It is unfolding. You will hear soon enough. We are near. When you draw upon the earth energies you also draw upon the human body, its cell memories and emotions, emotions such as fear.*

Draw upon the celestial energies and your soul is free of the human body. Free of fear and emotions associated with the human animal form. With celestial energy you may feel pure bliss and love of the soul without the body. With the earth energy you may enjoy the bliss while feeling your human form but risk the range of cellular emotions."

I fell asleep after writing this and I woke up a little later. It was still early in the morning and the room was barely illuminated by the rising sun. I knew there was more to write. I picked up my pen and allowed Yellow Dog to finish his lesson:

"Let's travel farther with this concept. Let's look towards the human past. The religions of multiple Gods and forms of worship...Follow the Pagan teachings. Evoke and draw power from the earth energies and you risk the 'dark energies'; energies of human emotions, deep primal energies of the animal within, the animal that was, the animal buried within the cells of our human, cellular form.

Humans are at a struggle with their two beings; the celestial soul and the mammalian form. Find peace in the stars. Enjoy the heavenly pureness of love and bliss. Yet humans need to function within the animal body. Humans are living their life in a quest of experiences, experiences as a mammal.

Last night you drew upon the deep seated cellular memories. You drew upon the original energetic memories; the vibrations of early life, the vibrational love energy of Mother Earth. Later, during your sleep, you were still pulling on the earth energy. Your body was still bathing in her healing comforts. Yet your celestial mind needed comfort too.

As your dream turned to violence your consciousness woke you up. Fear of the violence returning, guilt for allowing fear to surface, these negative emotions struggled with your frustration of this frightening dream.

Rest assured that this is not evil or wrong. This is the unfortunate path of the in between; the mixture of the earth energy through the human cells while the conscious soul is reaching to the heavens, bathing in the knowledge of the celestial energy.

Your dream is common for a human dream from within, a dream common for the mammalian form and existence. Unpleasant, yes, but violence is part of being a carnivore. Accept and limit its existence but do not be frustrated or ashamed. Honor the natural path. Accept the emotion as brief and ultimately beneficial. Experience the human body to its fullest.

Remember-the choice is ultimately your own. We are only exposing you to the possibilities. Choose the energies YOU wish to work with. CHOOSE your own form of healing and repair. The most important goal is to find happiness in every day, happiness without hurting others, ultimately happiness that can be shared by all.

Do not judge the faults of the human being. Accept. With acceptance you can develop understanding. When you understand you will be better able to accept, shape or even change how you work with energy. How you benefit, draw upon and heal with the available energies of the Universe.

Good Day and Namaste."

December 27, 2005: I decided to try another meditation with the fox crystal early this morning. I placed my seven quartz points over my chakras, held the eighth point in my right hand and the selenite point, or fox crystal, was in my left hand. I could feel the presence of Fox. I felt the nose twitch, the nervous curious energy but something didn't feel right. I reasoned that I might be holding the crystals in the wrong hands so I swapped the selenite with the quartz and held the quartz crystal in my left and the Fox selenite in my right. With the exchange I tried once again to meditate but couldn't sense the animal at all. I switched the stones once again and definitely received the fox's energy. My crystals were laid on my chakras and as I held the selenite in my left hand I prepared to journey with the fox spirit.

I wasn't with the fox but rather sensed the presence of higher vibrations around me. I opened my third eye and saw the Nubian Guardian, Yellow Dog and Hidden Deer. I could sense Hidden Deer working on me. Curious I pulled out of my body and watched from the ceiling. From that vantage point I could see that Hidden Deer was touching each of the crystals lying on my body and with each touch the crystal covering my chakra would glow as if activated by some magic source. The scene reminded me of the animated Tinkerbelle at the beginning of the old Walt Disney TV show but unlike Tinkerbelle Hidden Deer didn't use a wand. I simply saw her leaning over and touch the crystal point that laid on each of my chakras and simultaneously I felt an energy being activated, a loving stimulation of the chakra and a painless spark of electricity.

Once again I was surprised at how Angelic Hidden Deer appeared. Similar to the time I saw her in my bath she glowed with so much energy that she appeared to have wings. Satisfied as to what was going on with my body I allowed my consciousness to travel into the journey. I fully intended to travel with Fox and was eager to once again establish the low healing energy I discovered in that deep primordial place. I saw Fox enter the "Other World." I Watched Fox drop into a swirling hole of energy, Fox dropped down, down, down. But I stayed up with my spirit guides. I tried to follow Fox. I was eager to experience this energy again. But Fox stayed away from me.

In an effort to make my energy lower like the Fox I moved my consciousness down through my body. I left my third eye and placed my consciousness in my solar plexus. Now this was a weird feeling. I felt like the image portrayed in the Meryl Streep & Goldie Hawn movie titled "Death Becomes Her." I felt as though my head was displaced from my neck and reattached improperly to my body but instead of being on backwards, as in the movie, my head was growing out of my diaphragm.

I still couldn't tap into Fox's energy. He was in a tornado like vortex and I could see him, down, down below me. But I couldn't join him. So I moved my consciousness down further. I was in the process of moving my consciousness towards my root when I felt something intervene. I felt as though all my chakras were being pulled by an outside force. This swirl of energy was above me. I felt like a puppet on strings with the center string, or my solar plexus chakra, being the tightest. It felt like my back was arched but I didn't feel uncomfortable. I simply felt a blissful energy flow.

When I was able to process what was happening to my body my conscious mind once again looked for Fox. There he was! He was in the same deep energetic hole of a vortex and I could sense the deep energy pulsating upward. I could feel this energy on my legs. My legs appeared separate from the rest of my body. I tried to get to that Fox and feel that wonderful, low, low energy and was almost able to bring it up higher into my body then I was back into the higher energy being supplied by this being of light in front of me. The same being that was pulling me, energetically, by my solar plexus chakra.

I battled this energy for awhile then I started to return to a conscious state. I started to think of my plans for today and to hear the noises of the room and the noises of the house. I knew I wasn't going to achieve the state I was hoping to reach. I was not in charge of the outcome of my meditation and the greater forces to be were not helping me. I pulled out of the meditation and started my day. As I was placing my crystals back in their nightstand I heard, or rather I knew, a phrase; "*Look Beyond the Universe.*" I am not sure of the meaning but I am grateful for the experience. For now...Namaste

December 30, 2005: I went to a workshop last night geared towards helping me to learn how to market myself as a medium who reads Angel cards at home parties. I still have doubts regarding my ability to channel. When I use cards to do readings I wonder if I am channeling messages from spirits or if I am simply saying what I feel the sitter wants to hear. Could I be tapping into my ability to feel what a client needs? I am appreciative for last night's instruction but I am still unsure if I will ever be employed as a psychic or a medium.

What I did learn last night through casual conversations after class was that many of the "Angel Light Messengers" or people who want to do mediumship home parties had complaints of headaches and physical pains. When I took the Angel Light Messenger Course last summer I was taught that eating healthy was very important; no chocolate or caffeine, no alcohol, some even avoid meat. Yes, these workers appear thin and fit, but yet they have physical pain. Last night some of the ladies in the group attributed their headaches to a nutritional imbalance. I wonder why the Angels these mediums work with wouldn't be bathing them in healing energy? Why were these people having physical problems?

Many of the traditional Spiritualist Mediums that I have met appear to suffer from obesity, which could be due, in part, from their habit of fasting before doing energy work followed by feasting afterwards in an effort to ground the physical body. Yet the mediums I know don't seem concerned with the types of food they eat when grounding themselves. Many seem to be drawn to sugar.

I wonder if both these groups of individuals function in a higher vibration too much without tapping into the earth. My early recognition of the loving, healing, energy of the earth, first through horseback riding and now more refined in my journeys with beings such as the Delphi. Are these the energies that formed a foundation of health for my body? By recognizing and honoring the human body, the physical vessel I am contained within, will my physical body more easily adjust to work with the higher realms?

"First heal the body. Then teach how to sustain and continue to heal, pamper, and nurture the body. At this point pursue the Heavens. For here you will harbor no resentment for your cellular restraints. Rather you will relish the changing energies. The love and bliss of the Heavens, coupled with the warm, motherly love of earth."

Thank you for that wisdom. Namaste.

December 31, 2005: I was invited to a friend's home to celebrate the New Year by participating in a psychic circle. We all ended up doing past life regressions with Joseph leading the circle. As I type this into the computer I find it odd that sitting in circle to relive one's past lives has become somewhat common place. We were led into a meditative state then, one by one, we all told of our experiences. Sometimes we could even participate in the other's reality. I was a cowboy at a rodeo and Joseph led me to the point when I died. The group listened as I saw the light and my reaction to my family that greeted me. Then the group grew bored with my experience and another was reliving a life. Attention left me but I wasn't finished.

I was experiencing the floating happiness of being bodiless, lighter than air, diffuse. I was vaguely aware of the other's in the room. The room was dark except for the black light that illuminated the whites of the eyes and the teeth of those sitting in the circle. The light offered an interesting contrast at first but quickly proved distracting so those who were sitting in the circle chose to keep their eyes closed. My eyes were closed and I was floating then I felt my body contort, I started to condense. I actually felt myself getting squashed and stuffed into a very, very small space. I was as small as a pea. I fell silent and couldn't talk but could hear the next person sharing impressions of their past life. The focus of the circle left my experience. But I wasn't through. I was trapped in the space of a pea!

I was trapped in this pea and for some reason my voice was paralyzed. Then I could feel my body starting to coil, physically moving into an embryo position. I sat amongst my friends in a collapsed pose. No one knew that I had moved and that I was bent over for the circle of people all had their eyes closed. For some reason I knew I was safe and had no fear. I allowed the sensations to progress and was curious as to what it was I was experiencing. Then, little by little, I could feel myself becoming larger. This was when I understood…I was experiencing being an embryo! I was experiencing being created in the womb! I had died many times over the course of this past year. But this was the first time I experienced being recreated. Cool!

I explained what I had experienced to the group the best I could but they were unimpressed. Words can't describe the sensations or the progression of me experiencing a reality BEFORE I understood what was happening. What a wonderful experience! For now…Namaste.

~ CHAPTER 9 ~

ALIENS...THE CORONA - JANUARY 2006

January 3, 2006: I've started to read yet another book, *Talking to the Dead* by Barbara Weisberg, which is a biography of Kate and Maggie Fox, the sisters that experienced phenomena that led to the rise of the Spiritualist religion. The Fox sisters discovered that there was a "ghost" in their home and learned that they could communicate by using raps. They heard knocks or taps echoing through the house and by tapping a response they developed a means of communication. Weisberg's story allowed me to wonder...people that lived during the mid 1800's didn't have access to the internet, television or even the telephone. For centuries the only means of long distance communication between two people was either by messenger or by the written word in the form of a letter. According to Wickapedia.org, technology intervened when the concept of the telegraph was perfected by Samuel F. B. Morse in the United States in 1837. Morse received funding from the U.S. Congress for his experimental telegraph line from Washington, D.C. to Baltimore which was completed in 1844 and the Fox sister's learned to communicate through "raps" in 1848. Could the girls have "discovered" this unique form of communication because the human mind could now grasp the possibility of the telegraph as a means of communicating with the unseen?

I wonder if the Fox sisters ever witnessed a "movie" in their head like I have been waking up to lately and if their 1840's brain could understand the moving images and be able to process it. Without ever seeing a movie could a person living in the mid 1800's understand a full blown vision? I wonder if the ability to see spirit, or clairvoyance, became more prevalent later, when the average human had access to television and movies. By the same token could the ability to hear spirit, or clairaudience, become more readily acceptable to people after the advent of the radio within the human culture? But then again man had been telling stories to each other for years so the ability of the human mind to grasp and interpret words had been well developed. (I can sense Yellow Dog near and I'll allow him to finish my thoughts.) *"And man had the memories of existing, living from day to day, would these not be a basis for experiencing clairvoyance Little One...Yes, man saw and heard spirit for centuries and beyond. It was the new technology and the proof that allowed the Fox Sisters to become famous for although mediumship was understood for the centuries it was a private experience, one that relied on the impressions and interpretations of the medium. What the Fox Sisters demonstrated through the raps was a vehicle of a shared reality; knocking and a language that all could hear and learn to understand, a development for the masses and an opening to the unknown."*

Thanks for the wisdom Yellow Dog. Before I finish this journal entry I have one more observation about Weisberg's book. When Weisberg was discussing the ability to automatic write and spirit writing, she talked about how *"Messages were often scrawled in hieroglyphics or foreign languages...and they generally were philosophical or theological in content, elaborating, for example, on the seamless connection between matter and spirit."* I was excited when I read this passage because this has happened to me too! I thought I was unique in the ability I developed to write with symbols or hieroglyphs last year and this morning I read that this was documented to have happened to the early Spiritualist. Funny how you think you discover something new and wonderful, only to find out that someone else has already had the experience. The only thing "new" was the idea to me! For now...Namaste.

January 4, 2006: I woke up in the middle of the night and felt compelled to write the following: *"There were peoples who lived a most glamorous life. They had technologies advanced beyond your wildest dreams. They had the comfort of many kings. They had the knowledge of many priests. They had the compassion of the gods. Here my story just begins. This was a time before time in a place where we now live.*

The beings were loving, the fathers of the race. They taught us their ways. They instructed us on how to live a beautiful and full life. Yet we didn't listen. We did not want to follow their teachings. We chose a different path. For this we were shut off. We no longer basked in the light of their workings. We no longer felt the warmth of their magic. We were abandoned-set free. Free to live life like an élan in the woods.

These peoples have now returned. They're once again sent to enlighten humanity. They want to share their knowledge. They are curious if we have evolved enough to fully understand and appreciate their guidance. And now we are hopeful. They are hopeful. Let the story unfold."

As I am typing this into my computer I am struck by how this sounds like an "Adam and Eve" story and I'm curious as to whom these beings are, and how they want to "enlighten humanity." Perhaps this was simply a story that I tapped into through some greater consciousness? I don't know...but I am curious as to why I scribbled the word "élan" in my dream journal for I've never heard of this word before. I allowed my computer to define the word only to discover that élan is a French word meaning "energy and flair." What are the odds that I would scribble a word that I never heard of before and find out that it is French for energy which makes sense in the context of my late night writing? I am still amazed by my ability to channel knowledge that is truly unknown to me. For now…Namaste.

January 10, 2006: I did another healing session on my UFO friend tonight and want to jot down some observations about the healing before I forget. My friend lay on his belly when my hands started to work in the aura above his solar plexus. At first I felt a slight tornado type vortex opening and then a bright beam from above, a cylinder of strong energy, shone down and I knew the healing energy had started. This energy cylinder then became linear and formed little flames of energy all along the spine which then morphed into protrusions from my friend's spine. The impression of the energy I was receiving was that little fins, many fins were forming down his back which I did not understand at first but then it became clear. This was not one layer of fins, but three or four layers thick of back fins, staggered along the length of the dorsal side of my friend not unlike the armor carried on the back of the ancient dinosaur called a stegosaurus. My mind toyed with these images and searched for an interpretation as to the significance of the symbols I was sensing when I felt a sudden change in the energy. I was brought out of the images in my mind and I knew something, someone else was in the room with us…at my friend's feet!

I turned my head to look towards his feet and behind my closed eyes I saw nothingness, a black hole. I knew an invisible being was working at his feet just as I now understood that watching the energy changing into stegosaurus fins was a way of spirit keeping my mind busy. Was an unseen being(s) keeping me occupied while he or they worked on my friend's feet?

Curious, I slowly walked to my friend's feet to analyze the situation. I pushed energy through my third eye but could sense nothing behind my closed eyes other than my friend's feet which appeared as though they were transparent. I then laid my hands over his feet in an effort to detect any energy changes that may explain what was happening. Immediately I knew that this energy was different than what I felt over my friend's midsection and once I started to feel the new energy I could access the sight within my third eye. I saw square boxes which looked like large shoe boxes covering each of my friend's feet with three "knitting needle like" protrusions sticking out of each "shoe box." When I scanned his feet with my hands the energy bounced my hands out almost three feet away from the feet. The aura around his feet was huge!

With my curiosity temporarily appeased as to what was at his feet I turned my head to view my friend's body. I noticed that his body appeared out of proportion, as though it was very, very long and his head was missing! That same black hole of nothingness I sensed over his feet just moments before now engulfed his head! I knew I needed to return to my friend's midsection to channel energy so I walked towards his belly and allowed Hidden Deer to channel energy out of my hands with a sing-song chant melody. I felt a fluid sack forming around his body that was as transparent as a dragonfly's wing. I channeled information about seeing a jellyfish or was it a man-o-war? I shared that these fish can give off an electric charge yet they also exist in an ocean environment where they may choose not to give off a charge. I also remember sharing that it was the thick fluid of the animal's body that conducts the charge. I knew I was finished standing at the torso and returned to work over my friend's head, or at least where the head should be.

Once at his head I sensed an amplification of the energy. I could feel vortexes opening up under my palms and a large black hole of energy was pouring out of his crown, the top of his head. I peered through my third eye and could sense that the crown energy was shrinking to a smaller stream and two new vortexes of energy coming out of each of his ears were opening. Then all three vortexes resembled little tornados that twisted and looped around as if from the cartoon pictures from a Dr. Seuss book only to merge as one swirling vortex of energy spiraling up and a few feet away from my friend's body.

I verbally questioned the logic of such elaborate twists and turns of the ear vortexes and wondered why the energy would not travel in a straight line and maximize the shortest distance between two points. As I was pondering these questions in my mind I saw the image of a shell of a snail and at the same time knew the mathematical equation behind what configured the coils of a snail's shell. I had read about these spirals of nature, the Fibonacci spiral, when I had read the novel, *The Da Vinci Code*, last year. I did not understand the correlation between the spiral of the shell and the twisty vortexes protruding out of my friend's ears but somehow I did understand. As though on cue to still my hurting brain, I began to see little sparkling gold flecks within the vortexes and found myself sharing that these were either memory chips or a way of maintaining the vortex. I couldn't tap into the proper answer but I did sense it was time for my friend to change positions.

He flipped over and I stayed at his head and allowed my hands to work on his third eye. I could feel a large vortex being constructed over his forehead and this tornado of energy was pushing directly into a nickel sized opening in his skin. The vortex spun in a funnel shape for less than thirty seconds then the vortex started to close. As it shrunk the tornado turned into a linear laser like beam and with the understanding of the laser's existence I watched as the color changed from red to a blue violet. I then saw the beam blink on and off, on and off at which time I channeled information to my friend that he controlled this beam. He could turn it on and off and whenever he wanted to question these guides all he needed to do was activate the thought, the beam, and the answer would return to him via his own crown/ear vortex.

I then sensed smoke, no, it was a mist or fog that was spreading from the head and settled over his body. I saw the water droplets that were forming in the air around my friend and noticed that the area around him, his aura, was confined so it appeared as if the water was condensing on a glass. I channeled that this fog was a way of suspending the fluid until my friend required it to communicate with these beings. The last image I received that night was a white sheet being put over my friend and I found myself physically laughing as I explained this to my friend. I then assured him that they were simply putting a dust cloth over him as a sign that the healing was complete and that the cover could be removed when my friend wanted to re-engage these guides and use their knowledge for his project. I believe that the water dwelling aliens that I call the Delphi worked on my friend tonight. I wish I could have observed how they appeared. Oh well…For now…Namaste!

January 12, 2006: I've been experiencing such a numerous amount of strange dreams at night that I've been waking up tired from the lack of a continuous, uninterrupted sleep. So this morning, when I was enjoying a peaceful early morning dreamless rest and Greg woke me up before 6AM I wasn't very happy. But the enthusiasm in Greg's voice was infectious so I stirred myself to a full awake state and listened to the vivid dream he needed to share with me. As I listened to Greg's story I found out that it was not the content of the dream that was fascinating to Greg, but the reality of the obscure images: *First he saw a bi-plane circling, circling, and then it landed in a* *suburbia setting. A strange creature exited the plane which appeared to be a mixture of a horse and a wild pig. The animal got out of the plane then walked away.* That was the dream.

After hearing Greg's story I felt that there was a hidden message in his dream meant for me. Greg got out of the bed to start his day and I stayed in bed with the intention of experiencing a journey with the crystal that I associate with the boar; I held my large quartz point in my left hand, I held the boar crystal in my right and placed a cloudy quartz point over my third eye. Intuitively I knew that the horse in the dream represented me and that the stone held in my right hand was the boar. I knew that the mixing energies of the boar crystal with the horse within me was the message. I settled in for the journey:

I traveled back in time to a memory of a place that I had recently experienced which was the home of a friend that I visited just before Christmas. Then I followed Boar in a tight slice of light which I can only describe as a dimensional shift of color and movement that I have seen duplicated on science fiction programs. I was in this plane of light that was like being in a low ceilinged never ending building for the light was very thin going up and down but endlessly stretching out from side to side.

I was then at the foot of a tall building. When I looked up I saw a very, very tall, rectangular building that had no noticeable windows and was constructed of a rust red stone like material. I was wondering where the door was and how I was to get inside this building when suddenly I found myself inside the building. I looked to my side and noticed that I was with my boar animal guide and a human like guide. The human felt like the Nubian that had visited me in dream last week but he was no longer dressed in a leopard loin cloth. He now wore a flowing, hooded robe and instead of carrying a spear he held some sort of a scepter or a staff. He told me that he was a Hathor. (I learned in my lightbody merkaba workshop that the Hathors were believed to be a species of aliens that helped the Egyptians.)

We were now contained in a large open room, a cavernous pool area not unlike an ancient roman bath. The Hathor, I and the boar were standing on a sidewalk that bordered this still, indoor pool of water. I stepped into the steaming pool's thick, warm waters because I knew the Delphi were in these waters. I wanted so much to communicate with them. I could sense the lower part of my body going numb and I didn't want to get out of the pool until I could speak with these beings. I heard the phrase; 'fountain of youth' and realized the Hathor could communicate with the Delphi without entering the pool. I, too, wanted desperately to talk with the Delphi.

I analyzed how to best communicate with the Delphi and considered emerging my head into the water. I wondered if I submerged my head into the pool if I'd be able to talk with the swimming Delphi. As I was pondering this question I sensed being pulled back into the thin plane of light, the plane between realities. I slid above my body, hovered over myself, then dropped into my body and opened my eyes.

As I am writing this into my computer I wonder if it really is so difficult to speak to me that spirit needs to involve my husband, through a dream, in order for me to feel compelled to journey.

YD: *"Yes Little One. You are wise to our methods. The path of communication can be difficult, the teaching difficult, the understanding difficult. Many thanks for understanding and sharing. Namaste."*

Still January 12th: I had an appointment to give a friend some energy work today and when I arrived I shared this morning's journey with her because it was her sister's home that I first traveled to in that journey. She thought the memory of visiting her sister was curious because her daughter mentioned having a similar dream this same morning. What was odd was how her daughter described me as the "Suzy" in her dream. It wasn't a memory of Suzy, one of your clients. Or Suzy, the Mom of the girl who I go to school with. Or even Suzy, the woman we went to the mall with last month. Instead my friend's daughter recalled the mundane memory of being at her Aunt's house when I was there. I wonder why the two of us tapped into the same shared memory.

Back to my friend's healing today…After Hidden Deer and I initiated the energy my friend experienced a journey similar to what I had described from my morning dream. My hands stayed above her solar plexus and I did minimal chanting while my friend described where she was and what she was sensing. My eyes were closed and I could see images that where similar to my friend's experience; sometimes identical and sometimes slightly different. We were traveling together in a journey with the only apparent outside influence being Hidden Deer's occasional chanting and her channeled energies.

It is hard to record exactly what happened this afternoon but I'll share what I can remember. At first my friend saw an elephant then somehow we progressed to another place, time or dimension. Then my friend saw a deer like creature which resembled a spiral horned antelope. A very, very tall being in robes was present and we followed this guide and the antelope creature. Similar to what I had experienced this morning we came to the building and then we were inside the building. But instead of walking to the pool of water our path was blocked by the bald heads of a line of smaller beings. My friend couldn't make out the faces of these beings and the image that I saw was somewhat blurred. My friend shared that the antelope jumped over the smaller beings and I listened to her description of moving beyond the little bald guides because I was eager to return to the pool of water. But it wasn't meant to be.

The scene changed and we were no longer in the building but were with the small bald beings. We were in a place of mirrors that were not manufactured mirrors but the opaque mirrors of ice or crystals. (I knew this place! This was the Ice Palace or Crystal Palace I traveled to last January when I was at a workshop. I was holding a piece of light blue Celestite when I experienced this mirrored place last year.) I asked my friend if the mirror/crystal/ice that she was experiencing was light blue in color. My friend saw the place as being white and she saw the little beings as being white. Behind my closed eyes I saw the beings and ice as baby blue and knew these were the same child like beings I played hide and seek with last year. I told my friend briefly of my previous experience and she disagreed with my interpretation. She felt the purpose of these beings was more than playing a game of Hide and Seek. Then my friend felt the beings were working on her arm. She had been experiencing pain in one of her tendons and my friend sensed that the beings were, somehow, healing her. I can't recall what else happened in that half hour of time. It all seemed to fly by so quickly and then my friend needed to close the healing and prepare for her next client. Regretfully we pulled out of the journey and we were both curious as to what and why we experienced this journey/healing. For now…Namaste.

January 15, 2006: I woke up and scribbled a channel in the dark last night: *"We have been making you warm. We want our story told. We are the Corona. We too are a species from far away. We have been visiting here for many, many years. We visit now because the stars are aligned in such away so we can.*

Many centuries ago we also came here. At that time your civilization was not so involved with the technologies of communication. This is a good thing. How you are now able to communicate with peoples all around the globe.

Yes, our forefathers knew Yellow Dog. He had the ability of knowing. Like you he could understand our existence. Please tell of us. Please enlighten. We want peace. We offer peace. We are curious. We love anthropology. We observe.

I understand about your sleeping patterns. We will wait until closer to morning in the future. Good night and thank you for listening."

When I woke up this morning and read what I had written I was intrigued and decided to research the word Corona on the computer and was surprised to read that the word Corona was used to describe more than a brand of Mexican beer. According to NASA's "Imagine the Universe" website corona was described as *"the rarefied gaseous envelope of the sun or a star."* I read further details about the mysteries of the sun's corona and learned that physicists don't fully understand the mechanism at work that allows the corona to re-heat. The surface of the sun registers 5,000 degrees and the corona that surrounds the sun registers over one million degrees and scientists believe a magnetic carpet somehow provides the source of heat to the corona. I found the mystery of the sun's corona confusing but there were synchronicities to what I've been experiencing.

Could my mind have designated the title for an alien species as the word Corona when I did not consciously understand a definition of the word? And I have been sensing what I thought were hot flashes whenever these new beings were around. Could my inner mind be complex enough to draw out a definition of heat as a title to an alien race that my conscious mind does not register? And all this talk about light and heat. My tea bag as I am writing this reads: *"The job of the human being is to radiate through the finite self the infinite light."* And now that I've read my tea bag…what are the odds that the content would be related to, once again, an image of the field around the sun. Could all of this be a coincidence or is there an outside force at work? Are there really aliens in my bedroom?

Intrigued about the information about the Corona that I could glean from the computer I researched the word Delphi through the internet. I read about the Delphic Oracle, an ancient site in Greece, situated over an ancient spring where natural faults in the earth's crust caused gases and ground water to mix and emerge around the springs. Again, my mind and dreams created the name Delphi to describe an alien race that existed in heated waters and I learned through the computer that emerging springs run under the Delphic Oracle site in Greece. Could this really be a coincidence?

And the third alien species that I've journeyed with is called the Hathor and I have heard about this race of aliens during the light body activation workshop I took on November 12th. If I knew of the title of one alien race why would my mind create two more alien species? I must be channeling this stuff which means that aliens really do exist and frequent my bedroom!

Q: "Yellow Dog, can you please explain about the Corona?"

YD: *"Good morning, or rather afternoon, Little One. The Corona have been with you as they have been with me many, many, years ago, when I walked the earth plane. Yes, they are the smaller bald looking beings you have seen with your friend during her healing session on Thursday. Also called Star children, they are a mature race. They simply resemble human children of 8 or 9 years.*

They are a loving, playful race. They want to see others achieve a state of bliss, a state of peacefulness, a state of pure love. Unlike the Delphi they don't require any specific environment. Not of water, they can breathe your air. However their body temperature is much warmer. Their touch or contact can echo a warm feeling. This is why you may travel to the Ice Crystal Place to communicate where humans can contact the Corona without the interference of the heat. The human mind processes the cold of the ice crystals. The human mind cancels out the body's reaction to the Corona's heat production.

They vibrate to an extremely high level. This is another explanation of the heat. When they contact you your vibrations, too, accelerate. Your human form processes this as heat. The homoeostatic mechanism within the human body causes the human vessel to process and the brain to react by sensing the heat."

Q: "What do they want? Why are they visiting with me?"

YD: *"They want to help enlighten you and to help the human race. The Delphi have a hard time communicating with you. This is why the Corona have stepped in. Even with their accelerated vibrations they feel they can acclimate to you, Little One, your human vibrations."*

Q: "I hope they understand that my sleeping mode is not always, well, hospitable. I do not want to offend them by not journaling when they wish to talk."

YD: *"Do not worry Little One. Your intent is pure. The Corona sense this. They have observed you for some time. They understand your past trials and struggles. They understand the animal-ness of your human body. They understand the struggle you have successfully made in achieving a spiritual logic. They feel you are ready. The process will unfold. They will find a successful venue for communication."*

Q: "Can they communicate right now? Like the way we can Yellow Dog?"

YD: *"Not yet. They have to keep trying while you are in a semi-dream sleep. They have a hard time with human activity. When you are fully conscious you have many foreign energies that cycle throughout the human body. Foreign, that is, to the Corona. Your human hormones are primitive, your emotions detrimental. A way will be discovered. A process will unfold. Be patient."*

Q: "What about the power animals. Does the boar and horse help the Corona understand our human evolution more fully?"

YD: *"Yes Little One. Tapping into the pureness, the unspoiled instincts of the earth mammals is a way of further understanding the human race."*

Q: "Will you or the Corona let me know if I need to journey again? Can you do this without involving or bothering Greg?"

YD: *"Yes, we can try."*

Q: "When you want further contact or when you require me to journey can you please give me a signal. Maybe you can invade **my** dream state with the animal which you want me to journey with. Then I will find the time to meditate with my crystals and absorb any communications."

YD: *"Will do Little One. We will find the path. Be patient. Namaste."*

January 18, 2006: Early this morning I felt the bright lights behind my closed eyes and felt that familiar suddenness of heat. I knew that the Corona were near so I asked them; "What do you hope for humans to achieve?"

A: *"A source of reaching a state of oneness, wholeness, agreement with all. No more hating, killing. No need for* regions. Live together as one community, united peoples. Keep your individualism. For this is the beauty of self. But respect and draw off of each other. Allow the pieces to become the whole. Then the world can progress into the next stage of her development."

Q: "How do we achieve this?"

A: *"Enlighten as to the existence of other beings. Enlighten as to the existence of other dimensions and worlds. Enlighten as to the cosmos of possibilities. Then man will learn to broaden his horizon. He will learn to expand his psyche beyond the small world he is structured to live within, for within a broader understanding of the possibilities of life and the life force. Then man can adapt to peace."*

Before I channeled this conversation this morning, I saw a strange image behind my closed eyes. I saw a purple outlined cartoon face of a lion that morphed into the almond eyed face of an alien, then the image once again was a lion, then an alien. Then it faded. Now that it is morning and I am fully awake I am curious about the image that I woke up to behind my closed eyes.

Q: "Yellow Dog...Any ideas of the purpose of this image?"

YD: *"Good morning Little One...release, release your mind, and allow the words to flow...allow the senses to take over...allow the mind to blanken...the purpose of the line drawing is to illustrate, illustrate the possibilities to you. The lion's strength, the lion's bravery, this is what you must call upon when working with the Greys. They only respect you if you are self assured. Do not falter in your convictions. Do not falter in your decisions. Be honest, brave and true. Then the most feasible outcome will be achieved. The Greys are like the lions; brave, fearless and yet merciless."*

Q: "What am I to do with this information?"

YD: *"Respect. Respect what is out there. Respect what is. Learn to work with that which demands respect. Learn to accommodate that which you do not understand. Learn to adapt and bend."*

Q: "Am I not already doing this?"

YD: *"Yes, you are. But you are still applying human logic to your actions. Like the lion documentary.* (This was a story I watched on television about a lioness that tried to "adopt" and nurse a baby antelope and the antelope eventually was eaten by another lion.) *Not all things are as pleasant as they seem. The antelope baby did die. The lion intended the best but had to rely on its own instincts, its own DNA, its own soul. Do not expect the aliens to all have the soul of a human. Do not expect all of the same rules to apply."*

Q: "Now you are frightening me. How do I stay safe while addressing these beings?"

YD: *"Their existence does not only rely on your acceptance. They exist now. They have existed for years. Rely on us. Rely on your acute senses. When you feel something is wrong. When you feel the presence of what is not right. Acknowledge that feeling. Ask me or ask the beings for which you have developed a close human bond. Ask these Saints, spirits, ascended masters for conformation, support, protection."*

Q: "Can you explain to me? Are the Coronas those you call the Greys?"

YD: *"Open your mind, allow the words to flow... yes, they are a similar species. They have good intentions, those that you are currently working with. But like humans, they may harbor ill intent if they feel justified. They do not regard humans as equals, simply a curiosity."*

Q: "How do I stay safe?"

YD: *"Remember how to meditate. Remember how to ask for verification. Remember to trust your senses. Do this every day. Do this if the energies you are feeling are not familiar. Then you will begin to understand. Understand the intent of those that are new to you. Understand those that may or may not be safe."*

Q: "What about the friend that appears to attract aliens when I channel healing to him? Am I putting him in danger by being a channel for the Delphi?"

YD: *"Do not worry. The man is very, very well protected. He has been chosen; chosen as a vehicle to understand, a man to work for the unseen. He is allowing his pre-chosen path to unfold. He is allowing the information to download. Those that surround him are strong. They will not allow him to encounter any negative forces."*

Q: "Then why do I have a risk?"

YD: *"Your path is different. You are more of an ambassador. You are not chosen to allow information to unfold. You have chosen to enlighten. Your natural curiosity makes you the ideal vehicle to unfold your future. A future of meeting, screening, and learning about all that is unseen. Even this brief encounter with the negative is documented. You will go on to enlighten others. You will write this down, others will read, they will learn as you have learned. You are a teacher, a teacher by example. This is why you need to have exposure to what is considered negative. For through you walking this path, through you solving these issues, through you identifying these problems. Then you will teach others. You will enlighten more than we can. This is the purpose."*

Q: "Any other wisdom I should know about this topic?"

YD: *"Just find the time to cleanse yourself. Find the time to shield yourself. Find the time to communicate with those that you feel protect you. Then you will be fine. You will enjoy this path. Do not let fear stop you from learning. Do not allow the possibility of what is negative to close your eyes, your heart, and your mind. The end result for this journey of enlightenment is rewarding. It is what you choose. Live it, love it, cherish every minute of your living on the earth plane. It is such a special experience, a special gift of love."*

After I wrote this down I read my tea bag; *"The purpose of the being is to receive love from the Unknown."* The Unknown...why can't I just blissfully accept things? Why can't I be like some of the ladies from development class? Why can't I just trust in God and the Angels to take care of everything? Why must I remain acutely sensitive to what danger may be lurking around me? If I cease to worry, like some of my friends do, will the danger not exist?

I can't help but feel this perspective is that of an ostrich. I can't bury my head in the sand. If I experienced a negative force, a negative being, a negative feeling, then they exist. If I pretend it doesn't will it really cease to exist or am I shoveling off the responsibility of righting the negativity to someone else?

Q: "Yellow Dog, do I create my own reality or am I a being that exists in the reality of all? If this is the reality of a group of beings, the reality of the human race, a reality controlled by fate, or even controlled by one God, then should we not all take responsibility? Shouldn't each human search to discover the truth? Shouldn't each human accept responsibility to expose the negative? Isn't it irresponsible to ignore the negative? Irresponsible to feel that if it is not thought of, then, it will not exist?"

YD: *"Little One, you ask much about the creation of reality. You control your life by what you perceive in the world. You now understand that there are factors that are unseen; such as the energy of your aura, such as your feeling, and how they affect you, your life, others around you. You contribute to your* own reality but it is not simply a manifestation just for you. Reality is an existence created for the group to explore, interact and learn. Reality is created for the enjoyment of learning. Life is a reality. Your biological being is a reality.

There are other dimensions. Within each dimension there are concurrent realities existing. You may learn and then you may choose to experience an alternate reality; a reality existing in another dimension, a reality existing at a different speed, a different time. The creation of reality in this plane is not up to you. You can choose your reactions. You may, at one time, learn how to cross into the other dimensions. Then you may choose a reality, a dimension, different than your own.

You may choose this out of curiosity. You may choose this as an escape. You may choose which reality to exist in. But the ultimate orchestration of reality is not your decision. The ultimate orchestration is a group decision; a decision of many, many beings as a whole. A decision of one group consciousness, a decision of what you call God.

The choice to search for the truth is individual. Some humans aren't able to handle the truth. Some individual's bodies are not adaptable to the stress of the truth; the stress of being afraid, the stress of the unknown. Be patient with their ignorance, short sightedness, inability to cope. This does not make them lazy. This does not make them, as you say, irresponsible. This just makes them…them.

Do not apply your strengths as a judge of other's weaknesses. Be patient. Be patient in the knowledge that you know the truth. Be patient in the knowledge that the truth is known by those who care; by those who ultimately protect, by those who silently govern the workings of your reality."

Q: "Then, if you 'silently govern the workings of my reality', should I not fear anything? Should I not fear driving my car? Should I simply close my eyes and let the car drive itself? As the country song says; "let Jesus take the wheel?"

YD: *"You are challenging me Little One. This is why I enjoy working through you so much. To your question...you already know about the hardship of crossing the realities. If you were to put yourself in danger than you are risking the fact that we may not be able to detect the danger before it is too late. Or the fact that we may not be able to cross into your reality and enforce the proper energies to rectify the situation.*

Do not test us, do not risk harm to yourself to prove a point. This is not a positive motive. This is not a way to prove the truth. Simply trust. Trust that the best will unfold. Do your best. Live your life to its fullest and happiest. Learn what you can and share your insight. This is the purpose."

Thanks Yellow Dog. Thank-you for your patience, honesty and endless knowledge☺

Still January 18th: It is now just after 8PM. I was just re-reading Yellow Dog's entries and still trying to understand, trying to absorb this wisdom. One more thing that I need to ask...

Q: "Are the Grey's considered 'bad fairies' in some cultures? Are fairies and aliens and angels all separate beings? How do you classify them Yellow Dog?"

YD: *"Another lesson unfolds...The ancients had limited understandings. The phrase alien was not within their realm of thinking. They understood gods, goddesses, angels and fairies. In your modern culture you understand the concept of aliens. Through your TV shows, comic books, literature, the concept of aliens is well understood. Aliens are believed more commonly than fairies now. Let me explain this another way.*

Those that come from worlds not of Earth, these beings are Angels. Angels are not of your world. They come from a system far away. They can exist without body. They have developed this function so, so, long ago. They are extremely advanced. They love, cherish and enjoy helping the human race. Their intent is all knowing, all good, all pure in intent.

The fairies, these are beings in another earthly dimension. They exist in another plane of reality. Their rules and physics are of another plane. They can be helpful if they are enlightened. They can be harmful if they feel threatened. Like you in your dimension they are trying to evolve, develop, some at faster rates than others.

Those from the fairy realm that are advanced enough to cross into your dimension can achieve great things. They can fuse the powers of the two planes and exchange helpful energies. Their world is a mirror of your own. Their realities can complement your own. Their truths may not be the truth of your world. Care, care must be practiced when venturing into the other dimensions.

There are some beings that are not truly of the fairy realm. They have ventured from other worlds and now exist in the other dimension. They are alien to the earth. Yet they have existed here for centuries. Are they now considered fairy? I do not know. Those that can come and go freely from their world into the fairy realm...are they fairy or alien? As you see the truth is somewhat clouded.

As for gods and goddesses...to the early earth peoples any extraordinary being was considered a god. Look at your human rulers of Egypt, then later Rome. They used the phrase god liberally. Yes, superior beings of all races, dimensions and worlds were considered gods. The line here is very clouded. I do not have a clear definition for you. I hope you understand."

Q: "The beings I think of as the Delphi. Are they from another world? Are they able to travel to and from Earth at will?"

YD: *"Yes, the Delphi are a very sophisticated and very, very old race. They have seen many, many things. They choose to keep their form. They enjoy the sensation from their bodies too much to forfeit a bodily form. They tried being bodiless, but they felt so saddened without the feeling of touch. It is a strong sense that is the center of their communication.*

They enjoy seeing the early forms of planets. They enjoy the stillness of a planet without many life forms. They know how to time travel. They choose to go back, back to the early forming of the planets. This is where they love to exist. This is their choice; a world of solitude and peace, a world back in time, a world of existence within their beloved body, an existence free of diversions of other life forms, their own home of solitude in time."

Q: "Then why would they want to help my friend that I channeled healing to?"

YD: *"Many species of what you call aliens have contracted to help this man. This was an agreement he entered into when he was in a bodiless form. This was a decision, a task, his soul chose to make."*

Q: "Are the Delphi a 'safe' group of beings for me to work with?"

YD: *"Do not disturb their solitude. If they choose to help you then appreciate their wisdom and their abilities to channel the lower vibrations of existence; the vibrations of the fluids, the vibration of the water, like whale sounds, the low, low, pitches of adjustment and ultimately healing of the human form."*

Q: "Please explain to me about the Corona?"

YD: *"They are a species, too, from another reality. They come from far away. You are correct in that they enjoy warmer temperatures. They can get careless in their appreciation for the human body and its limitations".*

Q: "Are they the beings in the plane where I see the multifaceted crystals?"

YD: *"Those of the Blue Ice Palace that you experienced last year. These playful beings were beings on a quest. Like a vacation they were simply in a playful mode. You happened to fall into the dimension the same time they were there, akin to you stumbling upon a cruise ship in your world, a place of unrealistic fun."*

Q: "Do they have healing powers? Were these the same beings my friend experienced last week?"

YD: *"Your friend stumbled upon those in charge of the play time. They understand how to help and cure. Yet they do not seek you. You and your friend stumbled upon their dimension. This is where you must take care. If we come to get you and lead you into our dimension then all is right. If you stumble across us while traveling into the other dimensions then please take care. Not all that are happily enjoying a dimension that is different from yours will be able to assist you. Not all of what you call aliens are enlightened. Those that your trusted guides show you are safe."*

Q: "But wait...Hidden Deer guided my friend and me on that journey?"

YD: *"No Little One. Hidden Deer opened the door. You and your friend stumbled along on your own path."*

Q: "Should I not journey this way? Is it safe?"

YD: *"The two of you are exploring, learning. You both are protected. This is the path for which you have chosen. Do not worry about being safe. Feel, sense, you will know when things are wrong. Hidden Deer will not allow you to go down a dangerous path. She is simply exposing the two of you to the possibilities."*

Q: "Why was my friend not able to tap into the Delphi like I was?"

YD: *"We are trying to understand your friend's capabilities. We are trying to find her frequencies. We know yours. When she travels with you she can go to some of the places you go to. When she tries to drive, the possibilities are more limited. Keep playing, keep experimenting. You are protected. You will discover much, much for both yourself and human kind. Enjoy."*

Q: "How can I tell the difference between the Corona and the Greys?"

YD: *"They feel different; the Corona feels warm, the Greys are cool. Cool like death. But not all Greys are negative. Like the dark fairies, they simply don't follow the same rules of existence as humans do. For that matter neither do the Corona.*

The Corona are more Scientifically driven. They are so consumed in the search for their truth that they may not put the human needs first. Your world is a temptation to many, many races of beings. We in the united circle want only what is best for you humans.

Our races are developed; our needs have been met so long ago. We need so little. We are simply happy providing for you humans. We enjoy watching you grow, expand. Like a rose flower. We weep with joy when a new plane of understanding is reached. To us time is endless. Watching your race develop is just a hiccup in time to us."

Thank you again for all your wisdom...Namaste.

January 22, 2006: Today I was speaking with a woman that enjoys reading about the Mayan culture and together we shared insights regarding the legendary continent of Lemuria, the changing of the constellation formations in the heavens recorded by the Mayans and the mysteries of the ancient people of the Americas. She has been worried about some information she read in a book so when I explained my ability to confide in you she asked me to ask you, Yellow Dog, if the Maya had an understanding of what my friend calls 'the evolution of consciousness?'

A: *"Little One your friend is wise, her insight keen. The Mayan are an advanced race, advanced because of their association with the unknown, their association with those that understand and know of many, many things. The ancient peoples themselves were of simple challenges. It was their association with the Others. This is what fed their curiosity. This is what allowed them to explore what is unseen, allowed them to wander into the other dimensions of reality as we have discussed before.*

Yes, the Maya did venture into the unknown. First they simply allowed the Others to assist them. Then, when they learned how to see the unseen, then they learned how to transcend the unknown. They shared this knowledge with fellow Maya that showed the ability to learn, the capacity to transmit the ideas of the Others.

The general public was a simple loving people. The average people did not require any fantastical advancement to exist, to remain happy. It was those that had the talents, those that could tap into the unknown. Those that you would now call shaman, priests, psychics. These peoples learned and listened to the Others.

They learned how to assist their peoples by working with the unknown. They learned how to tap into their hidden resources with the help of the unknown. But not all of the peoples were naturally gifted or physically able to adapt to these abilities. So this treasured gift. This ability to talk with the Others. This was reserved to those with the ability. Just like the general public understood that not all people were adept at being a gifted runner, or a gifted weaver, or a gifted person in working the stone, all people were not gifted in working with the Others.

So, in answer to your question, only those who were chosen were led into an "evolution of consciousness." With time the Others taught them many techniques; many ways to transcend time and space, many ways to move beyond the boundary of their physical bodies. But the people that were adaptable to these talents were few. The interest was held sacred and revered. For this reason only a small percentage of the Maya ventured into these interests."

Q: "Thank you Yellow Dog...Can you provide a modern definition of the Others?"

YD: *"This is a difficult task for I am merely conversing with those that have lived during those times. They don't require a classification. They never heard of Aliens, Angels, Fairies or Saints. To them the helpful beings of the unseen were simply, and lovingly, referred to as the Others. No classification was needed."*

"Thank-you Yellow Dog. I'll relay your insight. Goodnight and Namaste."

January 23, 2006: Yesterday, during church service, I was chosen to be a healer and a pleasant older woman, one of the matriarchs of our church, was the first to sit in my chair. WOW! The energy was so strong! I am used to Hidden Deer's pattern of movements but today when I allowed my hands to motion something was stopping my right hand. It was as if a powerful spirit had transposed his hand over mine. I smiled at the loving embrace of this new spirit and allowed the superimposed hand to gently move with me as I chanted in my mind, allowing my mouth to quietly follow along. I didn't want to end this healing and apparently neither did the lady sitting in my chair, for she appeared startled when I gently touched her shoulders as a signal that we were finished and the healing energy was done.

The second and final person to sit in my chair was a smaller woman with short cropped hair who I've channeled healing energy to before. I expected to sense the same energy that I had remembered from her last healing which was the playful fairy like energy of little dancing beings. I started to motion then…WOW! Again I felt the strong energy and the sensation of a hand transposed over my own. I motioned very little and allowed this new energy, this new being, to heal and as the healing energy was working I wondered. Was this healer spirit associated with the older woman I had just channeled healing to? Believing that this new energy was associated with my first sitter, I allowed her guide to channel through me in healing the new sitter in my chair. I still sensed some small beings or fairies but they seemed far, far away. After the healing chairs were closed and I was placing my healing chair into its stored position at the front of the church I wondered why the older woman's people, her spirit guides, chose to stay for the healing of this second woman.

The church service progressed to the time for "Messages" which was when a medium would share impressions that spirits wanted to share with the congregation. The guest reverend that was the medium on the podium turned to me as said; "Did you feel the presence of a hand guiding you during today's healings?"

"Ooo-freakie!" I thought and responded sheepishly; "Yes."

The reverend then informed me that this was a new guide that is willing to work with me, if I chose. His eyes were large, relaying that the power of this being was strong. He stared through me as he said; "That I must find the time to explore working with this new guide." I understood his message yet I was perplexed as to why I needed another healing guide. Much to think about…for now…Namaste.

January 24, 2006: I am writing this for the second time because my first attempt to record these words disappeared after I typed them into the computer. I hate these stupid machines but journaling directly into the computer seems more efficient than hand writing my insights and later transcribing them into typing. More efficient, that is, until the computer "gets stupid!" I wonder if there are unseen beings affecting my computer or if I am just being paranoid. At any rate allow me to share what happened today.

I was enjoying my weekly massage when two friends dropped by from my development circle. I briefly explained the energy that I had with the Delphi and they appeared to understand what I was talking about for an impromptu circle led to all four of us traveling on a journey together. During the time we were journeying I was lying on the massage table while my masseuse and I talked with my two friends seated in the small massage room. One of my friends from development circle experienced a journey that was eerily similar to the experience I had with the boar after Greg's dream. She shared her experience as we were sitting in the confines of the small massage room.

My friend first sensed traveling with the light that she described as existing in and around other planes of reality. Then she saw the sandstone building. She was outside the building, then inside with a mythical centaur type creature. Then she saw the bald headed short beings. Then she was whisked away to where a mutual deceased friend was. Here she started to channel a message from this deceased friend.

That was the last I remember from her journey for I lost time. I realized that the clock that hung in the massage room said we were in circle for over thirty minutes but my reality was different for I felt as though I only experienced five minutes! Where did the time go? Where was I? I hate losing time when I journey. I feel I missed out on something, and this especially sucked because I missed out on sensing my massage as well!

When I entered this into the computer just thirty minutes ago I asked Yellow Dog to explain why the similarities between the three journeys? My two friends and I didn't discuss our dream/journeys, yet these all followed the same pattern; the light, the animal/mythical guide and the sandstone building. Once inside this building we all branched off into different experiences; I went to the Roman baths and met with the Delphi. One friend went to a place of crystal like mirrors and small white glowing beings that tended to her sore arm. My other friend went to a place where a mutual deceased friend existed.

Yellow Dog explained that we all went to a place where we were seeking answers or assistance. I wanted contact with the Delphi and their healing energies, I received it. One friend was seeking a cure for her ailments and received it. My other friend had just met with a psychic and was in search for better mediumship and she received it. Now that I've retold what I had just typed that was zapped away by this computer...allow me to continue with my questioning.

Q: "Is this place, this sandstone building, a Genie's bottle, a place where our wishes are granted? Or is this a place where spirit can understand and communicate to us our desires, a Shangri-La of sorts?"

YD: *"Yes Little One. This pattern of journeying is a tool. More so than the journey you take with the animals to the Other World. This place is of a dimension deeper out of your reality; a dimension where time and space collides, a place where you can imagine and materialize the proper answer, a place where all can co-exist and re-route to the most logical end."*

Q: "What is the purpose of the light we see at the beginning of the journey?"

YD: *"There is a travel to this place. It is not as close as the Other World. Like a star gate, you must jump from your reality to this reality of assignment, with your animal guide. Then you will be read by those which you call the "bald beings." They will process your desires and forward you to an appropriate reality."*

Thank you Yellow Dog, you gave me much to think about. Namaste.

Still January 24th: It is now just after 10PM and as I rethink my experiences of the day I still find the similarities between mine and my other two friends' journeys too coincidental to be coincidence. I remember an old, original *Star Trek* series episode where the characters were "beamed down" onto a planet of barren, blowing desert where they find a single building being watched over by a sort of "gate keeper." Inside the building was a gong like device that was actually a time machine. The characters in the *Star Trek* story each entered the machine and traveled to a place back into time. The story unfolds and they need to locate the vortex that will re-establish their pathway back, through the time machine, back to the original building in the blowing desert.

I know our experience was not identical to the scenario in the television series, but what are the chances that we would all experience a rectangular upright building that stood alone in a desert-like setting? And how coincidental is it that this building represented some sort of gateway into another reality? Could the creator of the aforementioned *Star Trek* television episode have somehow dreamed or journeyed to this same place of the tall red sandstone building that my friends and I experienced?

I am tired and want to go to bed but I need to journal one more strange event. Today Greg and I went to the grocery store together and arrived home around 3PM. We were getting out of the car when we both looked up and saw a spark in the sky that turned to a bright round light. We stood there in our driveway and discussed that the light was simply a jet plane high up in the sky that was reflecting the brightness of the sun. Then the too bright orb narrowed into an upright rectangle shape and disappeared. In unison Greg and I turned to each other and smiled. Did we just witness a UFO? The mystery continues to unfold…for now…Namaste.

January 25, 2006: "Hi Yellow Dog. I know you're with me. I can feel your philosophical mind coursing through my fingers. You and your friends really did download a lot of information into me lately. Is this why I was missing so much time during that impromptu circle I did with my friend's yesterday?"

YD: *"Yes Little One. Your human mind cannot function with consciousness while understanding our thoughts. This is why you lose the time. It is an unfortunate problem with your brain. However it is developing, growing, changing. With time you will be able to understand us better. You will better be able to communicate our thoughts, our input to theirs. This is the purpose of these time-loss episodes. This is a good thing, a natural progression in your ascent into enlightenment."*

Q: "A friend of mine channeled that I need to find a special frequency; a phone line or code, for which I talk with you Yellow Dog. I need to be sure that you are near. Then I will be assured that only the best beings can communicate through me. His concern made me think of how I know it is you when I channel words and I believe it is my clairsentience that self-assures me. As you are beginning to type through me I first feel a warm sensation in the base of my spine, my root chakra. Then a pressure in my head, behind my eyes, starts and at this point I can push energy through my third eye. When I push the energy out I can empty my mind or "zone out" and let my fingers type without my mind interfering. When I am typing I can then feel a warmth in my heart; a feeling of love, a feeling of fatherly love, and/or a feeling of pride and protection. Then I hear in my mind; "Hello Little One." It is at this point I know Yellow Dog is here and the wisdom to be shared will start. If I rely on these sensations and this method of channeling wouldn't you filter out the beings that talk through me so that only the beneficial beings are channeled?

YD: *"Yes Little One. On the computer we have found a comfortable and efficient way of communicating. The problem lies in the evolution of your learning. You must not panic when you do not have access to the computer or a writing implement. You no longer require a crystal to channel healing. Now you no longer require a computer to communicate with me. This is what your friend was trying to allow you to understand. The next step to you being a medium is to allow us to use your body as a keyboard. Before you can do this you must be assured that I am there, in control, orchestrating the beings which will be in contact through you.*

This is the purpose of today's information exchange over the telephone. This is the purpose of what you need to work on now. You must become more aware. Just as you are aware of the....do not drive please....feel me working through you. Feel my presence next to you. Concentrate on my presence. Then I will better be able to use you as a true channel."

Q: "I don't want to interrupt but I understand what you are saying Yellow Dog but do you fully understand my earthly concerns with my family and my body's limitations? I can't afford to fully trance out and do...God knows what! I must not embarrass my children. My two younger children are teenagers, living at home. They deserve to blend into society. I don't want to appear unusual, eccentric or...crazy! I must not infringe on my children's rights to "fit in."

YD: *"Yes, Little One. I too, was a human form once. I understand the complex rules of society."*

Q: "I guess I do expound on your wisdom some. Sorry."

YD: *"Not to worry for it is not me that you are hearing. I allow the wisdom of many to reach your fingers. I also can allow the wisdom of many to talk through your body. But first we must practice, practice slowly, and understand the boundaries of acceptability. For now...Namaste."*

January 29, 2006: I spent today at an event held at a hotel on the other side of the state which was a gathering of holistic practitioners called an "Alternative Expo." I traveled there with friends from my development class and the day was not only enlightening but fun! I listened to many speakers. The first was a woman who talked about crystals. I felt I knew more than she and was somewhat bored through her presentation, but I did learn that I have traveled deeper into my own understanding of the subject. The second lecture I attended also concerned crystals but this woman used the stones to assist in her healing work. I took notes and was intrigued by her strict rules, but I know I have used similar stones and have felt different results. I suppose that crystals work differently through different workers and perhaps it is the practitioners belief that is more powerful than the crystals.

I then attended a one hour lecture titled "HUNA! Ancient Hawaiian Healing Technique." I listened to this man's stories of the island of Hawaii's intriguing link to a long lost past. I thought of my current belief in ancient Lemuria as a place in a time before recorded time. I was intrigued by this lecturer and his philosophy that the enlightened person accepts things that go wrong with the affirmation: "Such is the nature of things." I also listened to an explanation of the three levels of consciousness and how each level has its own corresponding energy. I am still unclear behind the meaning all of this man's teachings but I found the theories interesting. After the lecture I went to this man's booth in the lecture hall. I was curious to find out if he could understand Hidden Deer's language but I was unsure as to how to approach him.

I hovered around his booth looking at the bracelets and crystals that were on display when finally I saw a break in the people around his table. I introduced myself and explained about the Native tongue I have the ability to speak and before the man could intervene I allowed Hidden Deer to talk through me. The man said that it didn't sound Hawaiian to him then he tried to escape with his eyes darting longingly for others to drift towards his booth. I understood that this man was at the exposition to promote his business and his healing technique. I accepted his purpose for being at the exposition plus I believed the man was concerned that I might be a little crazy so I silently walked away from his booth disappointed that I was not to find a clear answer as to the language of Hidden Deer today. I am tired from the long day away from home. For now...Namaste.

January 30, 2006: Once again I found an interesting insight through watching TV. I was flipping through the channels and settled upon the travel channel's program called "Weird Travel Spots". What caught my attention was the mention of Sedona, Arizona and the reputed "vortexes" in the area. The program was scanning pictures of tourist sites in Arizona when the television screen showed a picture of one of the dwellings of the indigenous Sinagua peoples. Wow, this building was the sandstone building from my journey!

Early European explorers called this cliff dwelling building; "Montezuma's Castle." The building had nothing to do with the Central American ruler called Montezuma nor was it a form of a castle. It was cave like dwelling chiseled out of the mountain side that was believed to have been constructed 1100-1350 AD, presumably by the Sinagua people. If I isolated just the central tower of the conglomerate I would be viewing a picture of a building identical to the red earth and sandstone looking upright rectangular building in my journey!

The television program then talked about the nearby lake which was kept at a consistent temperature due to underground springs. I felt shivers down my spine when I reasoned that the underground springs was coincidentally similar to the underground springs I read about existing by the building at Delphi in Greece. And I did experience the pool for the Delphi aliens when I journeyed to the place where the tall rectangular building stood!

My mind wrapped around questions and explanations that I couldn't solve. Did I travel to Sedona in my journey? Or did the Sinagua people pattern their building after one they saw in their own journeys? Did the Sinagua travel to the same place I experienced in my recent meditations? Was I traveling to Arizona in today's time? Was I traveling to another planet that the Sinagua patterned their cliff dwelling after?

One more strange synchronicity that I learned from the documentary was that there was a river in this area where a strange tree existed that was considered the center of a vortex. This tree was actually two species of trees intertwined as one; half sycamore and half cypress. Upon hearing this I remembered the meditation that I was led through at psychic class before Christmas when I traveled down a river past either a Sycamore or a Cypress tree. I assumed after the meditation that cypress was an explanation for the sycamore tree and that the sycamore was explaining something about the mythical animal the Phoenix. But was this meditation's purpose to reveal things about Sedona? Come to think of it I am going to travel to Phoenix, Arizona soon. Was my journey a prophecy about this program I was watching on TV today? Too many coincidences to digest and I don't sense Yellow Dog near. My brain hurts and I'm tired so…for now…Namaste.

~ CHAPTER 10 ~

HUICHOLS AND EGYPTIANS - FEBRUARY, 2006

February 1, 2006: I woke up this morning to the light flashes behind my closed eyes. The flashes were almost understandable and I thought I was watching brief glimpses of a color movie. I could sense my daughter and somehow I understood that these flashes had to do with her. If only I could focus on just one image. If only I could slow this movie down…Then I saw a clear brief image! The image of a girl wearing a blue basketball uniform making a lay-up shot. I was experiencing the image as though seeing it through my own eyes. I knew that I needed to look to my right to see this image and I knew that this was during a basketball game. My recognition of the event stopped the images for as soon as I placed this scene as reality in my upcoming day the movie in my mind stopped playing and the flashes behind my closed eyes were gone.

When I was out of bed and eating breakfast I asked my daughter before she left for school about the game she was scheduled to play today. I wanted to know if she would be wearing her blue uniform with a little white or the white uniform with a little blue. She told me she was playing a "home" game today so she would be wearing the white uniform, then asked me why I wanted to know. I told her about my "vision" and how I thought she would make a lay-up shot at today's game. She doubted my prediction for she was second string, plays defense, and seldom gets to shoot the ball. Besides, she was wearing the white uniform today. I accepted her insight and forgot about my early morning dream until later today.

This afternoon I was watching her basketball game and it was the fourth quarter. My daughter was called in because her team was winning by a healthy margin and I was sitting on the bleachers in the right side of the gym. Then I saw it. The action was fast. My daughter had the ball. As she dribbled by me I looked to the right and saw her make a lay-up shot. From my view point, all I could see was her side and her uniform had a bold blue vertical stripe under her arm which made her shirt appear as though it was blue, not white. She made the layup shot just as I saw it in this morning's "movie." Boy that was weird! For now…Namaste.

February 3, 2006: Again I woke up with a flash of lights dancing behind my closed eyes. I waited and watched the lights flying by, wondering if I was to see another vision into the future. The scenes did not reveal any event in my real time but instead reviewed a clip from a movie I fell asleep watching last year called; *A Beautiful Mind* starring Russell Crowe. The scene was when a tall, thin, college roommate character who was actually the red haired ghost that communicated with the genius of the main character, was talking. This was the image I woke up with from the moving lights behind my closed eyes. I knew spirit wanted to communicate so I got my pen and wrote:

"The human brain's ability to understand advanced material…The human brain is so delicate, so limited in its ability to absorb knowledge. This is why you must not push knowledge; like the images you are trying to process behind your closed eyes. The images will form with time, as will the knowledge. With time it will come. With time the brain will understand.

The soul already understands. The soul is in complete understanding of all there is. For such is the knowledge of pure energy. It is the mammalian body that has limitations,

limitations of the reality of its current senses. This is the block, the obstacle that you must overcome if you are to learn how to process true knowledge.

Many have learned through art. Poetry and paintings are expressions of knowledge. Yet these expressions through love are only understood by those with the same level of love. To reach beyond emotion, this is the goal for you. To use the human brain to process logic without the art, there is the question at hand. Can the human body withstand this process without going mad?

For this reason you must bury pride and stubbornness. Bury fear and frustration. Simply trust. Trust that the unseen will channel the appropriate information at the appropriate time. Trust that we will relay the information through you. Trust that the information will come through. Trust that we understand what your mind can and cannot process. Trust that the knowledge will ultimately be shared.

You are protected. You sacrifice no free will. No harm is intended nor will it precipitate. Trust, trust without interpretation. Trust without analyzation. Trust with pure channeling. Be the device for this channel, this communication. Leave it to their talents to ultimately understand. With time your human mind MAY be able to grasp.

Do not lament. Do not feel ill at ease, for your soul understands. The purpose is not for you to define. The purpose is to channel."

Unfortunately my husband came into the room and turned on the light and my writing stopped. I was frustrated at having lost the channel but happy that Greg and I shared an interesting conversation about the movie called *"What the Bleep?"* that we watched a few evenings ago. We talked about the scene from the movie that questioned whether the human mind could accept the existence of an experience that it has never experienced. The movie illustrated this with a scene of Native Americans that were unable to see the Spanish ships in the ocean for they only would have seen these ships with their eyes. It wasn't until the Spanish ship was closer to the coast and the Natives could feel the ripple in the currents of the water AND see the water parting AND hear the sounds of the calling birds regarding the intruders when they COULD see the Spanish ships. The accumulation of all these human senses was necessary for the Native's brain to finally process the Spanish as a reality. My husband and I were kidding about the possibility that all sorts of UNSEEN beings could all exist in my bedroom at this moment. Aliens, fairies, dead people, could they all be walking in our midst even as we ponder this possibility and because we can't sense the unseen with our human bodies do we believe they don't exist and thus they don't TO US? I find these concepts…Confusing!

After my husband left the room I lay in bed staring at the ceiling and thinking. Then I felt compelled to write once more: *"Sight without the other senses does not always process what the brain sees. The human experience relies on touch, smell, hearing or even taste, for confirmation of what is in your reality. The human brain has learned this as a safety mechanism for all humans have given up peering into alternative realities in order to survive.*

In order to be able to feed the human mind, the human soul, the sight needs the reality of the human body to stay properly shifted in the dimension. With the human senses combined, the body can stay materialized in your current plane. Without your plane of reality there would be chaos.

The human body functions in the one plane it can survive. For the human mind will be cognizant of the human body's needs, wants and interactions. To shift too frequently is to give lack to the human body. To lack the body is to lack the brain. Without the brain the soul cannot process. Without the brain the soul cannot experience humanness, the human experience. This is a delicate balance; a balance assisted by those who are unseen, a balance that you are learning to master.

When you are leaving your body, you are leaving part of your senses. The human body concentrates, organizes for the soul. Without the body your soul is free, yes, but reality is confused, depressed. The feeling of bliss is the feeling of bodiless, a feeling of the soul without boundaries.

The human body is necessary for education of the soul. Stay on the path. Respect and honor the human spirit, the human mission. Appreciate your current existence, for the complex reality of its limitations is truly a blessing to experience.

Enjoy the naivety of it all...Namaste."

Still February 3rd: It is just after 8AM. The animals are fed, the children are off to school and I feel the need to continue with the channeling I started earlier: *"During sleep, while I am allowing my mind, my consciousness to travel, while I do not allow fears or worries to surface about my human body. This is the time that I can experience alternate realities. This is the time that I can start to understand the unseen. This is the time for the truth to unfold.*

The human, mammalian body is the limitation of the soul while it exists within, as one with the body. The human vessel is flawed. It must survive in its environment. The same mechanisms that allows this survival; these are the emotions, the fears, the worries, the protection of self. These are the emotions that limit the evolution of consciousness. For here lies that paradox.

To further enlighten humanity with what is unknown, man must forfeit his survival instincts. He must forfeit all of his instincts. For the instincts are tied to the human body. The instincts will draw in the mind. The instincts will activate the brain in such a way as to render the soul temporarily useless.

The mind must learn to let go of these instincts, these restrictions. The human who harbors this mind must rely on other humans for their sense of survival. By working in tandem, this is how the soul can surface. This is how the human body can survive without damage. The human must have a partner, a guardian on your own plane. Then you can progress without fear of what is unseen. Then you can consult and understand the human experience, the human opinion, when you are allowing your soul to blossom. Rely on your mate. Rely on a trustworthy individual. Allow them to rely on you when you are fully within your body. Then you can progress with ease.

For it is those that try to journey alone, it is those that isolate themselves to discover the true meanings. These are the individuals that risk the madness. These are the individuals that do, indeed, 'lose touch with reality.' These are the individuals that ache to return to that which is unseen. These are the individuals that neglect their human form in search of the unseen. These are the individuals that evolve in a warped pattern.

A pattern that is not understandable to fellow humans. A pattern that is not fully acceptable to the unseen, a sort of hybrid existence that is not reality in either world. To avoid this confusion, consult. The development of the seeing the unseen is not to be hidden. This is not for you to be embarrassed, afraid, awed or to draw upon any other of the myriad of human emotions. The development of the unseen is for those that are able to experience. And it is the responsibility of those that are able to share their experience with others. Not only to enlighten, but to preserve the humanness of those that are vessels for communication.

Trust, rely on others for your safety, your sanity, then you can overcome this final hurdle; this fear of the unseen, this fear of the unseen causing harm, doing evil, tricking your human form into damage.

We are here. We are guarding you on the other side. We are monitoring that which we can see and interact with. We understand your humanness. We understand the limiting effect of your human emotions. We understand your intuition. For this is the purpose of this channel.

What is intuition? It is not the sensing of us for we are separate from the soul and body. We are the unseen. You are hearing us. Your soul hears us. This is channeling, not intuition. Intuition is instinct. Intuition is the human ability to survive, the human ability to adapt. The human ability to preserve its bodily form, this is intuition.

You call it many things. When you sense anger in another...this is not, necessarily, us channeling this information. This is your soul, in union with your body, processing energy. You are sensing the energy of fellow humans in your plane. You are sensing their energies, desires, wants. Your human body is reacting to these sensations. That is intuition. It is the energy sharing amongst fellow humans. It is the acuteness of this energy sharing that allows for survival.

Think of the bird flock flying in formation. Why do they not bump into each other? This is, in part, their intuition. When the flock changes direction, when the bird not in the lead senses that the direction will change, senses the directional changes before they actually transpire. This is intuition.

When you sit next to a serial murderer you can sense his ill intent. You can feel the sadness of his past deeds. Yes, you may actually, subconsciously be channeling his victims that have crossed, but beyond this, the pure animal emotion that he emits. This is picked up by the receptors in your brain; the part of your body that wishes to fight, the part of your humanness that wants to survive. This is intuition.

Your friend doesn't display this willingness for self survival. He does, indeed, lack the human ability to sense, the human animal's ability to instinctually know about the animal energies around him. This underdeveloped sense of survival allows him to more easily jump into alternate planes of reality. But within your society he must sacrifice his individuality. He must sacrifice the ability to formulate solutions. The ability to sense, through his humanness, what is unseen. He does not have the animal-ness sight, the instinct, the intuition.

What he does have working for him is the channeling, the communication with the unseen. The ability to hear, discern, read what is thrown at him. For this is a more difficult path. This requires trust. For the human body cannot easily confirm the unseen. The human body can use its senses in your plane. The human body can activate its senses when traveling to other planes; can reason material through memories of the human senses.

What your friend doesn't have hindering himself is the doubt that intuition brings. He does not doubt, he does not worry about self survival, he just is. He travels into other planes and simply enjoys the experience. He exists with other humans and listens to the unseen channeling bits of information. He simply doesn't know how, nor wants to, nor needs to rely on his instincts, his humanness, and his intuition.

Intuition: the mind's ability to avoid a situation before it transpires. The mind's ability to prophesize an event in order to avoid a detrimental result, the human mind's ability to warn itself to avoid destruction, the human mind's ability to foresee in order to survive."

Q: "Is this not a multi-second form of time travel into the future?"

A: *"No, this is purely sensing energy. This is purely sensing the intent of others. Some people can see the aura. Some people can read the colors and understand the intent and process this information. The root of this insight is from the human body alone. Alone does the human body read the colors and process the intent. There is no intervention from other beings. Intuition is purely from within; a human survival technique developed within the human, a pureness of self-preservation."*

Q: "Then why doesn't my friend possess this ability?"

A: *"All humans have their strengths and weaknesses. When the earth was younger, when man was younger in his development, this is when certain traits became concentrated within society. Those that could survive produced. Those that didn't could not pass on their genes.*

This is what happened in some ancient civilizations. The enlightened also forfeited their instincts. With this inability to sense dangers they ultimately perished at the hands of other humans, humans that still relied heavily on their instincts. This is the troubling fact about humanness. They still feed the primordial need for competition; the need to compete for food, the need to survive."

Q: "Then, if competition is paired with intuition. Why does my friend enjoy sports?"

A: *"Do not lump together all primitive human emotions. Competition is also related to aggression. This is an emotion that runs pure in those that want to lead, those that want to be heard. Those that need to have others; others to take care of them, others to do their bidding and others to help them to survive. Intuition is more for those that enjoy battling within nature; those that enjoy feeling the humanness of the body and those that enjoy savoring the closeness to the animal side.*

Again the human body and its reaction with its soul are a complex and beautiful relationship. Ever varied, ever changing, and ever evolving. This is not a relationship that should be worshiped or feared. This is a relationship of love, harmony and co-existing.

Embrace your humanness. Respect the vessel you reside within. Respect its limitations and its vast array of abilities. Enjoy the vehicle. For through it your soul can learn much. Through living your being truly advances.

Learn, experience, share with others. This is your soul's purpose. Enjoy relearning what your soul already knows. Enjoy learning how to communicate your soul's understanding through human reality.

Enlighten those around you. Help them to better understand the unseen. For it is through this understanding that humanity will progress. For it is through communication that the human race will learn to co-exist. And it is through respect for the unseen that the world, your environment, will also survive.

When others realize about the existence of the unseen, when other humans realize the delicate balance of the environment, when others realize that the unseen are affected by the treatment of the world in your plane of existence. Then civilization will truly evolve.

The ages of quiet respect are through. The time of obedient religion is past. Your current civilization is damaging to the Earth. The unseen have accelerated our communications. We have opened the door to our realities wider. This is in an effort to enlighten. This is in a loving effort to assist, to assist those that live in your reality to preserve their existence.

Enlightenment, this is how man can progress. Acceptance, this is the obstacle you must overcome. Acceptance without fear; fear of past laws, fear of the birthrights of societies, fear of the unknown, fear of the written laws of the past.

Illustrate that you can work in tandem with others. A group of two or more people can become enlightened without "damning" them all. Appoint one being to be a seer. Appoint one being to the seer, the enlightened one and the communicator with the unseen. Then invite the group of others, the community of peoples to question the unseen through this seer. Let the group hear the words. Let the group discuss the unseen. Let the group weigh the logic. Let the group feel the true intent of love, peace and harmony.

Do not expect all within the group to share the desire to be a medium. Allow some in the group to be providers. If more than one exists within this group of communicators...then allow another to be the questioner. Assign all of your fears and worries to the group. Let these fears and worries be communicated. Allow the channel to, with the help of the unseen; develop solutions to the humanoid worries and concerns. Then you may come to accept us as pure of heart and intent.

We only ask for the chance to be heard. We have no desire to lead. We only want to enlighten. We only want to preserve the earth as it is, as it can be. We want to continue to use your dimension on the earth plane. We want to continue to develop our inner self, our only self, and our souls.

Enlighten, enlighten as to the many possible ways of respect. Enlighten that many paths of reality do exist. Enlighten that each human may choose. You may choose to exist without communication with the unseen. All we ask is that the word is made public. All we ask is that the world is preserved. All we ask is that humans jump a step in their evolution. We ask humans to abandon some of their humanness and question the existence of the unseen.

We do not look to lead. We do not look to experiment on humans. We do not look to control. We want the human experience to play out. We want the soul to develop as it must. We want the earth to survive. We want the human race to survive. We want enough enlightenment to secure this survival.

Continue on your path Little One. Continue to learn. Continue to journal. Continue to share. For with each human voice sharing we can communicate to a different source of people, for each human has a different perspective. Each human has different talents and abilities. Each human has different paths, different paths of understanding. And with each enlightened being that chooses to communicate, a different path of understanding may develop; a path of mutual respect of the Earth, a path of mutual respect of each human to the next.

The task is daunting. But the outcome is very important. Try Little One. Get these ideas published. Get the word out. And let the people decide. Try to examine the idea of enlightenment from many view points, from many sources of emotions. Then, perhaps, more humans will learn to respect the unseen. Respect the unseen without worship. Respect the unseen without fear. Respect the unseen without having any desire for communication. For again, we have no need to thin the veils between your reality and the unseen. We simply want to enlighten enough to save the environment, save the reality of your human existence."

Q: *"Why is this so important if the unseen are bodiless? Why would you care about the continuation of the earth?"*

A: *"As usual, this is complex...The earth exists in many realities, layered realities of existence. If one reality, if your environment should be poisoned, if humans ceased to exist on the earth, if the earth ceased to exist, then a domino effect of destruction would affect other realities, other existences within the world, other places that are unseen.*

Let us gently move humans towards a cleaner earth. Let us gently move technology towards a safer environment. Let us gently move human communications towards a more unified peoples. For with more unification comes peace. And with peace comes the time to truly experience the wonders of the earth, the beauty of the human experience. Namaste."

February 7, 2006: I slept straight through last night which felt wonderful! I stirred after Greg left the room and became aware that there were spirits near. Sleepily I rolled over and read 6:04. UGH! I don't have to get out of bed until 6:45 and it felt so good to not have to think so I turned over, stuffed the pillow into my belly, and started to drift back to sleep.

Behind my closed eyes I saw a shape forming. Curious, I allowed the colors to move like the molten center of a lava lamp until the elongated, hour glass form of a handset formed. This was the hand held receiver part of an old chord telephone, which is a distinct recognizable shape, not easily confused with any other forms. I smiled as I thought how clever these spirits had become. In the past I've heard mediums say that when one channels, the purpose is not to interpret the results but just be the telephone and relay the message. Understanding the rationale behind the telephone symbol has stirred me towards consciousness enough to start to write:

"Turkey. It was a country of great mystery; a country of wondrous advancement, a country where civilization prospered. Do not worry about its ancient name. I am talking about the modern location when I say Turkey."

Having no conscious interest in geography I drift in and out of sleep only to be stirred enough to write names and words. The information I was receiving did not feel the same as when I usually write in my journal because instead of a flow I just remembered words. *"Queen Zefratitic"* or was it *"Nefertiti?"*

Not understanding the word I question if my logical mind was trying to make sense of a name I never heard before. I received another name and a description; *"Arten, Strong, great wisdom, channeled from other beings."* Then I stopped receiving the sensation of spirit being near and any further messages.

When I came downstairs later this morning I noticed a hard cover book lying by my claw foot bathtub that was called *Ancient Egypt*. I picked up the book that I had just received as a Christmas present last month and noticed that the book marker was protruding between pages seven and eight out of the 246 page text. I don't remember when I last looked in this book. I wonder if my mind was regurgitating some information that I read earlier.

I picked up the book and turned to the index to see if anything looked familiar. The name Akhenaten seemed to pop off the page as my mind sensed a feeling of déjà vu. I flipped to pages 86-87, which is much further in the book than I've marked as having read before, to read about this Egyptian Pharaoh. *"Akhenaten was a ruler from the 'The New Kingdom' period of 'c. 1550-1069 BC'."* He presided during a time of change in the religious belief of Egypt. His father, the ruler Amenhotep III accepted the throne, c. 1390 BC. He *"defied tradition by choosing Tiy as his Great Royal Wife, the title held by the king's senior consort. As a non-royal Tiy..."* The passage goes on to explain the shift in religions explored first by Amenhotep III:

"The Aten (I wonder if this was what I was channeling when I spelled Arten?) *was often depicted as a solar disk with rays emanating there from. These took the form of outstretched hands, some holding the 'ankh', the sign of life associated with the royal and divine power."* The passage continues to explain that while Amenhotep III *"endorsed the cult of Aten"* his son, Amenhotep IV, believed in one god, not many deities. This

king, Amenhotep, whose name meant *"Amun is content"*, changed his name to Akehnaten meaning *"Glorious is the Aten"*

By the ruler changing his name he showed his alliance with his new religious belief of one god. With this belief he also created much turmoil in the power of Egypt for Akehnaten stripped the power of the priests who practiced the old way of worshiping. In short, by the king changing his name; *"The power of the priesthood was curtailed virtually at a stroke and a number of temples dedicated to the new sole creator god were built."*

Akehnaten sought a new capitol of Egypt to coincide with his new religion. *"The site chosen was Akhetaten-'Horizon of the Aten'-some 300km north of Thebes, near modern-day el-Amarn."* The king's city occupied the east side of the Nile. The burial place for the kings was to be on the same side of the Nile. *"This meant that the symbolic east-west crossing of the Nile would not take place, another major departure from Egyptian tradition."*

This ruler, Akehnaten, was a radical. By changing the religion and the center of Egypt's power he *"had a damaging effect on the economy."* It was a period of great artistic achievement, but the royal court had become insular and inward-looking. Akhetaten was so remote from the Egyptian people-both literally and metaphorically-that the king's popularity declined considerably.

I read further in this book about Akehnaten's chief wife, Nefertiti, who bore him six daughters and no sons. After eighteen years of ruling, Akehnaten's son from another wife, Smenkhkare, reigned for only a matter of months. His younger brother, Tutankhaten, took over.

This nine year old king was influenced by senior court advisers, *"who were now having misgivings about the entire cultural shift of the past generation...After only about thirty years in existence Akhetaten was abandoned in favor of a return to Thebes...Egypt's brief flirtation with monotheism came to an end."*

As an interesting side note: *"Tutankhaten...renounced the 'aten' suffix...replacing it with 'amun'."* This king's new name was Tutankhanmun, the king whose burial chamber riches were found by Howard Carter in 1922.

This book I've referred to was rich with photographs. I flipped to page 87 and saw a familiar silhouette and read the caption under the photograph: *"Eighteenth Dynasty relief of a Nubian slave, almost certainly a prisoner of war."* The passage by this photograph explained how peasants, through a sort of serfdom, not slavery, were the main workers for the pharaohs. I found this interesting because I have been visited by a Nubian in dream before and I never realized that Nubians were a culture of people that existed within the culture of ancient Egypt.

After referring to the book, *Ancient Egypt,* I picked up my old Collier's Encyclopedia to research Turkey. Geographically, Turkey lies north, on the opposite side of the Mediterranean Sea from Egypt. The cities referred to in the book, *Ancient Egypt*, appeared to all be on the Nile River with Egypt being situated across the Mediterranean Sea from Turkey. I wonder what Egypt and her ancient kings have to do with "the land where we now call Turkey?"

When I opened my encyclopedia to the pages about the country of Turkey, the book opened to a map of the Ottoman Empire, 1529-1789. I learned from this map that Turkey ruled over a large chunk of the known world during this phase in our world's history. From Hungary, the Ottoman Empire nearly encircled the Black Sea to Persia and dipped under the Mediterranean Sea. Part of Egypt was within the boundaries of the Ottoman Empire. Perhaps the spirit that was speaking through me this morning died before the borders of Egypt and Turkey changed?

What does all this mean to my dream? Ok Yellow Dog. I'm ready to channel any wisdom that you might share because my mind is overflowing with fact, ideas and possibilities. Can you shed light on the significance of my early morning channel/dream?

YD: *"Good morning Little One. I was wondering when you would let me come through. I marvel at the way your brain functions. At the way you fight the channels. At the way you require to prove to yourself what is unseen. The morning's channel is an old, old memory. Go back within your mind, to a place that you once knew, a place where you once lived. This is the meaning of today's channel. It is not about a period that you need to relay. It is about your inner self. It is a about familiarizing yourself with what you once knew."*

Q: "Then why the phone receiver?"

YD: *"We needed to get your attention. You are not always willing to let us in."*

Q: "Did this come from the Nubian warrior? Is he is around you."

YD: *"He is a guide that watches, enlightens and chooses those which are best. He is me in another lifetime. We are the same. Try not to process this too intently. Try to accept. Accept that which is not linear. For this is where you tend to fail. This is where you must learn to simply accept and trust. Trust that which your brain cannot fully understand. Trust the co-existence of many personalities. For the soul has evolved many times. The soul has a multitude of lifetimes coursing in his matrix. For this is the path of the soul; to evolve and learn, to develop and mature. You are starting to see the method. You are starting to unlock some of your own past. With time your brain may be able to make sense of this all. Do not lament. It* will all start to mesh. Your brain is shifting. It is starting to make sense."

Q: "Anything else you wish to share Yellow Dog?"

YD: *"Go forward. Develop and share. For this is the function of you during this lifetime. This is what you must show the masses. For this is the biggest **obstacle** of all. It is easy to convince a ruler. It is very difficult to appease the masses. It is very difficult to show a full society the beauty and the wonder of being one. Try to learn and understand our ways. Then chronicle these events. Avoid the failure of this ancient Egyptian King for he tried to educate. Communication with the one God, communication and oneness of the peoples, that is the goal we are trying to direct."*

Q: "Yellow Dog. With so many beings existing as unseen how do I know which ones I should believe? I mean which ones have intent that is for the greater good of the human race?"

YD: *"Little One...It is not a matter of choosing the unseen. It is the matter of believing that there is one creator. That all the other deities, all the other unseen are workers to this one God. The God who orchestrates all that exists on your world and in my plane of reality too. There is one God. What man needs is but one religion, one belief system, one path to respect and honor the one supreme being; the one supreme force, the unity of all peoples, the unity of nature. It is not about "politics." It is not about control. It is about harmony and love. It is about co-existence and evolution. It is about oneness."*

Q: "You are right Yellow Dog...My brain has to evolve or change just a little more before I can fully grasp your concept. I love and appreciate your words. Please do not give up."

YD: (I can feel him laughing with a loving undertone*).* *"Little One, I am with you always. I cannot 'give up.' I will help you to use your human vessel to understand. For through your* *understanding you may be able to illustrate a method for communication with the unseen...Namaste."*

February 8, 2006: I recorded some early morning dream journal entries: *"Familiarity breeds contentment."*... *"Fear of the unknown can be overcome by making it known."*... *"Face your fear with facts."* I don't have time today to ponder their meaning but thought them interesting. For now...Namaste.

February 9, 2006: I woke up and it was barely light outside. I knew that the Egyptian influence was once again at the top of my consciousness, or standing in my room as a spirit. I remember having a dream where I was learning about the mythological Egyptian God called Horace and the purpose for mummification of bodies. In my dream state the spirit was referring to a healing I channeled to my friend that believes in UFOs last Tuesday:

"Grounding, the healing you did last Tuesday was very beneficial. The mixing of an assortment of energies allows for the ability to channel an assortment of beings. We are grateful, grateful for the opportunity to help. We are eager to be heard. The energy field you helped us to achieve will be useful. Many thanks.

The information is necessary. The reasons are just. The man will be safe. The man will succeed. Hon na ee ah tay, Hon ae ee ta nay, Ee a too ma to now. Ee a con te' tay, Ee na toy, ee an toy to now. Horace the deliverer of ideas... (I draw a picture of bull horns in my dream journal and continue to channel an explanation of why leaders use crowns of precious metals.)

The crown too is used for information. The gold bands too allow the brain to understand; the hollow top to allow the crown chakra to stay open, to allow the elliptical waves to connect. Connect with the feet to form the current, a current of knowledge, a unity of truth.

The bands through the crown exist in an altered dimension, its meaning hidden from the masses. For it is with acknowledgment that jealousies arise. It is with the exposure of gold and certain metals that pillaging arises also.

Eternal life is true. The life is that of the soul, not of the flesh. By keeping the riches intact, by keeping the crown in place, the tools can be accessed from the other realities."

Q: "Why would a crown be needed by a soul with a dead physical body?"

A: *"Imprint. Information imprinted within the metals of the heart necklace and the crown. Matrix fields established. Like a living machine. The preserved machine can still be activated."*

Q: "Why can't the bodiless soul just travel and speak with the gods/deities/aliens?"

A: *"Not all unseen can interact! Some are stuck in a dimension as you are encased within a body. By preserving the body with the tools, with the jewelry intact you insure further communications."*

Q: "Can't the bodiless soul use merkaba/chakra activations to travel through dimensions?"

A: *"No...No body, no concentration of energies. The bodiless soul must stay in a plane of like energies. If it chooses to stray in your dimensions, then its reality, its consciousness, becomes altered, confused. In the dimension where the dead reside, here the like energies of all can support each other. Support and enjoy the existence of bliss."*

Q: "Why the mummification?"

A: *"To more easily draw to those still living, to more easily channel to the advanced races, to remain in contact with planes of realities that is usually lost with the loss of the human body, as a type of ancient radio for continuing communications from the crossed-over state. That is all-thank you."*

Now that I have transcribed my early morning interactions I find myself still thinking about this channel. During breakfast I began receiving more information. I grabbed my journal and started to write:

"It is not that the people blindly followed the Royals as gods. It is more the knowledge; the knowledge that they could channel, the knowledge of the dead, the knowledge of the God, the knowledge from the all-knowing. This was the purity of the Royals, their abilities to channel for they channeled many who could lead and guide the peoples.

Not all that is unseen has an intent that is pure. And here with lies the problem...To filter out that which can be bad. So this is the purpose of the crown, a wavelength that connects to specific beings and ideas. Much like the buildings, the churches, that was the venue for the circuits, the venue for communication."

I went outside to do my morning chores and still felt the need to channel more information. This was written while my bath was filling:

"Wearing colors filter energies. For the colors, you see, affect your own energy patterns. When self vibrates in specific ways, specific waves, your energy attracts like. Black, the absence of color, allows the human to call upon whatever energies are chosen. Call upon the energies without interference. White allows all energies to permeate and allows the crown chakra to open and to be accessed. Must have previously established guardians and communications for this color is open. Open to all the frequencies. Color, or rather the

human eye's ability to perceive color and to harmonize with color, this is a vehicle for communication, or rather harmonization with a form of the unseen.

The morning bathing rituals of the priests of Egypt or the Native American Indians utilize water and how its energy can pattern with the human vessel. Communication and understanding can coerce better within the presence of water.

With the ancients they would cremate their beloved. The ashes would return to the earth. The ancients worshiped the four elements. The beloved, by turning into ashes, returned to the elements through fire, blown by air, into the earth or water. The Pagan worship mirrored talking with the deceased beloved.

When man started to bury the dead, peoples returned to graves to talk to the dead. The remains, coupled with the metal or stones of any jewelry act as transmitters for information or ideas.

The cremated body buried with any belongings such as jewelry would have energy. Ash dust as energy plus the jewelry as energy, even common household dust is a mixture of particles, a mixture of energies. Dust can comfort some people by providing a combination of energies, a blanket of safety in the mixture. While this combining of many energies may be confusing to others, too much dust, too much of a mixture of energies can cause a single energy to be lost. Dust can contain multiple energies but is not a reliable source, alone, for communications.

(I am out of the bath and once more this channel resumes with a final thought.) *The crystals, the amulets, the medicine bags, the herbs, these are all ways of communications. These are all ways of ensuring the proper line, the proper connection with the unseen. These are all ways to blend the energies and feel the oneness of that which is not tangible.*

Develop your own ways. It may be a feeling you can derive, a familiarity of certain energies. This is a perfect way to communicate from your vessel, your human body. With time you may require tools. With time you may develop yourself as a more efficient tool. Time will tell, the story will unfold, the meaning will come clearer. Enjoy!"

February 13, 2006: I was away all last weekend. I've been curious as to what exactly a Shaman was and what they do so when I saw an advertisement for a weekend retreat titled; "Huichol Indian Shamanism" I knew I had to go. Surprisingly, I didn't get any last minute jitters or regrets at committing to a weekend away from my family, my horses and my obligations. I wasn't exactly sure why I was going, yet I was eager to attend and it was with optimism that I drove out of my driveway Friday afternoon, alone.

The drive to Springfield, Massachusetts was routine for me. I did, however, get off the wrong exit from the "Mass. Pike." The old Suzy, the way I used to behave a few years ago, would be swearing and cursing at my idiotic mistake. My shoulders would be tight, my guts in a knot with worry and anger. But I have changed. I simply asked the toll booth operator; "Did I mess up and get off an exit too early for route 91 North?"

The lady in the booth very patiently gave me directions; "Continue on this road for around four miles and you can find the expressway's entrance."

Thankful that I found a kind toll booth operator I drove off with renewed optimism. Time passed, the miles went by and I started to worry that it was almost 4:30 PM on a Friday afternoon and rush hour traffic would be starting. I began second guessing myself and wondering if I should simply turn around and return to the exit I came off of, and just as I was allowing these doubts to run through my mind, a car passed by.

The license plate read 444-AFK. Seeing 444 and believing that this was a numerology sign from the Angels I knew I was heading the correct way and smiled and drove on.

    I drove for what seemed like too far and once again started to doubt myself. Thinking that I might have missed directions from one of the overhead green signs I checked my odometer to see how far I had traveled. My odometer confirmed that I still had a mile to go but I doubted and wondered if I was lost when I noticed a color off to my left. A RAINBOW! The beautiful beginning of a rainbow was arching up to the sky. The colors weren't the complete spectrum but just the first third of the spectrum with red, orange and a hint of yellow. Seeing a rainbow was unexpected because the sky was clear blue and it was, after all, February. I don't ever remember seeing a rainbow in February before and just when I was contemplating how and why a rainbow would be in the February sky I looked up at the green sign; "Route 91 North/Greenfield." I smiled at the coincidence that the rainbow lay just behind the sign.

    My trip up route 91 was uneventful. I found exit 26 with no problem and started my westward drive on route 2. As I was driving I was stealing glances at the "MapQuest" directions I held in my hand. Between glimpses of the road ahead, I read: "Follow route 2 west...about 18 miles to Charlemont." Ok, this part of the directions was easy. I flipped the page of my computer print out, to skim through the rest of the directions which seemed confusing because they were full of landmarks before the next turnoff and landmarks, if I should wiz by my next road.

    Once again I started to worry about finding my way because I was all alone, in the Berkshire Mountains, and it was getting dark. The road I was traveling on was on fairly flat ground and to my left was a river and on the other side of this river were Mountains. The sun was setting over the mountains and the scene was quite pretty. For a brief moment I thought about my trip, two years ago, to Hungary and how the Danube River looked similar to the scene off to my left. My father's family came from a little town in Hungary off the Danube called Nagymaros. I was remembering that trip with my father when we visited Nagymaros and our ancestral heritage when my SUV rounded a bend in the road. I caught my breath when I saw the sight lined up through my front windshield. The setting sunlight was shining up from behind the mountain and, to the left of the setting sun was, once again, that same piece of a rainbow I saw in Springfield. A prism of red, orange, and yellow, this small visible snippet of a rainbow was beautiful. I smiled and enjoyed the beauty of this strange winter sky knowing that I wasn't really alone on this road trip after all.

My journey ended without further incident. I found the center, the farmhouse where I was to sleep, and went inside to register. I was writing my check, chatting comfortably with the clerk, happy to have found my way and to not have gotten lost in the dark. Our conversation was light and friendly and I mentioned the rainbow I saw both in Springfield and just before sunset in her town. The clerk gave me a strange look and commented that she was outside late this afternoon and didn't see any rainbow. I felt my heart skip a beat when she told me this. I wonder...could spirit control who sees a rainbow?

After I was settled into my room and met some of my roommates we all walked up the winding dirt road to the Recreation Hall where thirty of us gathered to enjoy the workshop on Huichol Indian Shamanism. I don't want to journal a treatise on this subject; rather it is my hope to journal my impression of this workshop.

Our teacher introduced us to the peoples he spent many years with. He told us of his adoptive grandfather, a respected Shaman who died at the age of 110 years. Throughout the weekend we were to learn of this race of Native American people; of their isolation from technology, of the purism of their beliefs. This living model of ancient traditions was indeed special. I am grateful to have learned of the Huichol.

Friday night we learned an exercise on how to work with Grandfather Fire. We were told stories about these native peoples and their impressions of how negative emotions were attached to energy centers in the body. We were told Huichol names for these energy centers. I will use the chakra names I am familiar with in describing the exercise.

I learned that the throat chakra was associated with fear. The heart chakra harbored the negative emotion of jealousy. The stomach, what I would call the solar plexus chakra, could hold anger. We learned that these three emotions; fear, jealousy and anger, were the root of all negative emotions and that any negative feelings could be traced to one of these three chakras.

We learned how to stare into the flames of a fire to release our negative emotion. We were then coached to continue to stare into the fire, staying in a meditative state, while a positive emotion would find us, thus replacing the negative. And the positive emotion would be offered as an answer to us by the spirit in the candle flame, Grandfather Fire.

My mind, my personality can be, at times, challenging. I tend to worry that I am not following a "ritual" properly and I worry so much that I don't allow myself to fully enjoy the task at hand. I felt awkward in following the directions I just received. Awkward in believing I may be doing the sequence improperly. I felt "clumsy." To add to my feeling of awkwardness was a sense of isolation because this was my first time here and I came alone. I understood that some of the other members of our group attend these workshops often. Many have traveled all over the world to participate. There was even a man from Germany. I felt like a rookie amidst a room of followers.

The worst part of attending the opening ceremony for me was the "dance of the deer." This was what I would call a "drumming circle" but instead of the thirty of us forming a large circle where we sat and drummed we were now required to get up and dance. We all spread out into a large circle inside the cavernous Recreation Hall and four people started to drum. Their drums appeared to be made of wood and deer skin and fit comfortably between each musician's folded legs. The drum stick was a rattle made by the native people we were here to learn about, which consisted of a hollowed out gourd with a reddish wooden handle adorned with a pom-pom of colored yarn. Every rattle was handmade and had markings burnt into the gourd's side and the gourd head itself had small holes drilled into them. We were each given a rattle when we first arrived which we were expected to shake while we danced.

Not only was I not crazy about the idea of having to get up and "dance" in a circle with a bunch of strangers but I had a problem with the idea of shaking this rattle. I was diagnosed with carpal tunnel in 2002 and was warned to try to avoid repetitive movements such as hammering a nail, playing the piano or SHAKING A RATTLE! My mind held fear as I thought of what my neurologist, and later my physical therapist, cautioned me to NOT to participate in. How was I to safely participate with shaking this rattle?

I just went for it. Damn the doctor's opinions! If I "screw up" my nerves, my shoulders, my back, I could always work at "fixing it" later. I wanted to experience this Native way. I wanted my guides to show me if this was my path. I took the rattle and shook it as I danced around the circle. All weekend long we would dance. The group's leader would be singing a native song. The drums would be beating. The people would be moving, sweating, laughing.

I felt concern the first few times I participated in the "dance of the deer." Not over the rattle shaking but rather concern that I would step on the person in front of me or that the guy behind me would step on me. For not only did we dance forward but, every time we'd hear a "whoop, whoop," we were required to reverse the direction. This helped to relieve the repetitive aspect of the dance and lead to some good laughs at our misinterpretations.

As the days progressed I actually started to enjoy these dances. I became comfortable participating with a group of strangers and I did not feel isolated. I felt I belonged as part of a drumming, moving, dancing and rattling mass of humanity. I no longer worried about the rhythm of my feet, or about the nerves in my neck and shoulders and wrists that were supposed to be damaged. I simply learned to enjoy the sound, the movement and the moment. I learned to let go of my physical fears and to just…be.

I experimented and found that I actually enjoyed rattling. I found that if I allowed the rattle to swing close to one ear and listened to the beat of my own rattle when I danced I could get lost in the rhythm. I could sense myself more in tune with the song of the drum, the chanter and the vibrations of the floor. As the weekend progressed the songs seemed to grow shorter and by Sunday afternoon I was enjoying the "dance of the deer" immensely!

We also used the rattles while we sat still in a circle. This was usually done prior to us getting up to dance as a sort of building up of the energies. Here too, I experimented and learned that if I gripped the rattle lightly I could hold the rattle like the reins when I would ride the horse. I could relax my upper body and find stability through my lower back and I could open my root chakra and allow the energy to flow up. Then I could sense the energy coming up from the ground with the vibration of the drumming against the ground. It felt as though the beat of the drum would travel up through by bottom, up my spine into my hand and I could shake the noise out of the rattle. This was fun!

I'm not sure if I would rattle and dance when I returned home but I did purchase the rattle that I used all weekend long. I sort of felt like I bonded with it or that it had become part of me.

February 11, 2006: Early Saturday morning I woke up in my "dorm room" to the sound of the rest of the women breathing heavy in their sleep around me. I felt the need to journal and quietly transcribed a dream as it progressed in my mind:

"The girl met the spirit, met the spirit during dance, and met the spirit during celebration. Celebration of life, celebration of deer, celebration of faith and the girl was happy. She was happy for the energy, happy for the dance and happy for the opportunity to share the oneness with spirit.

For two days they enjoyed the dance. And now it was done. But the dance of the heart, this will continue on. Continue with thought. Continue with memory. For the dance of the heart is never ending. Always loving, always moving, and always beating with the rhythm of life all around.

What needs to be done is to 'plug in.' Tap into the energy of love. Feel this natural beat of life. Know the human body will be able to understand, heal, purify and vibrate with more harmony with all that is around. Vibrate and synchronize with that what is. Vibrate and heal with the comfort from the comfort of Earth's energies. This is all-Namaste."

After I read what I had written, I thanked spirit for this lovely story and felt touched by this prophecy of what I was to enjoy Saturday and Sunday. Then I rolled over and fell back to sleep only to wake up with the rest of my roommates to a quiet knock on the door followed by a man poking his head into our room while singing; "Good Morning, Good Morning." I couldn't be angry or grumpy after that alarm clock for the smiling bearded face of our serenader was so sincere and happy. I ate breakfast in the dining hall side of the farm house and joined my roommates in putting on our winter gear in preparation for the walk up the long, snow covered road, to the Recreation Hall where we learned another ceremony on how to pray to the spirits which reminded me of the "releasement ceremony" I learned at my Angel workshop this past summer. After a discussion and a break we were instructed about our next exercise then went outside to pray to each of the four directions.

It was cold outside and even though I wore an extra sweater under my polar fleece jacket, along with a winter hat, gloves and boots I neglected to wear long johns so my blue jeans alone offered little protection from the twenty degree temperatures. I pulled my coat down lower, over my butt and followed the rest of the adults outside into the cold where we were all instructed to separate into the sparse, snow covered woods. I hesitated and looked at my fellow students, the more experienced people who were already happily shaking their rattles, isolated in their prayers. The scene was somewhat humorous. A bunch of adults standing several feet away from each other, in the freezing cold, closing their eyes, shaking a rattle and smiling. I took a deep breath and thought; "What the hell…I'm here and no one cares what I look like."

Before leaving the warm comfort of the lodge we were instructed to shake our rattle while facing the East and concentrate on a negative feeling or emotion to release and after the negative was released we were to continue to shake the rattle and concentrate and wait for an answer. Then we were to rotate 90 degrees and proceed with the same ritual, praying to the South, then pray to the West and lastly pray to the North. I walked to a clearing by some birch trees and started to rattle. It felt natural to also chant so I allowed Hidden Deer to softly voice while I heard the shaking of my rattle.

    To the direction of the East I offered up my pain that I frequently still felt in my shoulders and my back. I was chanting softly with a familiar melody and the rattle appeared very, very loud then the energy seemed to change. Hidden Deer's melody changed and even the words seemed different. I listened to what was coming out of my mouth and then my attention was struck by the word "healing" and felt a sense of no more pain but rather a sense of bliss. I stood there rattling in the snow, a little stunned that this exercise actually worked! I felt the bliss like state fade and I knew I was to proceed so I turned to face the South.

    To the South I offered up my fears of the unknown that was challenging my progression into new realities. I heard the soft voice of Hidden Deer once again change and the answer I received was very powerful. The energy was so strong that I could no longer feel myself rattling and sensed that my consciousness was leaving my body. I saw a cartoon like figure moving behind my closed eyes that looked like a worm or perhaps a snake. This figure was wiggling or maybe swimming, it could have been a tadpole and I was not sure which animal the symbol was but when I saw the quick flash of this vision I heard the word "strength." The energy pulsed strongly for a few moments then faded and I turned once again.

    I was disappointed when I turned to face the West because the energy did not feel as strong as when I was facing the South. I searched my mind for another negative thing to release and became frustrated at having to follow the directions of needing to do this exercise with four different problems. That was it! I settled on releasing the frustration I have when I am with other people, a socially induced frustration. I searched for a word to go with this emotion and suddenly thought of "cynicism." Smiling at having the knowing put into me I allowed Hidden Deer to quietly chant to the rhythm of my shaking rattle. My chant varied as the energy seemed to shift. TRUST was the word. Or was it TRUTH? Perhaps both energies, both words, both truth and trust? I accepted both feelings to replace the negative "cynicism" that I just released. One more direction to go I turned for the last time.

    The fourth and final direction was north. I struggled with a fourth emotion to rid myself of and my struggling produced the answer; "WORRY." My chant changed after I knew that I was to release my worries and immediately I felt a new energy coming into me. I knew Yellow Dog was near and I felt that familiar sense of being wanted and belonging. I was still waiting for an idea to put with the energy when I felt the rose quartz pendant that was hanging around my neck. I saw a glimpse of the pink stone in my mind and what it represented to me and I knew the positive emotion...LOVE!

    Whew! Once I understood what I was sensing I didn't want to leave! I was enjoying the sensation of standing out there in the cold shaking my rattle immensely! I could have remained rattling and chanting in the love energy much longer but I noticed that the other classmates scattered in the forest around me were moving. I knew I had to return with the group so I allowed Hidden Deer to close down her chant. Hidden Deer did some gesturing of her own as I felt my hands moving as though honoring the four directions. Then I lowered my rattle and followed my classmates back into the lodge.

    When we returned to the lodge we all sat in a big circle and rattled while a few people played their drums. My shoulder and arm were tired from all the rattling outside and I was starting to feel concern for a faint back, shoulder and hand pain was pulsing down my arm. I started to rattle with the group inside the warm lodge and my mind was trying to block the pain. I was zoning out to the beat of the rattle and the pain was leaving when…ZZZIIPPP! I felt an electric jolt traveling down my left arm. The sensation was so unexpected that I almost dropped my rattle and my mind cleared into a state of full consciousness. I had stopped rattling and struggled for a few beats to regain my composure. Then I was able to rejoin the group in the drumming. My back and shoulder pain were gone!

After lunch we returned to the Recreation Hall to make a prayer stick. We were each handed a pair of feathers and a whittled stick which resembled a giant pencil. Then we were instructed to choose colored yarn that was piled in the center of our circle. Then we were to secure the pair of feathers at the end of the stick by wrapping the yarn around and around the stick. But this was more than a simple craft project for with each wrapping of the yarn, we were directed to say the same, brief wish. I thought of a personal desire I had and then repeated, over and over, this affirmation or prayer in my mind, as I wrapped the yarn around the stick. This repetition was intended to block out the chatter of the mind and set the intention of the prayer into the "prayer stick". After our group had finished wrapping the colored yarns around the sticks we were instructed to bring our prayer sticks back to the lodge tomorrow.

Before we closed for dinner our teacher was to do healings on a few people. I didn't know he offered healing and watched how he healed others with much interest. We all sat in a circle and drummed or rattled while the person that was to be healed sat in the middle of the circle, on a small rug, next to a single burning pillar style candle. Our teacher/shaman began to sing a sing-song-chant. His song had unusual high notes and our teacher seemed to go into a semi-trance state of awareness. He then got up and approached the person who was to be healed.

This was when I noticed that our teacher had several prayer sticks in the hat band of his cowboy hat that were decorated with large, dangling, hawk feathers. I watched as our teacher removed these sticks from his hat and held them in a bundle. He then used the bundled prayer sticks as if they were a single, healing wand. I enjoyed watching this healer work on the woman sitting in our circle.

Sometimes our teacher would touch the pillar candle briefly in the center of the circle and wiggle the feathered sticks as he approached the woman he was healing. It appeared as though the feathers were juggling to hold on to the energy from the Grandfather Light candle. Sometimes the shaman would use the healing sticks as straws by holding the feather end of the prayer stick towards the patient as he appeared to suck on the stick. Then he would turn his head and spit into a plate with a paper towel that was strategically positioned within the circle. It appeared that this action somehow was sucking negative energy from the patient.

Then I watched our teacher as he would touch the seated person lightly, with great purpose. First on the person's shoulder, then the sticks would be fluttering around the head, then they would briefly touch the back, and all the while our teacher appeared in a semi-trance state and yet he seemed so intent and precise in his actions. Occasionally our teacher would come back to full consciousness. I watched as his face registered acknowledgment and he would emerge to whisper a question to the seated person, or touch them on the shoulder, as if to ask if they were ok. Satisfied with the response the shaman would return into his trance, his healing. After healing three different people our teacher appeared visibly tired. His assistant announced that the healings were done for the day. The drumming was finished and the assistants removed the paper towels while the shaman sat wearily in his chair. He seemed to be grounding himself and allowing himself to recover. It was fascinating to watch him work. But now it was time to take a break before tonight's scheduled "sweat lodge" meeting.

Still February 11th: It is Saturday night, I'm experiencing my first sweat lodge tonight, and I am wide awake. Before I forget any of the details I want to journal my thoughts. Almost all thirty of us showed up to pile into the igloo shaped structure which appeared to be made of animal hides stretched over interlocking tree branches. The primitive, yet effective structure was built in the style of the Lakota people and sat alone in a snow covered clearing in the woods. I was instructed that we were to wear a bathing suit to this "sweat" so I layered as many clothes on as I could to ward off the cold. I wore my bathing suit under my polar fleece pants, heavy polar fleece shirt, winter jacket, gloves, hat and scarf and I was still cold!

Within sight of the sweat lodge was a huge bonfire that we all stood around, waiting and warming ourselves until the sweat was ready. I quickly became enamored with the fire itself and felt comfort not only in its heat but the way the powerful fire cracked and popped the huge teepee pile of wood contained within a circle of stones. This fire was carefully packed, carefully burning and the sight was somehow reminiscent and comforting. I watched the man who was appointed to tend the fire as he poked and prodded at the wood with a pitchfork. I then turned to allow my butt to warm up against the hot flames. I stared off into the snow covered woods and realized that we really were isolated this weekend. My eyes lowered and I looked down to where the firelight illuminated the perimeter of frozen, barren ground which, a few feet further out changed to pristine snow cover and just where the dirt turned to snow there were melted patterns of snow ice. I was fascinated at the crystal like formations that were melted and refrozen by the hot fire and the blanket of snow. Mesmerized by the patterns of the spiky symmetrical points and the dancing lights of the warm fire I jumped at the sound of our teacher announcing that it was time to disrobe in the twenty degree weather and go into the sweat lodge...UGH!

I filed in behind my classmates away from the comfort of the fire and towards the little dark sweat lodge in the snow. To the left of the sweat lodge a long piece of plastic was laid out on the snow and I noticed that those in front of me were standing on this plastic while they disrobed. I took off my boots and socks, my polar fleece sweat pants, my gloves, my hat, my two polar fleece jackets and stood there, shivering in my bathing suit and bare feet. I still had the beach towel I was instructed to bring with me and was torn between standing on my towel or placing my big towel over my shoulders. I opted to wear the towel as a stole and scurried closer towards the warm fire to wait for further instructions. God it hurt to walk barefoot in the snow!

Within moments that felt much longer, our teacher announced that it was time to go into the lodge. We needed to form a single file and some discussion ensued about the placement of people. Finally it was the women's turn to enter. The process took so long and my feet felt so cold! I discovered if I stood like a flamingo with first one foot balanced against my near warm leg, then the other, I could battle the painful tingling of cold under the soles of my feet. At last we filed into the dark low lying lodge.

Inside was a dirt floor with an open pit in the center and the banked perimeter of the structure was strewn with soft hay. The center pit appeared to be a significantly deep hole that was designed to hold the hot stones. Placed on the far side of the tent, opposite of the tent's flap of an opening, was a pail of water and a ladle of some sort. I didn't get a good glimpse of the interior because I only saw it from the glow of a flashlight which helped us to file in and to be seated. First the women filed in and made a semi-circle of women facing the pit then a second row of women filed in and sat sandwiched behind the first arc of women and the exterior wall of the enclosure. I was the last woman to enter and our teacher sat in front of me in the center of the lodge opposite of the entrance flap. As I looked straight ahead while seated behind our teacher, I could see the door opening flap of the sweat lodge as it was pulled back to allow the men in. The roaring bonfire that was warming me just moments earlier offered a faint glow of light into the lodge's interior. The men filed in as the women did moments before and formed two abreast layers of people but this time arcing to the left, mirroring the women. Through the flap that was opened I watched the man that was tending the fire outside. He had to stoop down when he entered the lodge with hot stones balanced on his pitch fork. The stones were brought in one at a time and I could feel our teacher in front of me as he directed how many stones to bring in. With every stone the crowd would say; "Welcome, welcome stone, welcome.", or some similar greeting to these glowing rocks. Our teacher explained that these were special lava rocks that were brought from California's Mt. Shasta. With around ten red hot stones carefully placed into the pit I heard our teacher give the order to close the door. The entrance flap was closed and the room darkened to nothingness.

 I felt panic start to set in because the interior of the lodge had turned to pitch black! I then heard a simmering sound as a ladle of water was placed on the stones. My eyes adjusted to the darkness and I could barely see the shadow of our teacher in front of me as he leaned over to use the ladle. I heard the hiss of the water again and felt a building wave of steam racing towards me. Claustrophobia coupled with a feeling of damp hot air filled my lungs and fed to my increasing sense of anxiety and my sense of panic was escalating when our teacher started to chant. He called out for us to pray and stated that we could pray in English, or any language. Simultaneously the crowd of people around me started to shout. They called in a loud confusion of words. The noise was confusing and I was curious as to why all the shouting so I concentrated on hearing just one person's words; "Hey, Mother Earth, Mother Earth hear my prayer, hear my prayer for Nancy, for she is in trouble. Hey, Mother Earth! Hear me, hear me Mother Earth, help her to overcome her illness. Help her to heal her wounds. Hey, Mother Earth, hear me. Help Nancy. Help her to heal, help her to be healed..."

Similar pleas were erupting all around me. I, too, tried to talk like the others. But I couldn't think of what to say in English and no words came out of my mouth. I was close to panic from the heat, the darkness, the wet dampness in my lungs. So I allowed Hidden Deer to come through and felt her soft voice praying as I started to call out in her native tongue and hearing Hidden Deer's voice quieted my fear and anxiety. I began enjoying the experience of this sweat lodge as I listened to Hidden Deer's melodic voice. It was a wonderful freeing feeling for I could feel the intent of her prayers. Then our teacher announced that this round was over and the flap was opened for more stones. A rush of cool air entered the enclosure and the light of the bonfire was visible once again.

There was talking amongst us as the new stones were brought in. With the presentation of each glowing rock the conversation would cease as the crowd greeted the stones. Then the conversation resumed until the next rock arrived. When our teacher seemed satisfied with the number of stones, the flap was closed and the prayers once again resumed.

This time I allowed Hidden Deer to surface immediately. I felt little discomfort from the damp heat and relaxed as I listened to my voice. I was able to understand the story that Hidden Deer was saying for as her soft words were forming I was seeing the images in my closed eyes. It was as if I was watching a documentary on the discovery channel but the image was vague as if I was watching a movie under water. I could also feel her emotion as she was speaking. No, I could feel the emotion of the event as Hidden Deer was telling the story. It was a warm and wonderful experience what Hidden Deer called a sweat lodge journey, a journey of a prayer and a prayer for the earth:

First I saw the stones of the fire in the pit. Then one of the stones was tunneling deep into the earth. Then the stone morphed and changed into a piece of coal. The coal multiplied and there were many pieces of coal; coal being mined by man and coal being taken from the earth. Then I could feel the energy of the earth which was a hollow energy and a sense of loss not unlike the sensation of a limb missing from the earth's body. Hidden Deer explained that this was like a chunk of flesh was taken out of her leg but this was not a feeling of pain but rather a feeling of loss, a feeling of missing a part or a sad feeling.

I then saw the coal nugget as it was shrinking down, down, down into a fine particle of dirt. Then this small grain of a mineral, a speck of a plant nutrient was being drawn up, up, up into the stalk of the corn. The mineral was feeding the corn. The corn stood proud and tall with many other stalks.

Upon seeing the growing stalks I had the knowing that the corn could produce oil that can be used by man and can be produced without raping the earth. This corn oil can be given by the earth without her feeling empty for the corn stalk will eventually go back to the earth. The energy of the corn will return to the earth. The corn's oil was given. But this was only part of the corn's spirit. The rest of the spirit exists and flows into the earth. This is a good and healthful way of producing energy for man. This is a good way for the planet. This can be a good way for man.

Then I sense wisdom being shared: *Learn, learn the technology. Learn how to make the oils of the corn work. Learn how to make the energies of all re-usable plants work. For the spirit of the plant is happy to help man. The spirit of Mother Earth is happy too. But man makes her weak. She needs help.*

Tell, tell this story. Tell many stories. Help man to understand respect. Help man to understand the many energies all around; the many spirits, the spirit of the plants, the spirit of the minerals and the vibrational energies of all. Help man to work with the earth. Not rob her of her parts. This is all.

When the round was over and the rest of the fresh rocks were being brought in our teacher asked that we each throw out a single prayer. I wanted to talk about my vision. I wanted to let the others know about the earth. But I couldn't get my voice heard because others were more eager to shout their needs and wants. In retrospect I do have one observation. The needs that all seemed to be throwing to the fire were negative pleas and I wondered why everyone was "dumping" their problems out to the heated stones. Prayers for making a sick person healthier were the most popular I heard in the sweat lodge that night. But I heard no prayers of thanks or hope but just lamentations of sadness for the negative happenings in our lives.

I had a problem with hearing all the negativity because I have been re-training myself to become an optimist. I want to see the glass as more than half full and wouldn't think of praying about the empty part of the glass. I wouldn't feel comfortable whining about how I want my glass filled. I wouldn't want to ask spirit to please fill up the glass.

I live more with the philosophy that others should want to help themselves and by actively wanting something wouldn't they then be helped. Am I really so lucky that I have no one to pray for? No one that I know is on a destructive path of substance abuse or the horrible path of a debilitating disease.

Is this because I will not recognize their pain? I will not acknowledge that others have negative aspects to their lives because if I acknowledge their pain, I too start to feel the negativity? Or is my reservations about publicly "dumping" my bad thoughts, my bad feelings, part of my own psyche's way of denial? I don't want to sense other people's pains so I deny that they exist?

I wonder how the stones, or Mother Earth, feel about us humans dumping their negative emotion upon her. But isn't this what we have been doing privately? Isn't this part of the purpose of the pray rituals we have been learning? Is it really about learning how to recycle? Learning how to let go of the worries and pains and allow the love to enter. Is the sweat lodge's purpose the same as my journeys?

I sense Yellow Dog waiting to speak: *"Yes Little One, you have understood this lesson well. You now see what to others is obvious. It is not up to you to shield everyone from the pain. There are times where you can dump your pain. Allow the earth to absorb the pain. Allow her to free you from the negatives. Allow the spirit of all to help you to exist in bliss.*

Use this tool of the sweat lodge. The tool of the prayer exercise is to release your negative energies. For with this release of these energies your spirit can prosper. This is the lesson. Spread the word so that others may understand and adapt to the ways. The ways that can help free their own spirit of negativity....Namaste."

Such an obvious reason for prayer...why didn't I see it before? Thanks Yellow Dog!

February 12, 2006: Sunday morning I woke up dreaming that I was the speaker for service at my Spiritualist Church. I was standing on the podium at the front of the church and at first I allowed Hidden Deer to speak briefly using her own beautiful language through the use of my voice. As I listened to her native words I started to see a scene behind my closed eyes and this glimpse of another reality lead me to understand the meaning of Hidden Deer's words. At this point I could switch to talking in English to interpret the scene. Then I would lapse back into Hidden Deer's language and pick up more about the unfolding story only to lapse into English to explain. Through this process a story would unfold.

(As I am editing this entry two years later I realize that this "dream" was a prophecy because I have been called upon to do mediumship and the sharing, or speech, during our church service many times over the past few years. I have developed the ability to lapse into "tongue" and reemerge as myself to interpret my impressions. This was how I've developed as a medium. At the time I wrote this down, on February 12 in 2006, I NEVER thought I would be standing in front of the congregation performing mediumship!)

Q: "Yellow Dog...Are you, or rather are the spirits around me, showing me a way to use Hidden Deer's channeled voice to allow my brain to process information from the other side?

A: *"You do know the answer to this. Use her voice now. Use her voice and you will be able to unlock all sorts of answers to your questions. Allow her energy to start to flow. And through her energy the answers will also flow, for you are placing yourself in the doorway between our dimensions."*

I tried what I had just dreamed. I asked a question to myself, heard native words in my mind and then received a direct answer! This was way cool! I've discovered a new way of using myself as a medium that doesn't require me sitting at a computer for an answer! I've been shown a more direct path to the other side for when I allow myself to channel a different language and I trust and allow the words to form then I am also allowing the wisdom from the other side to enter my body. This process allows for a clean and direct channel that I can be sure is not my imagination because when I allow the native language out of my mouth I know my consciousness is not participating. Any message I would receive as impressions while using Hidden Deer's native tongue, could not be my imagination for my imagination cannot form the words of Hidden Deer's language. Pretty Cool! Thanks so much spirit! In my mind's eyes I see my spirit friends dancing. I can feel their celebratory mood and a feeling of joy. A feeling of "finally, she's got it." I am thankful for this wonderful new insight!

I was excited after my early morning revelation regarding talking in tongues and mediumship so I didn't fall back asleep. I got up and prepared myself for the day then busied myself with visiting with my roommates while they got ready before breakfast. One of my roommates shared how she was healed from her Lyme disease after the Shaman gave her a healing last year. Another roommate then voiced her own anticipation for the healing she was scheduled to receive today and explained to me the form of arthritis in her hands that she suffers from as well as related pain in other parts of her body. Listening to the history of my roommates' ailments allowed me to wonder about my own mild, chronic back and shoulder pain. The pair of women I was talking to was still getting dressed when I heard that breakfast was served, so I decided to leave them and I walked down the hall to the dining room alone.

As I walked down the hallway I wondered if a healing from this shaman could be beneficial to me. Would I cause harm to myself by introducing a different form of energy into my body? Would I be wasting my money and time by receiving a healing that is not much more than the Reiki healings I've had before? I silently closed my eyes and envisioned Yellow Dog and received the sense that he approved yet I was still unsure. Could my mind be imagining that this was "safe" for me because I wanted it to be safe and beneficial?

I turned the corner in the hall I was walking through and almost ran into our shaman teacher and one of his woman helpers who happened to be the woman I was told by my roommate to speak to if I wanted to schedule a healing for myself. Before I could stop myself I blurted out the question; "Is it still possible for me to sign up for a healing today?" The woman smiled and said that she will be up at the Recreation Hall early if I wanted to sign up. I walked into the dining area stunned that I actually committed to this!

After breakfast I strolled up the hill to the Hall with my roommate. The snow was beautiful and the way it lined and spilled onto the road that wound-up to the Recreation Hall, made it picture perfect for New England. We walked in quiet camaraderie up the hill, each lost within her own thoughts and expectations. Once inside the building we stood in line to pay for our healing. At first I wasn't sure what to say when the assistant asked me what I wanted healed. Then I explained that I had back, shoulder and carpal tunnel pain and she jotted my answer down on a piece of paper presumably for later use. The Shaman was a healer after all so wouldn't he KNOW the problem? I started to have second thoughts but soon forgot my reservations when we all went outside to place our prayer arrows in the snow. Standing once again in the cold, snow covered woods while our Shaman chanted and we all rattled and I was starting to feel normal. I was going to miss this place and the curiously comforting aspects of the ceremonies I had the opportunity to participate in. We returned to the comfort of the warm lodge and again we talked, we chanted and drummed, we learned...the workshop was almost over. The shaman healed three more people and he looked tired as he announced he would heal the rest after we broke for lunch.

Great, I still did not receive my healing! Was there some problem with my credit card? Was there some issue about my psyche that required a later healing? My emotional mind was reeling. My intelligence stepped in and reassured me that the healer just wanted a break and that I am to be healed and I should just be patient. I participated uneasily through the rest of the scheduled activities and when the last planned exercise was finished and our circle was dismissed for the last time I was asked to stay for my healing. I waited uneasily as the majority of the students were in the hallway getting dressed for their snow bound walk down the hill to the dining hall. One more woman was to be healed with me so at least I was not being singled out for anything unusual.

The four people who stayed behind to help with the drumming sat in a semi-circle around the Shaman. The pillar candle still burned on its little area rug accompanied by the woman to be healed who was sitting cross legged with her eyes closed and a look of blissful expectation on her face. I was off in the perimeter of the circle with the drummers. The drumming started and my arm automatically shook my rattle. I laughed silently when I realized that I've been trained like Pavlov's Dog to shake my rattle whenever I would hear the drumbeats. Just days earlier I struggled through an awkwardness and fear of rattling and now it was so natural that my hand started moving before my mind asked it too.

The healing had begun for the woman seated on the rug and at first I was curious to watch the Shaman so I shook my rattle and watched him work. But I soon felt that it was more important to feel the beat of the drums so I closed my eyes to envision spirit which gave me a comforting and hypnotic sensation. I had a sense of bliss, a sense of shifting out of my current existence, my current reality. I lost time and then I heard the drumming stop...my companion's healing was done. It was my turn.

I moved to sit in the vacated spot, cross legged, on the carpet. I breathed a cleansing breath, closed my eyes and allowed my rhythm to relax into a slow normal breath. I allowed my chakras, my energy and my being to be open for the healing. I could sense my guides but curiously they appeared further away than normal, as though they were standing at the end of a long, long tunnel. I could feel the drums beating their rhythm through my body and I could hear the rattles shaking a higher pitch. Then I sensed the shaman draw near.

I could feel a vortex open around me. This wasn't the "beam me up Scotty" energizer sized beam I have felt before when I've facilitated healings with Hidden Deer. No...This beam was huge! I felt as though I was suspended within a six foot diameter tube. I mean, suspended, for I could feel no ground beneath me and I couldn't sense anything else around me. I was suspended in some sort of void of nothingness. The shaman's energy was flitting in and out of this pocket reality I was contained within. I could sense him near and feel his touch and then he was gone. It was as if I existed within two realities at once. I did not sense any other beings near me other than the Shaman but I did feel the presence of energy and a force I can't describe that surrounded me. I was surprised when the Shaman touched me lightly and brought me back. The healing was a strange experience and so hard to describe.

After the drumming had stopped the Shaman spoke to me and the other woman that was healed. We received instructions not to wash our hands, shower or even brush our teeth until dawn. We were also to abstain from sex and avoid shaking hands or hugging other people until the morning as well. The weekend's workshop was finished, the healings were finished, the drummers and the Shaman were finished. We all donned our coats and hats and gloves and boots in preparation for our last walk down the hill. I didn't wait for the group and slipped out the side door to walk down this snow covered path alone. I tried to evaluate how I felt as I heard the snow crunch under my feet once more. There was more energy going up and down my spine and I felt a little buzzed but overall I really didn't feel that different.

The original schedule was for the workshop to end after lunch on Sunday but a "Nor'easter" had blown in and a heavy snow was falling outside. Some of my classmates skipped their lunch and hurried to get to the expressway before driving off the mountain became too treacherous. I graciously accepted the hospitality of the Center and opted to lodge one more night in my dorm room. I lingered around the fireplace with my fellow students after dinner but I was feeling so tired that I decided to go to bed early. I wasn't sure if my sudden exhaustion was due to staying up late Saturday night after the sweat lodge or if it was the healing. It felt awkward not brushing my teeth before going to bed and it took a conscious effort not to wash my hands after using the facilities. I felt a little gross when I lay in my bunk bed but I was so tired that I quickly drifted off into sleep.

I was fast asleep in my darkened dorm room when I woke up to an electric jolt coming out of the muscles in my left shoulder down into my arm that literally moved my body in a quick wave of spasm. The release of energy shook my arm and my consciousness into an awake state. I saw strange images behind my closed eyes which must have been the dream state that I was so rudely pulled out of. I surmised that my body was probably reacting to the long weekend and that the spasm was simply my body's way of adjusting. I was tired and it was late and I wanted to return to sleep. I started to drift back to sleep and it did it again! But this time it was my right shoulder to arm that had the huge twitch that jolted me awake as I was seeing vivid colored images of crudely drawn animals and stick figures which resembled the artwork that hung in the Recreation Hall this past weekend. I must be recreating images from the past few days and for some reason moving in my sleep! I was tired and not too curious…I grumbled and nodded back off to sleep.

Once again I woke up to the archaic images and a spasm but this time it was from my left hip down my left leg. Reasoning that a pattern was forming I wasn't quite sleeping when the other leg decided to release an electric jolt. I smiled lazily as I realized that I ran out of limbs to jolt and NOW I FINALLY could sleep the rest of the night. I awoke one last time to bright colors and a whiplash jerk of my head. I didn't think that my neck needed to release its stored energy, or whatever it was my body was doing…I drifted back to sleep and didn't wake up again until 5:30 AM.

It was still dark when I opened my eyes. I wasn't twitching or dreaming, just ready to get up to a quiet stillness all around me. I dressed silently as to not awaken my roommates and because I was already checked out I decided to go ahead and drive home and enjoy a well deserved morning shower in my own house. I cleared the snow off my SUV and even though it was still dark out I marveled at the beauty of this area as the full moon reflected onto the snow. I turned my truck towards the east and drove down and off the mountain and onto the main road. I reached the spot where I had noticed the rainbow just three days ago and was treated to the sight of the sun rising up from behind the mountains on the other side of the river which was quite beautiful. Then I heard a country song on the radio; *"Oh when I get where I'm going. I know just where I'll be. I'll be inside a place that's meant for just you and me. Oh when I get where I'm going..."*

I listened to the words of the song playing on my radio and realized that it was about dying or rather the joy at "crossing over." The lyrics told a story about all of the loved ones you will meet on the other side of the veil. I started to cry. I am not quite sure the full meaning of the song nor was I sure of the significance of listening to this song playing on the radio as I drove home and watched the sunrise over the mountains. My consciousness was not sure why I was crying to a country song while it played as I drove home from this enlightening weekend. But something inside me understood the connection, the purpose. Maybe, with time, this mystery will unfold.

That's my story about my weekend away and as I finish typing this into my computer it is now Monday, February 13, 2006. I've been opening the mail that was piled on my kitchen table and sandwiched in between the magazines and junk mail was a card that had a picture of a rainbow on the front and inside was a poem that began with the words "Rainbow". I then opened a separate piece of mystery mail, a small box which held a pair of natural "rainbow" hematite stones that I had forgotten I purchased over the internet a few weeks ago. Too synchronistic to be a coincidence, I wondered what the meaning of the rainbow was. As I am writing this down I allow Hidden Deer's voice to chant within my mind. I start to understand. I write:

"The rainbow is a bridge; a bridge from what is seen to that unseen, a bridge from our side to the other side, a bridge from our plane to the next. Remember, be reminded, that we are always here. Reminded that we are always around, for like the rainbow we are not always seen. Like the rainbow our presence is not always detected. For you have to look for a rainbow to see it. You have to believe a rainbow will form in order to look.

So believe. Look for us. We will be there. Like the refraction of light. White light always is full of the colors of the rainbow. Trust, trust that the colors are there for they are not always visible from your plane, but the colors are always there, the rainbow always exist. Your eyes cannot always see. But the rainbow always exists. As do us...Namaste."

~ CHAPTER 11 ~

IN CONCLUSION

My computer crashed and I lost my journal entries from the end of February through March. Saying I am going to save information on a disc doesn't work...I need to actually do it! It was with a heavy heart that I accepted that the information I had channeled and recent memories of events that I had recorded were lost. I expected the laptop to be salvageable but I learned on April 1st that the hard drive had to be erased and with it all of my information. April Fools!

I tried to look on the bright side of all of this. I had some hand written notes and also, for some unknown reason, I had started to draw my impressions about healings, meditation and psychic circles instead of typing my memory of the event into words. I had copy on paper to work from in retrieving my memory yet all that typing and time I've spent on the computer was lost. This was depressing and frustrating and I considered stopping journaling all together but I knew I had to at least complete my thoughts...and this book.

***The Ancient Secret of the Flower of Life* by Drunvalo Melchizedek** was a two volume set of books that I first started to read on January 27th. The concepts behind these books were difficult for me to comprehend but there was something so familiar. I couldn't explain how I knew this information without really knowing it as I read about Melchizedek's personal experiences. Melchizedek learned information from an ancient being, an Atlantean called Thoth who shared that Atlantis did exist and that man had evolved into an advanced civilization before our current recorded history of the Sumerians. Thoth taught Melchizedek much about ancient history and shared his perception of the "flower of life" energy. I was fascinated with Melchizedek's explanation of how the human form was made up of atoms and that it was only our perception, our reality, that allowed us to exist in a three dimensional form. I understood these concepts but I struggled with a path of explaining this to one who has never experienced alternate realities of existence. Allow me to categorize the similarities and the path that Drunvalo Melchizedek outlined in his autobiographical story and how it paralleled my own experiences.

Ancient Civilizations did exist before Egypt, way before! Thoth was from Atlantis and appeared to Melchizedek to share ancient wisdom while my guide, Yellow Dog, was from an ancient civilization called Lemuria. In a time previous to that outlined in *The Skeptic Psychic*, in April of 2005, I was introduced, through dreams, to ideas about Lemuria which lead to me reading *"The Lost Continent of MU"* and *"The Children of MU"* by James Churchward. On page 91 of Melchizedek's books he also mentioned James Churchward's exploration into the possibility of Lemuria. Between Churchward's books and channels from Yellow Dog I learned that Lemuria was a continent in the Pacific that sank beneath the sea due to some natural disaster and that the remnants of the continent of Lemuria may include Hawaii and Easter Island. Churchward gave a convincing argument in his books that there was also a complex civilization in Central America more than 50,000 years ago whose remnants were discovered in quarries. According to Drunvalo Melchizedek man enjoyed a complex civilization that ended around 13,000 to 16,000 years ago which he called Atlantis. Melchizedek then showed mathematical equations and theories illustrating that time was cyclical. I wonder if Lemuria prospered then fell around 50,000 years ago only to have civilization once again peak in Atlantis which again fell around 15,000 years ago. Could man be following a repeating loop of civilization emerging, prospering and then peaking only to be destroyed to start all over again?

Egypt was the country where Akhenaten ruled during the 'The New Kingdom' period of 'c. 1550-1069 BC and it was this period in Egypt's history that formed a common theme in Melchizedek's books and my personal experiences as well. This past February 7th I received information about the Egyptian rulers Akhenaten and his wife, Nefertiti, through a dream/channel. Melchizedek devoted a chapter of his book about Akhenaten and Nefertiti and then proceeded to explain that these rulers were a bridge between the human race and an advanced race of helper aliens. What are the odds that out of all the rulers of ancient Egypt that I would receive in a dream state Akhenaten and Nefertiti and the same dynasty that Melchizedek refer to in his books?

Nubians were a people that lived during Akhenaten's rule and in his book Melchizedek mentioned that Nubian sorcerers were responsible for Akhenaten's death. I was visited by a Nubian in a dream on December 20th of 2005 where I wrote down; *"Umabala-the guardian with the sword, or is it a spear? The Nubian from the tribe of the cheetah sent to serve and sent to protect. Unakoot-will defend. Can run like the wind. Stab like the fangs, very strong protector."* On that date I also recorded that I saw a spirit that appeared as a tall, elegant, black man dressed in a simple loin cloth. Then on January 12, 2006 I experienced a meditation journey where I met a *"human* (that) *felt* (like) *the Nubian that visited me in dream last week but he was no longer dressed in a leopard loin cloth. He wore a flowing, hooded robe instead of carrying a spear he held some* *sort of a scepter or a staff. He told me that he was a Hathor."* (I attended a lightbody merkaba workshop this past November where I learned that the Hathors were believed to be a species of aliens that helped the Egyptians but nowhere in the workbook was the word Nubian mentioned nor anything regarding Akhenaten.) On February 7 of 2006 I researched about the Egyptians and learned that the Nubians were associated with the ancient Egyptians. This was also the day which I asked Yellow Dog about the Nubian Warrior that I had encountered in channels for which I received the answer; *"He is me in another lifetime. We are the same."* Melchizedek explained that Thoth was immortal and was alive during Akhenaten's rule and Yellow Dog explained that he was the Nubian Warrior "in another lifetime." I suppose that Melchizedek and I could each believe in an ancient race, such as Lemuria or Atlantis that fell just as we each could both feel a connection to Egypt but why would we both be interested in the same ancient dynasty and why would each be guided by spirits that claimed to have been from that same Dynasty as well?

Aliens that *The Flower of Life* books refer to were a species called the Hathors. In my January 12th meditation journey experience my Nubian Guide turned into a robed Hathor being. Paul Hubbert had mentioned the ancient alien Hathor race within the material of his merkaba lightbody workshop that I attended last November 12th so I have heard of this alien race before. Like Paul Hubbert, Melchizedek associated the Hathors with sound healing, the merkaba and ancient Egypt.

Melchizedek delved further into ancient alien visitations to earth through the interpretations of ancient cave paintings which illustrated the revolution of two stars; Sirius 'A' and Sirius 'B'. These same stars pictured in a modern astronomical chart were identical to an ancient diagram found on a cave wall. The odd thing was that the second star in the cave painting, Sirius 'B', was only "discovered" by our modern scientist during the latter part of the 20th century. The question remained as to how these ancient people knew of the existence of Sirius 'B' to accurately chart its path on the cave walls. Melchizedek suggested alien intervention has been affecting human development as far back as 200,000 years ago. I read about theories that are substantiated through the tales of ancient mythology and fables and wonder if ancient humans to alien contacts were the fodder for old fables? I now believe in aliens and although I went through alien encounters right after Christmas I have now reached a level of acceptance. I know that we are not alone and just as I understand I have a choice I also understand that I am at a developmental disadvantage to some of the unseen beings in my bedroom at night. But most of all I know that I am loved and protected. Just as Melchizedek talked about his teacher, Thoth, I know Yellow Dog is near me and cares deeply for me and my well being. It is this love that has empowered me over my old fear of unseen beings.

Back to Melchizedek's book...A common consciousness was explored through the "hundredth-monkey concept" which was a scientific experiment that chronicled how monkeys learned from each other to wash a sandy sweet potato before eating it. First one monkey discovered how to wash the treat, with time other monkeys, by watching the first monkey, then each other, also learned how to wash and enjoy the treat. After a few weeks the entire colony of monkeys learned this behavior. The scientists observed that after approximately 100 monkeys understood that they could wash the sweet potato in the ocean before eating it, all the monkeys living on surrounding islands began to wash and enjoy this treat as soon as they found it, as though it was instinct, even though they were not in contact with each other. How did they suddenly KNOW how to do this behavior when communication between the monkeys was not possible because they lived on various islands? This was a simultaneous imprinted pattern within the species that the scientists theorized must be due to a common consciousness. When enough of one species believes, that 100th monkey, then all of the species will experience this new belief.

Melchizedek's book then theorized that humans, too, could have a common consciousness. These explanations made sense to me and with it an acceptance of being a part of all humanity, as one consciousness, no longer appeared wrong or scary. I began to wonder if enough humans believed in a behavior or an acceptance, could this then manifest into a reality. I remembered the movie, *"What the Bleep Do We Know?"* that I saw last year. In the scene about the Spaniard's ship the Natives did not see the ship because they didn't believe it could exist. Could this be possible? Would I start seeing fairies with my eyes if all humanity believed that fairies actually existed? When enough people believe that an unreality could be a reality then would this new reality actually begin to exist? Could we really all be connected to one common consciousness?

When returning to the idea of Akenahten and his dynasty in Egypt I understand that this ruler was different in that he worshiped one god not the many gods of the dynasties before and after his rule. I paged back and read my channel of February 7th when I was questioning the religion, the belief system or mind set of the ancient Egyptians during Akenahten's reign. Yellow Dog shared; *"Little One...It is not a matter of choosing the unseen. It is the matter of believing that there is one creator. That all the other deities, all the other unseen are workers to this one God. The God who orchestrates all that exists on your world and in my plane of reality too. There is one God. What man needs is but one religion, one belief system, one path to respect and honor the one supreme being; the one supreme force, the unity of all peoples, the unity of nature. It is not about "politics." It is not about control. It is about harmony and love. It is about co-existence and evolution. It is about oneness."* Could this be Yellow Dog's way of saying One Common Consciousness? I wonder if all people are really interconnected.

Dimensions, realities and the flower of life are difficult concepts to understand. Melchizedek proposed many theories in his books that would be better left for others to explore first hand rather than for me to interpret. Other than what I have learned about sound healing through the merkaba and lightbody activation workshop last November I am surprised at synchronicities between what Melchizedek has experienced and what I have lived through. Melchizedek described the difference in scale once sensed while traveling from one dimension to another which was similar to what I experienced this past fall. When I was in the fairy realm I was a similar size to the fairies around me. When I stepped into my realm I felt very large, while the fairies appeared small. I felt a chill up my spine when I read that another person had actually experienced what I had and could explain it through a form of science.

I read in Melchizedek's book that the pyramid's purpose was more functional then a burial chamber. Ancient buildings were built for sound and for lightbody activations. While reading this theory I remembered a crystal meditation that I experienced back in March of 2005. I set out the intention of journeying with a power animal and found myself lying in a sarcophagus in an ancient Egyptian building. I wasn't being buried in this meditation/journey. Somehow I knew that I was placed in this sarcophagus as part of a ceremony, part of a teaching or learning. After I came out of that meditation I understood that not all pyramids were built for burials and that some were used as a complex form of learning what I perceived at the time as "psychic phenomena." I was not aware of sound healing or lightbody activations when I experienced that meditation last year. I find it curious that Melchizedek would echo my belief that the pyramid's purpose was more functional then a burial chamber. And the synchronicity becomes deeper when I researched the actual date of this journey from my hand written journal for when I turned to the page I noticed that under the date of March 10, 2005, I drew a picture of a Star of David over a flat topped pyramid. By this pencil sketch I noted that I saw the image while coming out of a nap. The Star of David is a two dimensional representation of the merkaba lightbody that I drew months before I even knew what a merkaba was and a year before I read Melchizedek's book!

I find it curious that I experienced much of what Melchizedek's *"Flower of Life"* books talk about **before** I ever read his books. I suppose I could say that there is only so much psychic-multi-dimensional-new age stuff out there. I suppose I could say that this author has just collected as much information as he could and stuffed it into a logical format. But his information was more significant than just organization for it holds a truth that I have experienced, learned and accepted. I am grateful for Melchizedek's books because they provided a confirmation that my own experiences were true. How can two people really "be crazy" if they had similar experiences and conclusions?

Dimensional Shift and the Ascension was the last topic from these books that I will address and I must say that I found these ideas to be both intriguing and yet unsettling. I read about a cycle of time that earth repeats every 25,920 years. I find the concept that time is not linear but cyclical somewhat confusing but if time does cycle then our current time is about to change. The Mayan calendar illustrates that the time for the next change would be our modern date of 2012AD. Because of our recorded history being limited man has no recorded evidence of when, if, and how, the last shift occurred. Many theories abound as to what will happen in 2012. Some fear cataclysmic changes to our environment, our earth and the ultimate end of our known civilization. Melchizedek theorized a few hours, or perhaps days, of confusion as our bodies would witness the earth changing and our atoms realigning. According to Melchizedek man made substances, such as plastics, would become unstable and "melt" and our eyes would not be able to perceive the new world at first because the colors would be from a spectrum totally foreign to us. Those people that understood about the change in time called the dimensional shift or the ascension would probably be awed but would understand. But those that were unaware of a change would probably lapse into a form of mass hysteria.

As I read about this "shift" of the earth in Melchizedek's books I started to think of the "Book of Revelations" from the New Testament of the Bible which warns about the end of the world, a time where only those who followed the teachings of Jesus would be "saved" or "risen up" into a new world. As a child I was fascinated with reading *Revelations* and found it more fearful than threats about the Devil or Hell. I was also fascinated with the Science Fiction movies that centered on the world after the devastation of a final nuclear type war such as in *Planet of the Apes, Terminator* or *Mad Max*. Yes, the pain of the earth falling apart around me was an ingrained fear of mine just as I was afraid of not being one of the few chosen ones to be allowed to survive. I wonder if I could have lived through a cataclysm of the earth before which was the last shift or cycle of change that could be adding to this fear.

Whatever the future of the earth is I feel helpless in changing the path of the physics I read about in Melchizedek's books. So I suppose what will happen will happen whether humanity is willing to understand the concepts or not. So, if I can't change it, then why worry? But I do find the possibility of a dimensional shift intriguing. Maybe this is because I feel I need to be prepared or maybe it is just because I hate secrets and want to know. Yes, I did enjoy these "Flower of Life" books for not only did I find them conclusive but they opened new possibilities to me. Now I find myself wondering about the possibility of a dimensional shift, ascension and/or an evolution of consciousness. For now…Namaste.

March 26, 2006: I attended another Alternative Connections Exposition today because I was curious about a presentation whose advertisement read: *"What is the 5th Dimension? We read and hear about this, but what does it mean? What are the pieces that help you attain this process? How do we change our beliefs? ...explain the components of this evolutionary shift."* A friend from my yoga class was interested in attending the Exposition as well so we car pooled and I was happy for the company. This morning I felt compelled to wear a necklace that Greg gave me for Christmas. It was a stone shaped in a spiral called a Nebula stone which felt right laying against my throat as I drove off to meet my friend and continue on to an adventure in Massachusetts.

When I first arrived at the Exposition I happened to see a woman hurriedly place a stack of informative fliers about her services on the table at the entrance to the exposition room. Something about her was interesting and I felt compelled to pick up one of her brochures whose cover was decorated with a diagram similar to the "flower of life." I looked up and searched for this lady in the ballroom that was filling up with patrons. I wanted to sign up for a "reading" with her but the woman had disappeared. Time was getting late and I needed to get seated for the lecture about "*the Ascension*" so I abandoned finding the woman and searched for the designated lecture hall listed in the program I was handed when I paid my entry fee.

I walked into the little room with my friend and smiled when I noticed that the woman standing in front of the room was the same woman I just saw in the hallway that was putting out the flyers. My mind rationalized the significance of me being drawn to this one woman. This was a fairly large exposition with three rooms of the hotel being used for lectures. Seven, one hour long lectures were scheduled for the day in each room. That would be a total of 21 different lectures during the course of the day. A fourth, large vendor room was crammed full of tables and people offering goods or services and many of those vendors did not offer lectures. What were the odds that, out of all the people doing business here that day, I was attracted to the one woman that turned out to be the lecturer that I went to this exposition to hear?

As I settled into my seat I took notes as to what this woman had to say. She shared; *"People won't move and won't change unless there is a lot of pain."* I thought this was the exact reason that I ultimately allowed myself to change. If I hadn't experienced the emotional and resulting physical pain of the stress of seven years ago, then I would never have changed my lifestyle, and consequently, my beliefs. Pain was my impetus for change. I listened on.

She talked about how; *"We need to clear ourselves so that we might hold the frequencies of the next dimension."* The speaker then talked about holistic practitioners such as chiropractors, psychic healers, mediums, and others that can help us to release blocks that we accumulated from our current, or past, lives. Her words reminded me that I, too, had learned to understand that phobias could be related to "past lives." I experienced my own regression and release in the spring of 2005. I've changed my perception on how to live by learning how to release my fear, anger, guilt and other negative energies.

She shared; *"We must change our core beliefs to change our reality."* This was a statement that I understood because I had to release my prejudice against other religions or beliefs and had to nurture my confidence in unseen beings. I had to develop new ideas, new ideals, and a whole new ideology. I nodded in agreement and listened for more.

"Manifestation is happening so fast it can appear scary. Time appears compressed now that we are approaching the next dimension." Many of the people that I've sat with in my psychic circles have shared that they have felt shifts in reality happening. And that time, the days and the seasons all just seem to fly by. Somehow time seemed much more relaxed just a few years ago. I remember, in 1997, how the winter just chugged along at a snail's pace. Now, this past winter seemed to go by so fast. Perhaps this was a sign of me aging? Since I don't remember a lot of my past lives I have nothing to compare this sensation too. I questioned this concept and listened for more.

I learned about this speaker's past. She has been a practicing medium for the past seventeen years, she practices Wicca and she enjoys and works with astrology. It was just recently that she discovered the theories about the ascension and wants to help others to understand. She has researched her facts about the ascension through many different organized religions and has summarized her own belief of what will transpire.

She told us that the next dimension, what she refers to as the 5th dimension, will be one of "Love Frequency." Living in this dimension will be enjoyable. Your job will not be work but rather pure love manifested. What you choose will always be bliss. She told us that this shift will be for the good of all. I wonder if this woman was portraying an idyllic, yet perhaps overly naive, perspective.

I left the room with my friend and we followed the speaker to her booth where we both signed up for a reading and returned to the lecture hall for our next lesson. We chose to see a shaman who spoke about Incan Energy Medicine. I knew why I needed to be there when I sat down. This lecturer was wearing the same exact nebula stone that I chose to wear today!

He talked about how; *"Shamanism is all about your personal experience and a path of the heart. Learn to conquer your demons through love and compassion. Conquer your anger and you conquer your need to have battles within."*

I learned that shamanism was not a religion but was about energy, light and vibration. This man explained that energy was not positive or negative, good or bad, but simply considered either healthy or unhealthy. We learned that energies in people could be balanced through the extraction of the unhealthy. He then demonstrated a healing that was similar to the Huichol Shaman I saw in February, yet different. This man called in the order of the directions different then the Huichol Shaman, he also drank from a bottle and spewed a spray of this substance when he worked, and he used a "mesa bag" and the stones it contained, to enhance his work. I found the demonstration interesting.

The third lecture I attended today was not very interesting. I snuck out early to shop before my scheduled reading with the lady that talked about the ascension. My friend had her reading first so I continued shopping and kept an eye on the reader's booth while my friend was having her reading. Finally after I saw my friend stand up and leave, I approached the woman's booth, we greeted, exchanged money, and I sat down for my reading. The woman seemed, well, awed, by my energy as she told me; "I chose to come back for this incarnation. I chose to come to this present lifetime to help others. I chose to be a light worker."

(Now that I am writing this into my journal I wonder. What is a Light Worker? I have heard this phrase used by Doreen Virtue and others but I really don't understand the implications. Yellow Dog, how would you describe a Light Worker?

YD: *"Hello Little One. A light worker is a being incarnated into the earth to show the way. Light the path for the general population. Help the consciousness of all to tip the scale of belief towards a new reality; a remembrance of the souls of many, a re-awakening of a new time, a new existence and an ascension into a new dimension."*

Thank you Yellow Dog. I am still wondering if I am really a Light Worker. Back to my story...) I was respectful as I listened to this woman as she told me I was a Light Worker who had lived many lives before here on earth. She felt I lived in Tibet then quickly added that I have resolved my past conflicts and that I was now balanced. She seemed very happy and said that she felt honored to be in my energy. She acted almost giddy.

I left her booth feeling somewhat cheated that I didn't receive any grand wisdom and no prophetic insight into the future. The reading was full of ego enhancing compliments that left the cynic in me to wonder whether the flattery was simply part of this reader's technique. By the time I walked to the cafeteria I surmised that all of this woman's "sitters" received complementing, uplifting readings and was eager to share my reading with my friend and hear about her reading as well. I approached my friend sitting in the cafeteria and immediately sensed that she was not in a pleasant mood and soon found out why. She complained that the reading she received dwelled on her unhappy past lives and she was told that she was repeating the same pattern of unhappy relationships and unresolved conflicts. My friend was frustrated. She wanted an explanation of HOW to break the pattern because she KNOWS what the problem is. What she was looking for was ANSWERS. I listened to my friend as she voiced her frustrations. I chose not to share the details about my glorious reading. I guess this psychic was actually impressed by the energy around me! I'll have to assess this more later, when I can think, alone.

I attended some more workshops and did a little shopping. The last series of workshops scheduled that day did not interest me so I walked into the vendor's hall once more. I wanted to catch up with the shaman that wore the nebula stone because he mentioned that the attendees to his workshop qualified for a free "healing." I had the time so I thought I would register at his booth.

After my experience with the Hawaiian vendor a few months back I was cautious about visiting. But I was happy that I went to talk with this shaman because we enjoyed a lengthy conversation. I don't remember how we got on the subject. It might have been the nebula stones that we were each wearing. But somehow we started to talk about aliens. The shaman, or rather his girlfriend that was working the booth who was also a practicing shaman, had a bad experience with aliens. After introductions she shared her story about how the aliens attached some sort of "homing device" to her. The pair then explained how a probe type device was stationed on her property.

A few years ago I would have passed these two off as total kooks. A few months ago I would have been terrified at the thought of intruding aliens and homing devices. But I can now accept the possibility that what once appeared as an unreality may actually be a reality. And I know that I am somehow part of all realities, mine and that of any unseen aliens. And that I am guided and protected by Yellow Dog and others. But in case

I was wrong and aliens could really be "evil" I listened to their story and tried to discern fear from fact.

We started to talk about different types of aliens. I mentioned the few that I have "seen" during meditations and healings. I told about the species of beings that I felt I had contacted when I channeled healing to my friend as well as when I traveled with the wolf in journey. I mentioned the robed being that looked like he had the head of a praying mantis insect. He and the woman became agitated at the description of this being, the man shaman called this species one of the "nasties." I somehow remained calm in the presence of their obvious discomfort. I knew this alien was safe for me. I was there, in the room when I was doing the healing on my friend a few months back. I did not sense alarm or evil. I sensed a positive purpose and an operation of intent when I saw the tall insect like being work on my friend last fall. I was surprised that my own self assurance was not wavered by the uneasiness these shaman were displaying. I found it very strange that I wasn't affected by their obvious fear.

I told the pair that I did not feel any negativity from the praying mantis type being but the man shaman would not readily agree and urged me to be cautious. He asked if he could check out my aura. I agreed and he swept his hands around me presumably checking the energy of my aura. He said that I felt ok and then excused himself because he had to leave to take care of an obligation. The woman offered to check me out more thoroughly but first wanted to discuss matters with the man before he left their vendor booth.

I used his impending departure to silently ask Yellow Dog if it was ok for me to receive a healing from this woman shaman. I quieted myself while the pair were involved in their discussion and searched my own energy for a sensation or a sense of well being. I felt no alarm or agitation, just a peaceful feeling within me which I concluded was Yellow Dog's way of confirming that the woman was ok. When the woman was through with her discussion I followed her behind the booth. She had me sit on a mat on the floor. She had her bottle of liquid and she started to motion with her hands and to spit a spray of liquid from the bottle in the aura around me. I closed my eyes and felt like I existed in a void, similar to what I felt last February, but this was less intense. I sensed this woman was doing no harm and was curious as to what she would find when she completed her "clearing."

When she said she was through she had me stand up. She ran her hand through my aura and seemed to find something odd. Her face contorted in a question as she motioned and announced that she felt a big cord of energy coming out of my heart chakra. She said that this cord was attached to something far away, something ancient and she didn't understand exactly what this cord's purpose was. I was wondering if the cord was connected to my spirit guides. Could it be a connection to Yellow Dog? Time was getting short and the Exposition was starting to close down. Other customers were milling around, eager to make their final purchases or requests before we were asked to leave the hotel's conference room. I had taken up enough of these people's time. I thanked them and left.

I left without my question about what the cord meant answered. But I left with a sense of peace over being exposed to the possibility that another person thought my praying mantis alien was evil for I **knew** that these Shaman were wrong. I knew the healing I did on my friend last year was with love and a purpose, that my journey with wolf was safe. I knew that this cord that the woman shaman detected as attached to me was through love. Yes, I felt assured that aliens weren't a threat. I had no more fear of unseen beings even when a stranger obviously doubted my well being. I knew I was safe and protected and loved.

It wasn't until I got home tonight that I made the connection regarding this cord of heart energy. The merkaba! The lightbody! That was what the woman shaman was feeling. Not a connection to Yellow Dog but a connection to all of the other Light Workers, a connection of the heart from the heart to the heart. This was the weirdest confirmation I could ever have received. A confirmation by a non-informed individual that my new found understanding, the understanding of the "flower of life," was actually, well, real!

The best way I can explain this is to refer to *"The 13 Phase Unity Merkaba Enlivened with Holographic Sound, level 2"* workbook where on page 8 I read; *"...project a beam of White Light from your Heart into the central shaft...As you hold this heart beam for a few moments, you connect simultaneously, into the hearts of all in the group...to the God/source and Earth Heart of the collective group..."* I offer this brief snippet of instruction to hold credence to my new understanding that I am connected through my heart chakra to others. But how did this Shaman FEEL this connection?

If I really do have a cord of light from my heart connecting me to others as the Shaman sensed and as I have learned about in my recent Holographic Sound Healing workshop, then am I really a Light Worker? And if I am a Light Worker, then why have I been incarnated or assigned to earth as a Light Worker? Could there really be a dimensional shift that is about to happen to this planet around 2012?

If there really is an ascension which could be described as a changing of dimension or an altering of time and space then my experiences, and this book, can serve as a tool; a guide through one year of one person's life, a development of perspective, and an evolution of the mind. Yet, if this was, indeed, a walk into a

possibility, a questioning of what might be. Then I may offer this book as a prophecy or a comfort for those who, like me, wonder of the possibilities. Because we are all part of the whole, we are all part of each other, the planet and part of God. In closing allow me to use Yellow Dog's words, an entry into my dream journal from late March;
    "I am in the heart. I talk to you from the heart. We are one."
    ...Namaste.

EPILOGUE

I've struggled with the length of this text. Yet there was a logical pattern, a reason for grouping the experiences of my journey. First, I marveled at Melchizedek's books; the similarity of his reality to my own, that his thoughts, ideas, and occurrences were but random coincidences taught through me and then my confirmation at the Alternative Connections Exposition in March of 2006; the lady who was awed by my energy and the Shaman who felt the cord of energy emerging from my heart. These were real people who I hadn't shared my belief of the merkaba or lightbody with. They were fully functioning within their own reality and yet they used their three dimensional senses to verify my new being. They confirmed that I was a light worker.

These two affirmations were the straws that broke my camel's back of belief. I no longer am skeptical or fear the unseen beings that are around me, I accept. And with this acceptance my world has evolved further. My journal entries continue as I learn to share a consciousness and an elevation of the earth's vibration. And I am also learning that I can, with time, manifest what I want in life.

Physically I am much healthier and am no longer tied to daily medications for my sinuses. I experience little if any back or shoulder pain and if I do feel pain or discomfort I have the ability to meditate and release the pain, literally. I calm myself, call in the energies, feel a sense of floating and a sense of bliss, then TWITCH, there goes the pain. I no longer have the need to use crystals to assist me during my meditations. Yes, I have evolved.

Sounds crazy, yes? But so did seeing ghosts in my bedroom. It is all a matter of desire, a base of perspective, and a realization of self empowerment. For now...Namaste.

DIARY OF RESOURCES

Please enjoy my exposure to these books which I was guided to experience. As always, I strive to be honest. In order to portray how deeply I absorbed the book's contents, I created a key on how I utilized these texts. This does not reflect on the quality of these works. Rather the path I was guided to pursue:

* Started to read the book but never finished. Only part of the text was what I needed to read.
** Again, I did not read this book cover to cover. I referred to its appendix as a reference.
*** Was guided to read this book from cover to cover.

*Jan. 2004: *"Tsvetaeva"* by Viktoria Schweitzer. First printed in Russian by Sintaksis in 1988, English translation 1992, HarperCollins Publishers Ltd.

**Jan. 2004: *"Hands of Light: A guide to healing through the human energy field"* by Barbara Ann Brennan. 1988 A Bantam Book, a division of Random House, Inc. New York.

***Feb. 2004: *"Lily Dale: The true story of the town that talks to the dead"* by Christine Wicker. 2003 HarperCollins Publishers, Inc. New York.

***March 2004: *"Psychic Pets: The secret life of Animals"* by JosephWylder. 1995 published by Gramercy Books/distributed by Random House Value Publishing, Inc., New Jersey.

***March 2004: "Psychic Development for Beginners: An easy guide to releasing and developing your psychic abilities" by Bill Hewitt. 2002 Llewellyn Publications, St. Paul, MN.

**May 2004: *"Animal Speak: The spiritual & magical powers of creatures great & small"* by Ted Andrews. 2004 Llewellyn Publications, St. Paul, Minnesota.

***May 2004: *"The Eagle and the Rose: A remarkable true story"* by Rosemary Altea. 2001 Warner Books, New York.

**May 2004: *"You Own the Power: Stories and exercises to inspire and unleash the force within"* by Rosemary Altea. 2000 by William Morrow, an imprint of HarperCollins Publishers.

***June 2004: *"The Little Doctor: And the magic power of her electric hand"* by Nellie Craib-Beighle. 1893-1911 San Francisco: The Hicks-Judd Co.

***July 2004: *"Eye to Eye: The language of energy and horse"* by Karen E. Nowak. 2002, Infinity publishing.com Haverford, PA.

***July 2004: *"Psychic Pets & Spirit Animals: True stories from the files of FATE magazine"* 1996 Llewellyn Publications, St. Paul, Minnesota.

***July 2004: *"Love, Miracles, and Animal Healing"* by Allen M. Schoen, DVM and Pam Proctor. 1996, New York, A Fireside Book.

***Aug. 2004: *"Healing for Horses: The essential guide to using hands-on healing energy with horses"* by Margrit Coates. 2002 Sterling, UK.

**Aug. 2004: *"The American Indian Secrets of Crystal Healing"* by Luc Bourgault. 1997 Quantum an imprint of W. Foulsham & Co. Ltd. The Publishing House, England.

*Aug. 2004: *"In the Shadow of the Shaman: Connecting with self, nature & spirit"* by Amber Wolfe. 1997 Llewellyn Publications, St. Paul, Minnesota.

***Oct. 2004: *"There Are No Accidents: Synchronicity and the stories of our lives"* by Robert H. Hopcke. 1997 Riverhead Books Published by the Berkley Publishing Group A division of Penguin Putnam Inc. New York.

*Oct. 2004: *"The Art of Psychic Protection"* by Judy Hall. 1997 Red Wheel/Weiser, LLC Boston, MA.

**Nov. 2004: *"Crystal Awareness"* by Catherine Bowman. 2003 Llewellyn Publications, St. Paul, Minnesota.

***Nov. 2004: *"The Druids"* by Peter Berresford Ellis. 1994 Constable and Company Limited, London, US edition published 1995 through Wm. B. Eerdmans Publishing Co. Grand Rapids, Michigan.

***Nov. 2004: *"The Druids"* by Stuart Piggott. 1985 Thames and Hudson Inc., New York.

**Dec. 2004: *"The Druid Animal Oracle: Working with the sacred animals of the Druid tradition"* by Philip and Stephanie Carr-Gomm. 1994 Fireside, Simon & Schuster, Inc. New York.

***Jan. 2005: *"Color and Crystals: A journey through the chakras"* by Joy Gardner. 1988 The Crossing Press, Freedom, California.

***Jan. 2005: *"The DaVinci Code"* by Dan Brown. 2003 Doubleday/Random House Inc. NY

**Feb. 2005: *"Crystal Enlightenment: The transforming properties of crystals and healing stones. Volume I"* by Katrina Raphaell, 1985 Aurora Press, Santa Fe, N.M.

*Feb. 2005: *"Secret Places of the Lion"* by George Hunt Williamson. 1977 Warner Books, New York.

***Feb. 2005: *"Beyond These Four Walls: Diary of a psychic medium"* by Mary Rose Occhino. 2004 The Berkley Publishing Group A division of Penguin Group Inc., New York

**Feb. 2005: *"Crystal Healing: The therapeutic application of crystals and stones. Volume II"* by Katrina Raphaell. 1987 Aurora Press, Inc. Santé Fe, N.M.

**March 2005: *"Love is in the Earth: A kaleidoscope of crystals"* by Melody. 1999 Earth-Love Publishing House, Wheat Ridge, Colorado.

***March 2005: *"The Lost Continent of MU"* by James Churchward. 1969 Ives Washburn, Inc., New York.

*March 2005: *"The Children of MU"* by James Churchward. 1968 Ives Washburn, Inc., New York.

***March 2005: *"Dawn of the New Age-New Agers-their search for truth"* (booklet) ??? UK.

***March 2005: *"Witch: The wild ride from wicked to Wicca"* by Candace Savage. 2000 Greystone Books a division of Douglas & McIntyre Ltd. Vancouver, BC, Canada.

*May 2005: *"The Goddess"* by Shahrukh Husain. 1997 Little, Brown and Company, Boston.

*May 2005: *"The Witches' Goddess"* By Janet & Stewart Farrar. 1987 Phoenix Publishing Inc. Custer, Washington.

***May 2005: *"The Book of Shadows: A modern woman's journey into the wisdom of witchcraft and magic of the goddess"* by Phyllis Curott. 1999 Broadway books, New York.

*May 2005: *"Green Witchcraft: Folk magic, fairy lore & herb craft"* by Ann Moura (Aoumiel). 1999 Llewellyn Publications, St. Paul, MN.

**June 2005: *"Goddess Guidance Oracle Cards: A 44-card deck with guidebook"* by Doreen Virtue, Ph.D. 2004 Hay House, Inc. Carlsbad, California.

***July 2005: *"Voyagers the Sleeping Abductees: Volume I of the emerald covenant CDT-plate translations"* by Ashayana Deane 2001 Wild Flower Press/Granite Publishing, Columbus, NC.

*July 2005: *"Voyagers the Secrets of Amenti: Volume II of the emerald covenant CDT plate translations"* by Ashayana Deane 2002 Wild Flower Press/Granite Publishing, Columbus, NC.

***July 2005: *"Divine Guidance: How to have a dialogue with God and your guardian angels"* by Doreen Virtue, Ph.D. 1998 St. Martin's Griffin, New York.

**Aug. 2005: *"Angel Therapy: Healing messages for every area of your life"* by Doreen Virtue, Ph.D. 1997 Hay House, Inc. Carlsbad, California.

***Aug. 2005: *"Earth Angels"* by Doreen Virtue, Ph.D. 2002, Hay House, Inc. Carlsbad, Calif.

**Aug. 2005: *"Angel Numbers"* by Doreen Virtue, Ph. D. 2005, Hay House, Inc. Carlsbad, CA.

***Aug. 2005: *"The Lightworkers Way: Awakening your spiritual power to know and heal"* by Doreen Virtue, Ph.D. 1997 Hay House, Inc. Carlsbad, California.

***Aug. 2005: *"Healing with the Fairies: Messages, manifestations, and love from the world of the fairies"* by Doreen Virtue, Ph.D. 2001 Hay House, Inc. Carlsbad, California.

**Sept. 2005: *"A Witch's Guide to Faery Folk: How to work with the elemental world"* by Edain McCoy. 1994 Llewellyn Publications, St. Paul MN.

***Sept. 2005: *"The Magic of Shapeshifting"* by Rosalyn Greene. 2000 Red Wheel/Weiser, LLC, York Beach, ME.

***Sept. 2005: *"Totem Magic: Dance of the Shape-Shifter"* by Yasmine Galenorn. 2004 The Crossing Press, a division of Ten Speed Press, Berkeley, Calif.

**Sept. 2005: *"Animal-Wise: The spirit language and signs of nature"* by Ted Andrews. 1999 Dragonhawk Publishing, Jackson, Tennessee.

**Sept. 2005: *"Enchantment of the Faerie Realm: Communicate with nature spirits & elementals"* by Ted Andrews. 2005 Llewellyn Publications, St. Paul, Minnesota.

**Sept. 2005: *"Faeries"* described and illustrated by Brian Froud and Alan Lee. A Peacock Press/Bantam Book Published 1978 by Harry N. Abrams, Inc. New York.

***Oct. 2005: *"Bushman Shaman: Awakening the spirit through ecstatic dance"* by Bradford Keeney. 2005 Destiny Books, Rochester, Vermont.

***Oct. 2005: *"Dragons & Unicorns: A natural history"* by Paul and Karin Johnsgard. 1992 St. Martin's Griffin.

**Nov. 2005: *"Magickal Mystical Creatures: Invite their powers into your life"* by D.J. Conway. 2003 Llewellyn Publications, St. Paul, Minnesota.

**Nov. 2005: *"The 13 Phase Unity Merkaba Lightbody Activation: Anchoring the 13 phase unity chakra system, introducing and activating the 13 phase unity merkaba"* (workbook) by Paul Hubbert, Ph.D. Published by Paul Hubbert, Ph.D. Austin, Texas.

***Dec. 2005: *"Talking to the Dead: Kate and Maggie Fox and the Rise of Spiritualism"* by Barbara Weisberg. 2004 HarperSanFrancisco a division of Harper Collins Publishers.

**Dec. 2005: *"Ancient Egypt: Kingdom of the pharaohs"* by R. Hamilton. 2005 Parragon Publishing, Bath, UK.

***Dec. 2005: *"When The Legends Die"* by Hal Borland. 1964 Laurel-Leaf Books/Random House New York.

*Feb. 2006: *"Deerdancer: The shapeshifter archetype in story and in trance"* by Michele Jamal. 1995 Penguin Group, New York.

***Feb. 2006: *"The Ancient Secret of the Flower of Life: Volume I"* by Drunvalo Melchizedek. 1998 Light Technology Publishing, Flagstaff, AZ.

***March 2006: *"The Ancient Secret of the Flower of Life: Volume II"* by Drunvalo Melchizedek. 2000 Light Technology Publishing, Flagstaff, AZ.

***March 2006: *"Living in the Heart: How to enter into the sacred space within the heart"* by Drunvalo Melchizedek. 2003 Light Technology Publishing, Flagstaff, AZ.